WILD CHILD

D1566929

Max and Carol in *Where the Wild Things Are* (directed by Spike Jonze, 2009).

WILD CHILD

INTENSIVE PARENTING AND POSTHUMANIST ETHICS

Naomi Morgenstern

UNIVERSITY OF MINNESOTA PRESS

MINNEAPOLIS LONDON

Copyright 2018 by the Regents of the University of Minnesota

Published by the University of Minnesota Press
111 Third Avenue South, Suite 290
Minneapolis, MN 55401-2520
http://www.upress.umn.edu

ISBN 978-1-5179-0378-7 (hc)
ISBN 978-1-5179-0379-4 (pb)

A Cataloging-in-Publication record for this book is available from the Library of Congress.

The University of Minnesota is an equal-opportunity educator and employer.

For my boys

It wasn't for love of having

children that I had a child.
Rather, I simply didn't know how a person

could cross, fully shoeless, a bed of coals
and not burn, and I needed

someone to pass this to.
I needed my obtuseness to survive me.

But I never accounted for our thwarting era.
Every day, the paper

runs a remembrance
of a child, the notice struggling to sing the few

years lived: *He never sketched the Earth without
its hatch of latitudes. She did*

not like to try new foods.

—Natalie Shapero, "Survive Me"

Contents

Introduction

The Posthumanist Wild Child

Here is a kind of question, let us call it historical, whose *conception,*
formation, gestation, and *labor* we are only catching a glimpse of today.
I employ these words, I admit, with a glance towards the operations of
childbearing—but also with a glance towards those who, in a society from
which I do not exclude myself, turn their eyes away when faced by the as yet
unnamable which is proclaiming itself and which can do so, as is necessary
whenever a birth is in the offing, only under the species of the nonspecies,
in the formless, mute, infant, and terrifying form of monstrosity.

—Jacques Derrida, "Structure, Sign, and Play in
the Discourse of the Human Sciences"

Hey weird little thing, I like you, you destroy things.

—Carol in *Where the Wild Things Are* (directed by Spike Jonze)

"Is anyone going to help me?" asks Carol, the first wild thing that eight-year-old Max encounters in Spike Jonze's 2009 film *Where the Wild Things Are.* "I'm the only one who cares enough to do this [crash!] or this [crash!]."[1] Carol is on a rampage, and the other wild things stand back as he destroys their dwellings. This destruction is "necessary," according to Carol, because K.W., another wild thing, has abandoned him. Max enters the scene in response to Carol, and, as a fellow wild thing similarly "abandoned" by a parent figure, he joins in the destruction. Carol smells Max, and Max smells back and growls. After extensive smelling, growling, and laughing, Carol declares, "Hey weird little thing, I like you, you destroy things." The wild

1

child is, among other things, a destructive child, as we shall see, but this destruction is inseparable from the *fort-da* work of survival, the work of surviving separation and surviving the other ("The subject says to the object: 'I destroyed you,'" writes D. W. Winnicott, "and the object is there to receive the communication").[2] Dressed in his wolf suit, Jonze's Max, like Maurice Sendak's Max in the book on which the film is based, hesitates between the animal and the human, yet he is also marked as a wild child of a different era who must negotiate both waning and newly insistent fantasies of paternal protection and the not always welcome gift of maternal care. Max shoulders the affectual burden of a profoundly uncertain future, for his apocalyptic anxieties concerning a seductive yet perilous destruction cannot be re-contained or diagnosed as appropriately developmental. Surely this wild child is onto something.

In the chapters that follow, I want to consider the possibility that a variety of late twentieth- and early twenty-first-century technological, political, and economic developments have helped to precipitate a posthumanist encounter with the ethics of reproductive choice and with the figure of the wild child. How might the intensification of the reproductive decision contribute to a deconstruction of the (hierarchical) opposition between "responsible" individual acts of procreation and nonteleological, species-driven patterns of reproduction? And how has contemporary literary fiction allegorized or theorized the extent to which recent developments have exposed more and more of us not only to the wildness of reproduction but also to the wildness of relation, decision, and human being? The posthumanist wild child often appears in a physical or ideological space in which the easy distinction between the wild and the civilized or rational has collapsed. The child in contemporary literature appears at the center of an ethical or ontological wilderness that allegorizes the relationship between parents and children and registers, in displaced fashion, particular forms of cultural anxiety about reproduction and futurity and about the relationship between the human and what has traditionally been quarantined as "the animal." The technological sophistication of advances in reproductive technology and the political "innovation" of post-heteronormativity often conceal from us some of the ways in which the transformations effected by such developments might take us closer to, rather than further away from, the world that we so often other as "animal." "What is called 'the family'?" asks Derrida. "I would not say without hesitation that the family is eternal. What is inalterable, what will continue to traverse History, is that there is, or that there *be, something of* a family, some social bond organized around procreation. What are called 'animal' families should also be analyzed in their complexity, as primatologists do."[3] The twenty-first-century wild child, as a result, belongs both to what is sometimes thought of as a disorienting or emancipatory future for human social organization *and* to what can feel like a past we have often tried to convince ourselves we have uniquely transcended or (in a romantic mode) lost. "We don't need to idealize the child as some noble savage or primitive poet ruined by the talking circle of culture," writes Adam Phillips.[4] The intensification of reproductive choice, whether it is generated by political post-heteronormativity or by advances in assisted reproductive technology (ART), might be said to give reproduction back to the human parent as if for the first time. But this is also to say that what was often confined to the animal—a reproductive "choice" that was commanded not by reason or metaphysics but by ecological "pressure" or "instinct," which is to say, by "the other"—will now come to describe human reproduction in a manner that could also return us to a more ethically demanding sense of *social* reproduction.

Since at least the end of the eighteenth century, the figure of "the child" has functioned, in Western thought, to protect and preserve the border between the "natural" world and the world of the rational and independent adult human being for whom Nature is at once reassuringly innocent and frighteningly other.[5] What Kant in his treatise *On Education* called "Practical or Moral training" is that instruction which no other animal receives and which, he continued, "teaches man how to live as a free being."[6] But as the primary target of this "moral training," the Kantian child has to occupy what Tamar Schapiro calls a "liminal condition . . . which distinguishes [the child] from both nonhuman animals and from full persons."[7] This liminality helps to construct the distinction it purportedly preserves, by shoring up our faith in the existence of a distinct realm of Nature and confirming the ontological and ethical superiority of the "free" adult human being. But it also produces the child as "wild" in a more profound sense. The child occupies and embodies a "demilitarized zone" located somewhere between a dangerous (if compelling) natural exteriority and the safe space of "civilization." It is this zone which, I want to suggest, has become increasingly delimited in the late twentieth and early twenty-first centuries, as the conceptual oppositions maintained by the liminal child become vulnerable to their own deconstruction.

Philippe Ariès, in what remains one of the classic intellectual histories of childhood, *Centuries of Childhood: A Social History of Family Life*, suggests that the child as such—the child with an immortal soul, the child whose singular death could be mourned and memorialized, the child who had to be carefully protected and cautiously trained for adulthood—gradually came into focus only between the sixteenth and late eighteenth centuries. "There was no problem for the Middle Ages," Ariès writes: "as soon as he had been weaned, or soon after, the child became the natural companion of the adult."[8] But this is also to say that "the child" came into his or her historical self (at least in the West) *as* an ontological "problem"—as a "wild child." And this is something historians of childhood seem to confirm. In a chapter on the legendary Victor of Aveyron in *Encounters with Wild Children*, Adriana S. Benzaquén suggests that "the new attitude to the wild child [in the late eighteenth century] signals the historical emergence of 'the child' as a privileged object of knowledge and intervention, and with it the inauguration of a space of inquiry and practice that is still our own."[9] The child that began to attract intense philosophical and disciplinary attention in the nineteenth century was the subject of a constitutive "freedom" that, for the first time, could be lost (and, therefore, nostalgically or romantically idealized) or that had to be carefully contained and managed. "The solicitude of family, Church, moralists and administrators," writes Ariès, "deprived the child of the freedom he had hitherto enjoyed among adults. It inflicted on him the birch, the prison cell—in a word, the punishments usually reserved for convicts from the lowest strata of society. But this severity was the expression of a very different feeling from the old indifference: an obsessive love which was to dominate society from the eighteenth century on."[10] This conjunction of affection and concern reached something of an apogee in the celebrated case of Victor, the "young savage caught in the woods near Aveyron," who became the subject of a highly influential account by the physician who attempted to "treat" him, Jean Itard. Victor helped to demonstrate what Itard explained was a "statement which . . . has been many times repeated," namely, that despite the "preeminent position which is his natural destiny," "Man" would be "one of the most feeble and least intelligent of animals" without "the aid of civilization."[11] Victor, that is to say, hyperbolized the condition of the Enlightenment child per se, the child as precarious border figure between the "animal" world and the "eminent station" of *Homo sapiens*. And, indeed, it is this border status, between the wilderness and "civilization," between nature and reason, that the present study will often refer to as "wild." Wildness adheres to the very conceptual instability and ideological precariousness of "the child" as a philosophico-ethical category of being. It is, in other words, the very idea that there might be a zone of indistinction between the human and "the animal," a zone that is required to be inhabited by some kind of go-between being, that introduces an irreducible wildness into every Enlightenment or humanist attempt to police the specificity and categorical superiority of the human. For Itard, as for many of his heirs in the scientific community, this wildness could also take the form of a specifically linguistic or semiotic aporia. The work of bringing Victor back into society involved repeated encounters with a certain wildness at work in language itself: was Victor learning to "speak," Itard wondered, or merely to imitate or repeat, in the manner of a certain kind of (domesticated) animal? Presenting himself to Victor with his hair in need of combing, and subsequently recording Victor's successful delivery of a comb, Itard thought he detected the beginnings of meaningful speech. "Many people see in these proceedings only the behavior of an animal," wrote Itard.

> [F]or my part I will confess I believe that I recognize in them the language of the human species, originally employed in the infancy of society before the work of ages had coordinated the system of speech and furnished civilized man with a prolific and sublime means of improvement which causes his thought to blossom even in the cradle, and which he uses all his life without appreciating what it is to him and what he would be without if he found himself accidentally deprived of it, as in the case which now occupies us. Without doubt a day will come when the increased requirements of Victor will make him feel the necessity of using new signs. . . . It will perhaps be neither more nor less than what happens to the child who first lisps *papa*, without attaching to it any meaning and who from then on says it everywhere and on all occasions, gives it to every man he sees, and then, only after many reasonings and even abstractions, succeeds in giving it a simple and correct application.[12]

The language of the child (like that of society in its "infancy") is unhinged from meaning and direction ("[he] says it everywhere and on all occasions, gives it to every man he sees"), but even so, Itard insists, it belongs to "the language of the human species." This linguistic wildness, in other words, belongs neither to the nonhuman animal nor to "civilized man" but to that strange being called the child, here isolated and magnified in the experimental person of Victor of Aveyron.

The impasses experienced by Itard in his treatment of Victor anticipate the contours of what the present study refers to as the posthumanist wild child. But what exactly does it mean to refer to a phenomenon or a way of thinking as "posthuman" (or "posthumanist")? This is at once a genuinely fascinating intellectual question and a tricky matter of professional nomenclature and field demarcation. Although the application of psychoanalytic and deconstructive theory in *Wild Child* might appear to distance its readings from those advanced by some contemporary scholars of the "posthuman," its interest in questions of ethics and relationality dovetails, at crucial points, with the work of certain "materialist" or "posthumanist" feminist scholars (Karen Barad, Rosi Braidotti, and Donna Haraway, to name a few). It is also worth pointing out that "posthuman" itself is a particularly unstable signifier. This somewhat fraught question is one that has been explicitly addressed by, for example, Cary Wolfe in his 2009 book *What Is Posthumanism?*: "Posthumanism in my sense isn't posthuman at all," Wolfe writes, "in the sense of being 'after' our embodiment has been transcended—but is only posthuman*ist*, in the sense that it opposes the fantasies of disembodiment and autonomy, inherited from humanism itself."[13] My approach to the conceptual and categorical question of the posthuman and the posthumanist is very much in line with Wolfe's (and, like him, I draw a great deal on the Derridean critique of humanist metaphysics). The articulation of posthumanism favored in this study, then, is constitutively unsure of the demarcation between the humanist and the posthumanist, and reads the child as situated precisely in this unstable, or wild, terrain. As Wolfe explains,

[F]ar from surpassing or rejecting the human, [posthumanism] actually enables us to describe the human and its characteristic modes of communication, interaction, meaning, social significations, and affective investments with *greater* specificity. . . . But it also insists that we attend to the specificity of the human . . . by (paradoxically, for humanism) acknowledging that it is fundamentally a prosthetic creature that has coevolved with various forms of technicity and materiality, forms that are radically "not-human" and yet have nevertheless made the human what it is.[14]

Wild Child will follow Wolfe by paying particular attention to the ways in which the child is both presented as and sometimes desperately shielded from a "prosthetic" humanity that has also been theorized by the discourse of psychoanalysis. Psychoanalysis names not a fixed set of ideas but an evolving body of ideas and practices that have been enriched and shifted by various refutations and expansions. The psychoanalytic theorists favored in this study, Jean Laplanche and D. W. Winnicott, do not prioritize Oedipal paradigms or intrapsychic accounts of conflict but, rather, emphasize irreducible relationality and opacity, both the breakdown and continuity that characterize (human) being. Psychoanalysis, I would contend, is nothing if not an exploration of all that humanism disavows, and it is with this kind of critical work in mind that I have attempted to combine psychoanalytic and poststructuralist reading protocols in the chapters that follow.

Like many of the scholars associated with posthumanist feminist philosophy, I also draw much inspiration from the work of Donna Haraway, whose work on posthumanist ethical relation (in *The Companion Species Manifesto*, among other publications) corresponds with my own approach to parent–child relations in *Wild Child*. And this despite Haraway's repeated insistence that she is talking about dogs and not (human) children![15] Haraway explores "co-constitutive relationships in which none of the partners pre-exists the relating, and the relating is never done once and for all."[16] At the same time, I think it is important to insist that the genealogy of feminist posthumanism resists any one intellectual narrative and remains, to some extent, a work in progress. Hence, aspects of Karen Barad's work on "relational ontology" are in sync with *Wild Child*'s critical approach to the ethics of relationality, despite her very different sense of the significance of "the linguistic turn." "Why do we think that the existence of relations require[s] relata?" Barad asks in a 2003 essay that, I would argue, makes a suggestive (but never explicit) case for the kind of (maternal) ethics I explore in the present study.[17] And Barad's account of "a specifically posthumanist notion of performativity" ("A posthumanist performative account worth its salt must also avoid cementing the nature–culture dichotomy into its foundations, thereby enabling a genealogical analysis of how these crucial distinctions are materially and discursively produced") is not as distant from the account of the materiality of the signifier that is so important for poststructuralist feminist philosophy (and for much of my own work).[18] I would argue, indeed, that Judith Butler (to name one of the most influential figures in this field) is concerned not merely with what Barad calls "iterative citationality" but also with what she calls "iterative intra-activity." Butler, that is to say, in my book, is already a theorist of a posthumanist performativity.[19]

Indeed, *both* poststructuralist and much recent posthumanist feminist work can be drawn on to contest conventional (and still very popular) accounts of the human and posthumanism, such as can be found in Francis Fukuyama's 2002 book, *Our Posthuman Future*. "[T]he most significant threat posed by contemporary biotechnology," writes Fukuyama, "is the possibility that it will alter human nature and thereby move us into a 'posthuman' stage of history." This is important, he continues, "because human nature exists, is a meaningful concept, and has provided a stable continuity to our experience as a species. It is conjointly, with religion, what defines our most basic values."[20] The human, for Fukuyama, has to be both epistemologically and ontologically stable, and we must do our best to ward off any violent or hubristic assaults on this status quo. This is an ethics of protection and preservation, committed to defying a constitutive otherness. Indeed, such thinking can seem, at times, to fear and ward off the very possibility of futurity. "What is coming?" asks Bruno Latour, with a nod to humanism's nervous defense of "continuity"; "What is it that is arriving unexpectedly, something they ["the Moderns"] seem not to have anticipated? 'Gaia,' the 'Anthropocene' era, the precise name hardly matters, something in any case that has deprived them forever of the fundamental distinction between Nature and Society by means of which they were establishing their system of coordinates, one step at a time."[21]

For the kind of humanism espoused by Fukuyama, the child is always a potential problem: the child harbors an uncanny otherness and an unpredictable futurity that must be reassuringly translated into the terms of a developmental narrative. "The conception of children's status which is implicit in our moral and legal practice," writes Tamar Schapiro, "is that children are persons, but not 'full ones.'" This conception concurs with Schapiro's neo-Kantian approach: "[L]ike nonhuman animals, children are objects, but not full subjects of duties."[22] But what happens to the child once we are no longer content to think of any human subject as "full" or when the opposition between an object and a subject begins to take on water? What happens, I want to ask, to the figure and function of the "wild child" when the confident distinction between the human and the animal, or between "reason" and "nature" (distinctions that the humanist child has been used to reinforce and that, in turn, have helped to define "the child"), begins to dissolve? In a recent memoir and work of critical theory about subject formation, love, and queer kinship, Maggie Nelson (here citing Adam Phillips) writes, "When all the mythologies have been set aside, we can see that children or no children, *the joke of evolution is that it is a teleology without a point, that we, like all animals, are a project that issues in nothing.*"[23] This study will ask, What does the posthumanist (or deconstructive) child look like, and what kind of ideological or aesthetic work does he or she do in a late-patriarchal moment of profound ecological, ethical, and reproductive uncertainty?

Reproduction and Ethical Relation

"The fact itself, of causing the existence of a human being," writes John Stuart Mill in *On Liberty* (1859), "is one of the most responsible actions in the range of human life. To undertake this responsibility—to bestow a life which may be either a curse or a blessing—unless the being on whom it is to be bestowed will have at least the ordinary chances of a desirable existence, is a crime against that being."[24] Mill's comment belongs to the early stages of a historical moment in which the child begins to be reconceived as, in the words of historian Viviana Zelizer, "priceless."[25] Between the 1870s and the 1930s, Zelizer explains, a "profound transformation" took place "in the economic and sentimental value of children."[26] "By the 1930s," she continues, "lower-class children [in the United States] joined their middle-class counterparts in a new nonproductive world of childhood, a world in which the sanctity and emotional value of a child made child labor taboo." To profit from the labor of children, Zelizer quotes Felix Adler as saying, "was 'to touch profanely a sacred thing.'"[27] As we shall see, this particular version of the "sacred" child continues to overlap with the humanist "wild child" in all sorts of more or less disturbing ways in our preapocalyptic moment. "Slumping along. Filthy, ragged, hopeless," writes Cormac McCarthy in *The Road*. "He'd stop and lean on the cart and the boy would go on and then stop and look back and he would raise his weeping eyes and see him standing there in the road looking back at him from some unimaginable future, glowing in that waste like a tabernacle."[28] McCarthy's out-of-joint child inhabits the border between a desperate Christian idealization and what the present study will refer to as a posthumanist wildness that the father (and the patriarchy he represents) has difficulty even imagining. In the chapters that follow, I want to try to think through the myriad ways in which technological, political, and ethical transformations in the way we think about reproduction and about the relationship between parents and children are being allegorized by contemporary narrative fiction.

If Mill's comments appear at the opening of the modern Euro-American era of the "priceless" child, the authors studied in *Wild Child* try to capture something of the crisis generated by the late twentieth- and early twenty-first-century reconfiguration of that era's guiding presumptions.[29] A widespread but far from universal expansion of reproductive choice over the last thirty years has been accompanied by rapid changes in the technologization and commodification of reproduction.[30] These developments, in turn, have exposed an increasing number of people to the complex ethics and politics of reproduction and to the unresolved question of whether or not there is a fundamental or natural right to have a child.[31] In an invaluable feminist history of sexual reproduction in the United States, *Pregnancy and Power*, Rickie Solinger pursues what she calls a "social-problem approach to female fertility."[32] Controlling the reproductive capacity of all women, but particularly poor women and women of color, she explains, has functioned as a symptomatic substitution for attempts to deal with any form of social ill: "Welfare reform legislation in the mid-1990s, for example, was built on the proposition that single pregnancy and motherhood is the chief cause of poverty in the United States."[33] Closer to our own moment, the politics of sexual reproduction and women's rights has been tied, via what Michelle Goldberg calls a "neat trick," "to the spread of Islam."[34] Allan Carlson, organizer of the May 2007 "World Congress of Families IV," for example, has suggested that the Islamic presence in Europe is merely a "symptom": "The [real] problem is that the Europeans have ceased to reproduce themselves, with a couple of exceptions, and have embraced a postmodern post child culture."[35] Goldberg categorizes this narrative of European population decline as a "classically millenarian one, in which Europe, like Sodom and Gomorrah, is destroyed for its sins of secularism and feminism"; but at the same time, she takes note of the fact that "the first world is about to get a lot older" and that this, if not a crisis of biblical proportions, certainly poses quite pressing social and economic questions.[36] The point, for Goldberg, is not to link reproductive choice to a classical account of the dangers of freedom: women do not choose not to replace themselves and not to reproduce the social because they are free to do so, she suggests, but rather because their broader social and economic choices are constrained, and this has resulted in "a kind of birth strike." "Further restricting their choices," Goldberg argues, "isn't just morally wrong—it's demographically counterproductive."[37]

Some of the ways in which reproductive choice has been ostensibly expanded mean, moreover, that it is no longer even as clear as it may once have been whether simply "causing the existence of a human being," to use Mill's phrase, makes one a parent. In 1988, the New York State Task Force on Life and Law suggested that "[a]t stake in the debate [on surrogacy] is nothing less than the psychological, social and legal content of the terms 'mother,' 'father,' and 'parent.' Surrogate parenting . . . challenges society to assess the process by which parenthood is recognized."[38] A posthumanist response to this transformation recognizes not only the need for new ways of thinking about parental responsibility and social reproduction but also that these transformations will have material as well as philosophical effects on what constitutes a child or what defines childhood. Donna Haraway registers something of the uncertainty as well as the utopian possibility generated by new reproductive practices when she articulates a "desire . . . not for a supposed natural mother over and against a violating father, but for a new world order in which women, men, and children can be linked in signifying chains that articulate the situated semiotic and material terms of reproductive freedom."[39]

Contemporary fictional representations of children and their adult caretakers register the changes that are taking place in the realm of reproduction in allegorical or otherwise displaced narratives of intense danger and almost unbearable ethical struggle. In this sense, these fictions also resonate, albeit hyperbolically, with everyday crises of reproductive decision making and parental responsibility. The new and perhaps not-so-normal parenting of the last quarter of the twentieth century and into the twenty-first has a certain panicked intensity about it (this is the era of "tiger mothers" and "helicopter parents") that has as much to do with the commodification of reproduction as with the child's dwindling capacity to signify a space immune to capitalization.[40] "Eternal vigilance about children," writes Paula Fass, "appears to have become the dominant western fixation."[41] *All Joy and No Fun* is the title of journalist Jennifer Senior's recent work on "the paradox of

modern parenthood." As Senior herself notes, this distinctive affect is itself
a kind of by-product of choice:

> Because so many of us are now avid volunteers for a project in which we were
> all once dutiful conscripts, we have heightened expectations of what children
> will do for us, regarding them as sources of existential fulfillment rather than
> as ordinary parts of our lives. . . . As the developmental psychologist Jerome
> Kagan has written, so much meticulous family planning "inevitably endows
> the infant with a significance considerably greater than prevailed when par-
> ents had a half-dozen children, some at inauspicious times."[42]

This new "significance" of the individual child translates, too, into an intensified sense of parental responsibility. This is how biotechnologist (and
father of an IVF baby) Andrew Hessel puts it in the documentary *Future
Baby*: "The fact that we have to take full responsibility now for the offspring
we produce, or maybe not full responsibility but greater and greater responsibility for the offspring we produce, is a very new way of thinking. Before,
it was much more random, much more chance, and if you got lucky and
had a perfectly wonderful healthy baby, great. Now, why gamble?"[43] But are
parents responsible for all that they transmit to their children? In the same
documentary, sociologist Barbara Katz Rothman suggests that this impossible ethical demand might be one of the collateral effects of ART:

> OK, the only thing that you actually know for one hundred percent certain
> about a baby that you are bringing into the world is that it will die. It's the only
> given. Everything else, there is a lot of wild chance involved. So the one thing
> you really don't want to have happen is the only thing that is going to happen.
> And then we present it as if you have so much control. And you choose which
> risks are acceptable. But you can't do zero risk, it's not an option. I honestly
> don't know how anybody would ever have the nerve to give birth to anybody,
> ever, if they could know all the things they are at risk for. . . . So the notion that
> somehow the burden of responsibility shifts to the person making the choice,
> and the language of choice [with new reproductive technologies and genetic
> screening, etc.] . . . so it's not like you are actually choosing the kind of child
> you want to raise, but you are responsible for any condition you didn't screen
> out, so, like I said, I don't see how anybody would have the nerve to bring any-
> body into the world.

What Rothman describes in terms of a shifting burden of parental responsibility is taking place even as we remain unsure about the relationship between reproduction and the rights of children.[44] In 1980, Joel Feinberg wrote of "the child's right to an open future," but exactly what kind of rights might this involve?[45] Is "protection" a right? Does a child have a right to be parented? Does a child have a right not to have been? What does a child have a right to know (about how, for example, he or she came to be)? If there are far more questions like this imposing themselves upon us now, it is not only because of feminist and queer attempts to critique and rearticulate theories of kinship, belonging, and family; in the United States and beyond, the child and the parent have also been at the center of a whole series of legal changes and cultural shifts that bring their own complicated histories to bear on the current configuration of the family, from anticommunist population panics, to *Roe v. Wade*, to the Hyde Amendment, to gag rules, to their repeal and reinstatement, to the specter of the welfare mother, to the rise of transnational adoption, to environmentalism, and so on.[46] These sociopolitical dynamics have, in turn, spurred and been shaped by developments in a range of contraceptive, imaging, reproductive, and genetic technologies. Advances in the science of ultrasound imaging, as Karen Barad suggests, have had profound effects on both the "subjectivation of the fetus" and the obscuring of the subjectivity of the pregnant "patient."[47] And, for all their fantastic qualities, as Rachel Bowlby notes, new reproductive technologies, from in vitro fertilization to embryo transfer, have "quickly become normalized" even as they have altered "the very 'facts of life' which engender parents as well as children."[48]

In *A Child of One's Own: Parental Stories*, Bowlby offers a fascinating critical reading of the contemporary and historical relationship between parental possibilities and reproductive technology: "Contraception separated sex from procreation . . . reproductive technologies separate procreation from sex. . . . Through IVF, a virgin birth is a real possibility, not a counter-realistic theological dogma."[49] "There has been," Bowlby continues, "a proliferation of new parents or proto-parents through surrogacy and egg or sperm donation." And, whereas the certainties provided by DNA testing may now seem to prove fatherhood to be something more or other than a legal fiction, "simultaneously, motherhood has acquired a new indeterminacy."[50] Bowlby places particular emphasis on IVF procedures and the way in which they have multiplied and hierarchized parental functions. In the old form of surrogacy, the surrogate mother was also the biological mother; now she is more likely to be "merely" the gestational mother, and the egg may or may not come from the mother who intends to become the child's parent and legal guardian.[51] And, of course, there may not be a mother at all. Bowlby writes, "One effect of the increasing normalization of gay parenthood has been to make arguments against new reproductive arrangements, including surrogacy, come to appear conservative; previously it was the other way round, with the technologies figuring as an extension of the patriarchal control of women."[52] Bowlby looks at the United States, where both surrogate mothers and egg donors can be paid, with egg donors receiving greater compensation: "A new kind of class division follows, with surrogates typically being women who are currently raising children of their own, while egg donors might be young women in college whose debts will be greatly reduced by the payment of the fee which their top-level eggs can command."[53] IVF also complicates how we think about prepersonhood and preparenthood. How, for example, are we to think about the status of frozen embryos, or so-called "snowflake" babies?[54] "This strange population," Bowlby writes, "is not about to take over the earth or rise in rebellion to protest at its inhuman treatment; but its presence disturbs."[55] If we have become somewhat used to arguments and questions regarding the rights of the fetus, now we must contemplate the "rights" of the embryo in its isolation from the maternal body. But to take such ideas on board is also to entertain posthumanist suspicions concerning what Karen Barad calls the "alleged spatial, ontological, and epistemological distinction that sets humans apart."[56] That is to say, these and other innovations in the realm of reproductive technology find their philosophical counterparts in various "posthumanist" accounts of "agentive" matter that is both "produced and productive, generated and generative."[57]

Turning to recent works of North American fiction, Wild Child asks how the particular narrative structures in which children are located register contemporary anxiety about postpatriarchal parental responsibility and about a posthumanist ethics of reproduction. How do these narratives figure some of the disruptive and disorienting transformations in our sense of what it means to "decide" on reproduction or to "choose" a child? How does this intensification of reproductive choice provoke a new understanding of what it means to be called into being by the other? And how might the child of this new culture of choice, like the child of international human rights

theory or of an intensified discourse of parental protection, inform a psychoanalytic and deconstructive approach to questions of ethical relation and
social reproduction at the beginning of the twenty-first century?

Wild Child engages with the ethics and politics of reproductive change
by following and interrogating narratives that depict adults and children in
extreme scenarios—adults and children at the social limit or on the edge
of disaster. Parental narratives, organized around the frighteningly intense
relationship between an adult and a child, have, to an increasing extent, displaced marriage plots in North American fiction and have become one of
the dominant forms in which novelists and film and television writers theorize personal and social relations.[58] Specifically, as I hope to show, both novelists and filmmakers have turned to the parent–child narrative in order to
register and process the promise and anxiety of a posthumanist future. The
fictional children I think about in the chapters that follow serve as the textual point around which adult anxieties concerning the ethics of reproduction and relation, the relationship between the human and the nonhuman,
and the future of and for humanity repeatedly circle. Hence, these children
sometimes function as symptoms of a new sense of ethical crisis and existential fear in the face of an uncertain future. But they often also belong
to (or gesture toward) a future that no longer confirms or conforms to the
confidence of patriarchal humanism. The posthumanist wild child, whose
function in selected narratives from the first decade of the twenty-first century I want to consider, figures or personifies the philosophical wildness of
a human being (and a being-in-relation) to come—but not of the future in a
teleological, modernizing sense. This new kind of wild child is, to a more or
less explicit extent, a child of the border between a liberal-humanist "world"
that might be coming to an end (a world that usually imagines itself doing so
in apocalyptic terms—as *the end of the* world) and a posthumanist, democratic future that not only might, in a certain way, come back to us from
what we had always figured was an evolutionary or historical past, but also
might not even arrive as a "world" in the sense in which we have often relied
on that concept.[59]

As will become clear in chapter 2, on McCarthy's *The Road,* the wild child
also presents as a kind of alternative to Lee Edelman's infamous "Child" as
"guarantor of futurity, a fantasy figure produced as the promise of secular
temporal closure intended to restore an imaginary past in a future endlessly
deferred."[60] Who, after all, is so sure about the future? At this moment, it can

feel as if only the end is reproducible, as with every new day comes a new fantastic apocalyptic scenario. But what if that future were something other than the past deceptively repackaged and regifted (something other than Edelman's future as "no future")?[61] Andrew Solomon's *Far from the Tree*, for example, risks embracing the "strangeness" of the child as part of a powerful attempt to render legible the work of thinking sexual and social reproduction together. Solomon describes parent–child relations in terms of horizontal and vertical bonds, where "vertical" names those aspects of identity transmitted from one generation to the next and "horizontal" refers to either inherent or acquired traits that mark a child's distinction from his or her parents and become the basis for an "identity." "Parenthood," Solomon writes, "abruptly catapults us into a permanent relationship with a stranger, and the more alien the stranger, the stronger the whiff of negativity. . . . There is no such thing as reproduction. . . . [O]ur children are not us."[62] Solomon's work addresses "our" desire for precisely what we must fail to desire, namely, a future that is beyond our own narcissistic projections. The wild child of this study is concerned with the ethics of precisely such precarious forms of relation and responsibility.

The "Child" that Edelman abhors is, of course, anything but strange, anything but queer: "For the cult of the Child permits no shrines to the queerness of boys and girls, since queerness, for contemporary culture at large . . . is understood as bringing children and childhood to an end."[63] Indeed, queerness and the child function as oppositional terms within the discourse Edelman analyzes, the child being the fetishized site of condensation or "imaginary totalization" that both blocks and conjures up queer negativity. So, is the "wild child" "queer"? Although the study that follows does not set out to be a work of queer theory, I would suggest that the wild child and the queer child are compatible enough to get along, and indeed that the project undertaken here bears a familial resemblance to queer work on the figure of the child. In *The Queer Child; or, Growing Sideways in the Twentieth Century*, for example, Kathryn Bond Stockton takes on "the century of the child" and offers an alternative to heteronormative developmental fictions with their accompanying theories, temporal imperatives, and other general armature. If "Edelman would like to smash this social order and, along with it, the child," Stockton suggests another mode of operation. "One could explore the elegant, unruly contours of growing that don't bespeak continuance," she writes. "I coin the term 'sideways growth' to refer to something related but not reducible to the death drive; something that locates energy, pleasure, vitality, and (e)motion in the back-and-forth of connections and extensions that are not reproductive."[64]

Stockton's queer children do not have to be conjured out of thin air, nor do they constitute an inaccessible futurity. Instead, they have a long history of sorts, a history (with a small *h*) that is inseparable from fiction broadly conceived. "The silences surrounding the queerness of children happen to be broken—loquaciously broken and broken almost only—by fictional forms," she explains. "I present this history of these queer children as a matter of fiction since this history has not taken shape in public ways outside fiction. Literally, these children—the ones I know from life and the ones I know from reading—lead fictional lives. I can only think beside the terms of History."[65] Although Stockton invokes the gay child and specifically that child's "backward birth"—meaning that a gay childhood can exist only after the fact, as a that-which-will-have-been, producing an "asynchronous self-relation" for the child who already feels queer—this "ghostly gay child" is one of a series of types of queerness that Stockton proposes are "braided" together and that can be disentangled only analytically: "the child queered by innocence, the child queered by color, the child queered by Freud, and the grown 'homosexual' typified by 'arrested development' and often rendered as a child (or animal)."[66] As Kenneth Kidd suggests in "Queer Theory's Child and Children's Literature Studies," Stockton offers "a queer theory of childhood as much as a theory of queer childhood."[67]

But if contemporary critics are rightfully wary of the sentimental, idealized, or essentialized child that anchors heteronormativity (if ever there were an effect posing as an origin by posing as an effect!), such a child, as this study will argue, has also been invoked to help secure the very idea of the human—the human of orthodox human rights theory and of much neo-Kantian philosophy. Human rights lawyer Jacqueline Bhabha, in a compelling essay on the figure of the child in international human rights discourse, proposes that "[w]e assume a purity and innocence in childhood that contrasts with the lack of those attributes in adulthood, as if childhood reassuringly guarded this aspect of humanness from the compromised, complex, materialistic environment in which adult life is increasingly played out."[68] The hegemonic "child," in other words, functions not to protect the child so much as to protect a set of Enlightenment ideals; the child, much like the animal, works to save the adult from him- or herself. The child, we might say, authorizes the adult to protect the child, who in turn protects the adult: "He knew only that the child was his warrant. He said: If he is not the word of God God never spoke."[69]

The wild child in this study may be inseparable from an intensive parental investment, but this intensity betrays, I suggest, a profound anxiety about the groundlessness of reproduction. Philip Roth offers a powerful fictional registration of one form of this reproductive anxiety in *American Pastoral* (1997). The novel's wayward daughter is responsible for a "speech act," the bombing of a post office and local store in rural New Jersey, that explodes the coherent dream of seamless Americanization and patrilineal descent and that leaves her father in ruins: "The disruption of the anticipated American future that was simply to have unrolled out of the solid American past. . . . The loss of the daughter, the fourth American generation, a daughter on the run who was to have been the perfected image of himself as he had been the perfected image of his father and his father the perfected image of his father's father. . . . [T]he angry rebarbative spitting-out daughter with no interest whatever in being the next successful Levov."[70] The posthumanist child, the child of a radical exposure to reproductive choice and decision, refuses to confirm liberal fantasies of contractual or consensual reciprocity and instead forces us to consider the constitutive desire of the other at play in every possibility of being or relation. The posthumanist child receives the gift of life as a gift of death and looks back at us not from the conceptual space of fantasmatic immortality but from the wilderness of what Jacques Derrida calls "survival."[71] This is the child as disoriented recipient of a flawed patriarchal gift, hesitating between omnipotence and disaster, so poignantly imagined in Spike Jonze's *Where the Wild Things Are*.

Love and Destruction in the Kingdom of the Wild Things

Jonze's film, based on a screenplay cowritten by Jonze and Dave Eggers, is a wildly imaginative extension of Maurice Sendak's famous and markedly Freudian book of 1963. The film was made with Sendak's approval, although the author hesitated over the manner in which Jonze's Max was shown to gain entry into the world of the wild things.[72] In Sendak's book, Max is sent to his room and the room itself transforms into the outside world, much to Max's mischievous delight: "That very night in Max's room a forest grew and grew—and grew until his ceiling hung with vines and the walls became the world all around."[73] In Jonze's version, Max runs away from his home and into the world of the wild things, worrying his mother, whose anxiety will not be relieved until Max returns and she can fall asleep. The spatial departure from the home in Jonze's film is important, I would suggest, because it marks a psychoanalytic shift of emphasis away from the internal and libidinal dynamics of the child's psyche and toward an embrace of what the present study will identify as a post-Freudian (Winnicottian, Benjaminian, and Laplanchean) emphasis on relational psychoanalysis, or on the priority of the other; as Winnicott would remind us, "There is no such thing as an infant."[74]

Jonze's Max (played by Max Records) is eight years old and lives with his exhausted mother and older sister; his father is no longer in the everyday picture. But if we don't encounter the father, we do see his gift and feel his absence. There is a globe in Max's room complete with a plaque that reads, "To Max / Owner of this World / love Dad." This gift is juxtaposed with a lesson Max's elementary schoolteacher delivers on the inevitable death of the solar system, a lesson that stays with Max and that he passes on to Carol, the father figure among the wild things he encounters:

> MAX: Did you know the sun was gonna die?
> CAROL: What?
> Carol looks up at the sun for a moment.
> CAROL (cont'd): I never heard that. (beat) Oh, come on. That can't happen.
> You're the king. And look at me. I'm big. How could guys like us worry about a tiny little thing like the sun?
> Carol looks up at the sun again, wondering.

Carol, in turn, shares his anxiety about annihilation with his fellow wild things. "K.W. is gone for good," Carol rages, "and now I have to worry if the sun is going to die."

Jonze's *Where the Wild Things Are*, in other words, portrays Max as the child of a distinctly doubled patriarchal inheritance: Max is promised the ownership and mastery that a certain father might (once) have been expected to pass on to his son, but he is also the subject of a lesson on astronomical catastrophe; this is the gift of death as an encounter with the hyperobject, as Timothy Morton might say.[75] Taken together, these gifts seem to present Max with both a frightening (patriarchal) power and a terrifying finitude, a state of indeterminacy and liminality that also materializes as the land where the wild things are.

One evening, when Max's mother (Catherine Keener) is having her new romantic partner (Mark Ruffalo) over for dinner, Max, dressed in his wolf suit, "displays": he stands on the kitchen counter shouting, "Woman, where's my supper?" and "I'll eat you up!" After a brief scuffle, Max bites his mother, who tells him he is "out of control!" Max later repeats this line to Carol, and the film's two "worlds" are indeed linked by numerous such repetitions. Max runs out into the night, finds a boat, and journeys to the land of the wild things (voiced incomparably by Lauren Ambrose, Chris Cooper, James Gandolfini, Catherine O'Hara, Forest Whitaker, and Paul Dano). He undertakes a series of adventures with them and passes himself off as their new king, only, in the end, to be found out:

CAROL: You're a terrible king.
DOUGLAS: Carol!
CAROL: What?!
DOUGLAS: He's not our king.
CAROL: What? Don't say that! How could you say that? How dare you say that?
DOUGLAS: There's no such thing as a king.
CAROL: Don't you say that.

As the film concludes, Max returns to his mother and eats his soup and cake as she falls asleep. This is the film's equivalent—with certain crucial differences—of the powerful end of Sendak's work, when Max returns to find his supper in his retransformed bedroom: "[B]ut Max stepped into his private boat and waved good-bye and sailed back over a year and in and out of weeks and through a day and into the night of his very own room where he found his supper waiting for him and it was still hot."[76] To anticipate a Winnicottian concept that I will deploy at other points in this study, Max's mother (and, indeed, the world itself) survives his "wild" destruction. ("This is the difficult part of my thesis, at least for me," writes Winnicott. "It is generally understood that the reality principle involves the individual in anger and reactive destruction, but my thesis is that the destruction plays its part in making the reality, placing the object outside the self.")[77]

If posthumanist theory moves beyond questions of subject formation to explore the production of the border between subjectivity and nonsubjectivity, the human and the inhuman, then psychoanalytic theory, I would suggest, shares some of this same terrain: it explores the vulnerability of coming-into-being as a subject, where such "being" is also always illusory, fictional, or enabled by a certain misrecognition. Psychoanalysis, like *Where the Wild Things Are* and many other literary fictions, might be said to allegorize some of posthumanism's larger claims (although allegories are complex structures and it can often be hard to decide what they "say" as opposed to what they "disavow"). With that in mind, I'd like to say a little more here about some of the ways in which the chapters to follow will incorporate a psychoanalytic approach to the parent–child relation before returning to the particular way in which such insights might resonate with aspects of Jonze's *Where the Wild Things Are*.

The two psychoanalytic theorists who will be privileged in this study are the English object-relations theorist D. W. Winnicott (1896–1971) and the French post-Lacanian analyst Jean Laplanche (1924–2012). What they have in common and what makes them theorists of the ethical as well as psychoanalytic thinkers and practitioners is their emphasis on an irreducible relationality. For Winnicott, this means that "[t]here is no such thing as a baby—meaning that if you set out to describe a baby, you will find that you are describing a *baby and someone*. A baby cannot exist alone but is essentially part of a relationship."[78] For Laplanche, this relationality involves rethinking the historical peculiarity not only of the Oedipus complex but of any existing and privileged form of mother–child relationship, for that, too, is "changing very quickly." "Without wishing to look too far into the future," Laplanche wrote in 1987, "it should be recalled that more and more children are being brought into the world by artificial means." Although, for valid reasons, psychoanalysis does not tend to be thought of as a historicist discourse, this is not the same thing as saying that it is ahistorical. Here, for example, Laplanche argues against the pretensions of certain historically specific formations to universality. For Laplanche, the "*primal situation* [and thus the starting place for psychoanalytic thought] is one in which a new-born child, an infant in the etymological sense of the word (*in-fans*: speechless) is confronted with the adult world," and this situation may take many different familial or sociological forms. "After all," Laplanche writes, "what will remain of the classic Oedipal triangle—not triangulation—in a few decades, or a few hundred years? Is anyone prepared to bet on the survival of the Oedipus on which Freud bases his arguments? Is anyone prepared to claim that human beings will cease to be human beings if it does not survive?"[79]

At the same time, both Winnicott and Laplanche could be said to anticipate or participate in a poststructuralist or posthumanist rethinking of the ethical: if relation is irreducible, in other words, it is also, as idealized communication between two subjects, impossible. For Winnicott, "destruction" might be said to provide one with a glimpse of the other, but this process is never a secure or final one. And for Laplanche, the subject is seduced into being by an enigmatic and forever untranslatable message from the other: "I speak of the concrete other. I don't speak in Lacanian terms, with a big O or a big A. I speak of the concrete other, each other person, adult person, which has to care for the baby."[80] In anticipation of the literary readings to follow, I want to unpack, briefly, Laplanche's account of seduction and Winnicott's account of aggression and destruction. As psychoanalysts, their accounts are at once developmental and structural, but this is also what makes their insights indispensable for thinking about childhood and for thinking about literary narrative.

One of the more familiar stories about the origins of psychoanalysis concerns Freud's reconceptualization of the etiology of hysteria. At an early stage in his research, Freud "abandoned" the seduction theory and relocated the "wildness" of its origins: its source was no longer to be sought outside of the subject, in the perverse and seductive father, but rather "inside" the subject, as polymorphous perversity, fantasy, and Oedipal desire. But it is precisely this story that Jean Laplanche would question, thereby reidentifying "wildness" not as a condition belonging to the father or the daughter but instead as the name for a primal vulnerability and for the traumatically unbindable and untranslatable excesses of signification and relation (including the relationship between the self and itself as other).[81] Wildness is not a social ill (patriarchal abuse of power), nor is it "sexuality" as a preexisting natural excess to be cured or managed. For Laplanche, psychoanalysis privileges a complex play between external and internal that must also be understood in temporal terms.

From the point of view of the subject coming into being, what comes first is an enigmatic inscription of the other, "a primal seduction," which the infant must attempt to master and translate: "I am, then, using the term *primal seduction* to describe a fundamental situation in which an adult proffers to a child verbal, non-verbal and even behavioural signifiers which are pregnant with unconscious sexual significations. We do not have to look far to find concrete examples of what I call *enigmatic signifiers*."[82] The subject, for Laplanche, is "Copernican," in the sense that he or she revolves around the other's message (or traumatizing, initiating address) but comes to misrecognize/recognize herself or himself in a "Ptolemaic" manner as he or she binds or translates this excess in the very work of self-constitution and self-representation: "[T]he small human being has to cope with this strangeness. And his way of coping with this strangeness is to build an ego."[83] Laplanche adopts (and extends) this astronomical terminology from Freud's own identification of the significance of psychoanalysis as a kind of Copernican revolution. "It is well known," Laplanche writes, "that on several occasions Freud compared the discovery of psychoanalysis to the Copernican revolution, and saw in them two major affronts to human narcissism."[84] The first of these "affronts" calls on us to acknowledge innumerable other human centers of consciousness, but the second invokes distinctly nonhuman othering forces—in posthumanist terms, other "agents"—including a diverse range of materialities, from the materiality of the signifier to the universe of organic and physiological materialities.[85] And if the infant "is bombarded by a range of signifying gestures and behaviours, of pre-linguistic and para-linguistic messages that, over and above their intentions, transmit an exciting but enigmatic meaning and force,"[86] this is not merely because the adult's language is foreign or complex but also because the adult's signification remains enigmatic to him- or herself. The infant will "translate" the adult message and misread it as meaningful address, but there will always be, according to Laplanche, that which is left over or resistant to such a binding process. This "remainder" is repressed and becomes what Laplanche calls the "source-object" of the drive. "Laplanche's 'source-object,'" John Fletcher and Nicholas Ray explain, "is a repressed, internalized fragment, the designified fragment of a signifying object (whether verbal, intonational, behavioural or gestural signifiers), an object that has *become* a source."[87] This untranslated excess, or ineradicable (material) wildness, marks the very intensity of our attachment to others and remains resistant to the calculations and decisions of reason. Laplanche's work, hence, offers us one valuable way to think about the irreducible relationality that has become harder to ignore in our world and for our species.

In 1939, pediatrician-turned-psychoanalyst D. W. Winnicott, along with psychiatrists John Bowlby and Emmanuel Miller, wrote a letter to the *British Medical Journal* explaining the detrimental effects on young children of the evacuation from London and, more specifically, the effects of separation from home and maternal care. This marked a decisive moment in Winnicott's intellectual trajectory, one that would, in its turn, influence the history of psychoanalytic thinking about children. The child targeted by these separations, Winnicott argued, was in the very process of coming into being (not that, for Winnicott, one ever finally arrives at this destination): "Only if someone has her arms round the infant at this time can the I AM moment be endured, or rather, perhaps, risked."[88] Here, Winnicott's concept of "holding" as well as his concern with "primary maternal preoccupation" becomes clear. Only a child whose bits are held together by a peculiarly devoted caregiver (a "mother") will be able to engage in "play"—a kind of "separation without separation"—and ultimately develop a capacity to use and experience the other. "Whatever I say about children and playing," writes Winnicott moreover, "really applies to adults as well."[89] Although it is difficult to account for one Winnicottian term without drawing on several others (the holding environment, the good-enough mother, the transitional object, transitional phenomena, the true and false self, play, and going-on-being, among others), I want to privilege the category of aggression (or primary love or ruthlessness or destruction—all almost interchangeable terms) insofar as this conceptual state can be said to constitute the primal or "wild" condition of the subject—the subject not yet in relation.

At stake in Winnicott's reconsideration of object use is a new appreciation for the importance of "environmental" factors in any account of being, relationality, and development. Winnicott outlines a process whereby what must begin as object relating (a relating that takes for granted a "ruthless" subject-coming-into-being, a good-enough primary environment, and the possibility of play) becomes destruction of the object, survival of the object and, ultimately, object use.[90] The omnipotent or ruthless subject without a capacity for concern is dependent on the good-enough mother so attuned to her infant that she can gradually fail him or her, allowing for the impingement of reality in manageable doses: "The good-enough mother, as I have stated, starts off with an almost complete adaptation to her infant's needs, and as time proceeds she adapts less and less completely, gradually, according to the infant's growing ability to deal with her failure."[91] The good-enough (m)other neither capitulates to every demand of the infant/child nor retaliates. Either route, capitulation or retaliation, would work only to confirm the illusory all-powerful nature of the emergent subject. What Winnicott describes, then, is a distinctive and idiosyncratic process of destruction and survival:

> The subject says to the object: "I destroyed you," and the object is there to receive the communication. From now on the subject says: "Hullo object!" "I destroyed you." "I love you." "You have value for me because of your survival of my destruction of you." "While I am loving you I am all the time destroying you in (unconscious) *fantasy*." Here fantasy begins for the individual. The subject can now *use* the object that has survived. It is important to note that it is not only that the subject destroys the object because the object is placed outside the area of omnipotent control. It is equally significant to state this the other way round and to say that it is the destruction of the object that places the object outside the area of the subject's omnipotent control. In these ways the object develops its own autonomy and life, and (if it survives) contributes-in to the subject, according to its own properties.[92]

Winnicott's account of the passage from object relating to object use suggests passage through certain progressive stages (destruction of the object becomes survival of the object becomes object use). But these steps certainly aren't surmounted once and for all; in fact, what remains and returns between object relating and object use is "an intermediate area of *experiencing* to which inner reality and external life both contribute," an area in which we might locate, among other things, the study of literature or all forms of (intimate) relation.[93] Moreover, destruction, for Winnicott, isn't a *response* to reality (as is Freudian aggression); destruction *produces* the very possibility of reality for the subject. "This," comments Winnicott, "involves a rewriting of the theory of the roots of aggression. . . . [T]he assumption is always there, in orthodox theory, that aggression is reactive to the encounter with the reality principle, whereas here it is the destructive drive that creates the quality of externality."[94] Revising both Freud and Melanie Klein, Winnicott suggests that destruction, or the death drive, isn't, in any privileged sense, an inborn aggression. "It is not necessary to give inborn aggression more than that which is its due in company with everything else that is inborn," Winnicott writes. "Undoubtedly inborn aggression must be variable in a quantitative sense in the same way that everything else that is inherited is variable as between individuals."[95] Hence, Winnicott usefully distinguishes destruction from both "annihilation" and "anger." "Annihilation" is more "primitive" and conveys "no hope," whereas "anger" is "sophisticated" and postdates the account of destruction that Winnicott theorizes: "*There is no anger* in the destruction of the object to which I am referring, though there could be said to be joy at the object's survival. From this moment, or arising out of this phase, the object is *in fantasy* always being destroyed."[96] That is to say, Winnicott's notion of "destruction" is closely allied with the present study's deployment of "wildness"—both terms name a force that makes relation and, indeed, futurity possible—even as it also risks, by definition, ontological security and the very continuity of the world.

The concept of Winnicottian destruction, and of the relation between violence and communication more generally, will return elsewhere in this book, as, for example, in my discussion of Lionel Shriver's *We Need to Talk about Kevin*. "There's a consensus," says the husband to the wife in Shriver's novel, "that violence is no way to get your point across."[97] The wife, Eva, and the narrative itself are less certain. When, this novel implicitly asks, is violence meaningless and when is it an act of address, a kind of "primal apostrophe" or "the turning into signifying form as such"?[98] Might not a certain violence also function as the precondition for relation? These questions, provoked by Jonze's film and by some of the other adult–child narratives I will look at in this book, trouble the classically humanist opposition between violence and reason or violence and language, and, as the Afterword will suggest, these questions are also taken up in contemporary narrative accounts of the adoption of a nonhuman animal, usually a chimpanzee, into a human family.

Jonze's *Where the Wild Things Are* also engages explicitly with the violence and enchanted thinking of infantile omnipotence. It deploys a magical vocabulary and portrays various wild-thing modes of conflict resolution and political power ("You know what I say, if you've got a problem, eat it!" remarks Judith). The king of the wild things is he who makes the heads of enemies explode, but he also has the capacity to make everything all right. At Max's "coronation," he is asked mournfully by one of the wild things, "Will you keep out all the sadness?" The wild things are strange grown-ups, and Sendak has said that they were originally inspired by his childhood sense of his adult relatives as peculiar, primitive others: "They're foreigners, lost in

America, without a language. And children who are petrified of them . . . don't understand that these gestures, these twistings of flesh [kissing, hugging, pinching], are meant to be affectionate."[99] As such, they also recall Alice Munro's representation of a six-year-old child's perception of adults (in a story I will return to in chapter 5): "It had to do with my parents. Adults in general but my parents in particular . . . the size, the lumpy shapes, the bloated power. . . . Their big, stiff, dressed-up bodies did not stand between me and sudden death, or any kind of death."[100] Crucially and ambiguously, the film's wild things, in all their strangeness, are both children and adults.[101] Carol is Max *and* his missing father, and Alexander, one of the other wild things, longingly suggests to K.W. (the stand-in for a mother when she intermittently reappears), "You could carry me like a little baby." Where the wild things *are*, that is to say, is on the uncontrollable border between the allegorical and the literal and between the adult and the child.

Max's arrival among the wild things coincides with a disorientation in the community precipitated, it would appear, by K.W.'s friendship with Bob and Terry and by the resultant betrayal of Carol. The Carol–K.W. conflict clearly functions as a displaced version of whatever might have happened between Max's parents, but it also suggests the psychoanalytic story of the child's relationship to the mother's desire as articulated by Freud and, in augmented form, by Lacanian and Kristevan psychoanalysis (see chapter 3, on Toni Morrison's *A Mercy*). One is sad, such accounts suggest, because one isn't all for the mother, one doesn't entirely complete her and satisfy her desire; but one is also sad because this incompletion coincides with a sense of having been insufficiently called into being. "You summoned me into being," says the child, "and now you refuse to entirely justify my existence by recognizing and wanting me with every cell in your body!" In a striking and highly coded scene, Max flees from Carol's rage and hides inside K.W. (he crawls into her mouth and down into her interior). The scene inevitably recalls myths or fairy tales in which the mother protects the child from the father by hiding the child in the womb, and in which the child subsequently needs to be reborn. But, as Otto Rank long ago suggested, these stories also register a "trauma of birth" more fundamental than the Freudian accounts of either Oedipal desire or castration anxiety: "I noticed that in the end-phase of the analysis the healing process was quite regularly represented by the Unconscious in the typical birth symbolism. . . . The analysis finally turns out to be a belated accomplishment of the incompleted mastery of the birth trauma."[102] The crisis for the child, in other words, isn't the trauma of sexual difference-as-lack, as a certain trajectory of psychoanalytic thought would maintain, but the trauma of being, the catastrophe of being-separated and being-mortal. No kidding![103]

As such a crisis narrative, *Where the Wild Things Are* bears comparison with another text that I will consider in more detail in chapter 2, namely, Cormac McCarthy's enormously influential 2006 novel, *The Road*. Here again, the world a father gives to his son is barely distinguishable from the end of the world, and the world in which the child has to survive is made up of those who might eat others and those who don't—those who are "good guys" and those who aren't ("No, no. I can't be a bad guy," says Max in *Where the Wild Things Are*. "I'm the King. I'm a good guy"). In many respects, *The Road* is the "adult" version of Jonze's film. The former gives us a father trying to work through his relationship to his son and to the gift of death, whereas the latter depicts the world from the perspective of a child who is not sure of what he has inherited. Max comes to renounce omnipotence and destructive rage and (like the baby in Alice Munro's "My Mother's Dream") chooses "survival over victory."[104] "You're not really a king, huh? You're just regular. I knew it. I don't even know if there is such a thing as a king who can do all the things you said," says a disappointed but simultaneously resigned Alexander. "He's just a boy pretending to be a wolf pretending to be a king," offers Douglas, in a pronouncement that deserves to be read alongside a range of Western philosophical formulations. ("One understands a philosopher," writes Derrida, "only by heeding closely what he means to demonstrate, and in reality fails to demonstrate, concerning the limit between human and animal.")[105] Max isn't a king, and his father wasn't a king, and he is going to go home to a mother who is vulnerable and who is incapable of providing fantastic and all-encompassing protection. If the posthumanist, postpatriarchal child is a new kind of wild child, as I hope to demonstrate, it is because he or she is at home after the end of "the world," which is also to say, after the end of the patriarchal-humanist "end of the world." This wildness is what McCarthy's dying father encounters as an "alien" strangeness, comparable to a sacred otherness but recognizable, finally, only in the form of a future he cannot command.

Within a contemporary context, then, the notion of "wildness" that this book will repeatedly privilege takes on a new set of associations. Rather than designating the space of exteriority with respect to the civilized, the educated, or the law-abiding, "wildness," as I use the term, will come to designate a space of ethical and ontological undecidability that helps bring beings into relation and that is inseparable from any attempt to render justice or protect the possibility of a future. Wildness names the child's absolute otherness with respect to any version of human being or human relation that has come before, but, as such, the "wild" child also names the very possibility of a future for something like a human being. Wildness is thus another way of referring to the *iterability* of the child (in a Derridean or Baradian sense) and to the opening onto the other that makes relation possible even as it threatens the very possibility of a self that could simply relate to another.

Hence, the present study will emphasize parenting both as a deeply material/discursive production of the other (a form of "posthumanist performativity") and as an encounter with a "maternal ethics" that shares much in common with a feminist posthumanist ethics of relationality. "The very nature of matter," writes Barad, "entails an exposure to the Other. Responsibility is not an obligation that the subject chooses but rather an incarnate relation that precedes the intentionality of consciousness. Responsibility is not a calculation to be performed. It is a relation always already integral to the world's ongoing intra-active becoming and not-becoming. It is an iterative (re)opening up to, an enabling of responsiveness."[106] The wild child is the materialization of a "mad" decision on the being of an other (the decision to reproduce) that undoes complacent accounts of consent and responsibility and offers, instead, the difficult thought of a (maternal) gift of death "[T]he only thing that you actually know for one hundred percent certain about a baby that you are bringing into the world," to recall Barbara Katz Rothman, "is that it will die. It's the only given. Everything else, there is a lot of wild chance involved."

Parenting at the Social Limit

The narratives under consideration in the pages that follow participate in one of two distinct allegories of the parent–child relationship. One responds to the violence of separation and the imposition of the social by defending and sanctifying the parent–child relation. In such scenarios, it can be difficult to tell whether the child is an other at all or whether, instead, it is merely a fantastic narcissistic extension or doubling of the self. Such narratives depict the difficulty of bringing a child into social and relational being (which is also to say linguistic being) as a struggle to the death with overwhelming force or terrifying evil. Such narratives not only participate in late-patriarchal terror at the prospect of its own imminent demise but also register a specifically antidemocratic panic concerning what is vaguely perceived to be the promise of a more egalitarian community to come. As with much contemporary apocalyptic fiction, these narratives of parents (usually fathers) and children allegorize democratization itself as a kind of deathly threat to the sovereign self and his immediate family.

The other kind of narrative I want to look at also allegorizes the violence that can affect a parent–child relationship (by, for example, figuratively invoking the historical violence of slavery or the all too familiar horror of rape and captivity), but it does so while telling stories about the necessary ordeal of separation and loss that every parent–child relationship has to submit to in order to bring being into relation and in order to reproduce the social. These latter narratives describe what I still think is useful to refer to as a maternal ethics, even as the account they give need not apply exclusively to female parents or caregivers. "To describe mothering as a work out of which a distinctive thinking arises, I develop a somewhat eccentric way of identifying 'mothers,'" writes Sara Ruddick. "Briefly, a mother is a person who takes on responsibility for children's lives and for whom providing child care is a significant part of her or his working life. I *mean* 'her or his.' Although most mothers have been and are women, mothering is potentially work for men and women."[107] Both kinds of narrative register the wildness of the parent–child relationship, be it the wildness of a reactionary refusal to give the child up to the social (figured, for example, as the desperate refusal to respect the law or even human rights in the pursuit of protection for one's child) or the wildness of a painful renunciation, an abandonment of the child to the world, or to another world—a giving up of the child to its own relation to language and the social, its own relationship to finitude and hence its own part in whatever world or worlds it may come to belong to or help to construct.

These parent–child narratives are, in turn, also readable as accounts of any subject's vexed encounter with relationality and with the social. In this respect, the child characters we will encounter have a wild relationship to their ostensible parents: they are and are not the simple reproduction of their parents and their parents' world; they are the living site of an encounter with the limits of the social. For those (male) parents who retreat from the social into a utopian world without loss, the child must be protected and kept close at all costs. David Vann offers such a portrait of paternal pathology in his 2010 novella, *Sukkwan Island*. Roy's father, Jim, seeks to (re)invent the social from the ground up by going off with his son into the Alaskan wilderness, even as such a trajectory is ironically borrowed and well worn (and even as Roy does not survive his father's "dream").[108] Such a protected child (sometimes fatally protected) is deployed in an attempt to seal the (patriarchal) individual and to guarantee its immunity from the other. For those parents, however, who are not yet willing to give up on the future or on community, the child becomes the bearer of finitude and a representative of the social per se. The posthumanist child lives on the ever-shifting border between these two models of subjectivity, and it is this theoretical and ontological space that I also want to call the space of the wild child. The posthumanist wild child inhabits a liminal zone between a form of parental protection that would collapse all relationality into the fantastic space of a paternal identification (the space of an idealizing repetition or immortalization without loss or contamination), on the one hand, and a socialization (an entry into language and relation) that might look like abandonment or even a kind of murder, on the other. "I am become wilderness," writes Morrison's protagonist in *A Mercy*, "but I am also Florens. In full. Unforgiven. Unforgiving. No ruth, my love. None. Hear me? Slave. Free. I last."[109] Parenting, in the twenty-first-century works under consideration here, often takes the form of a kind of mad or incalculable commitment to another that bears no relation to reciprocal or contractual models of intersubjective responsibility. Any and every socially oriented ethical code might be suspended in this wild parental moment and suspended in the name of, or for the sake of, a child for whom the parent claims a kind of irresponsible responsibility. "Yeah, it's called being a mother," says *Room*'s Ma—or, rather, as the novel puts it, "Ma nearly snarls it"[110]—but what does it mean, now, to be a mother or a parent? Does the wildness of caregiving consist in practices of absolute protection or in forms of abandonment or abuse ("It is as though parents daily said, '. . . You must try to make out as best you can; in any case you are not entitled to call us to account. We are innocent, we wash our hands of you'")?[111] Is the "wild parent" the one who renounces responsibility for children or causes them to suffer, or the parent who promises a care that he or she will inevitably fail to provide? Perhaps parenting is the art of the broken promise: "I'm right here" are the father's first words to his son in *The Road*. How can the parental narrative *not* be one of failure, even as this "failure" takes on a critical intensity in contemporary narratives? "There is so much I want to do and experience and give to kids. Time going by so quickly, kids growing up so fast. If not now, when? When will we give them largesse and sense of generosity," asks the hapless father and narrator in George Saunders's "The Semplica Girl Diaries."[112] In the narratives I will focus on, child figures are suspended between worlds, in a wilderness of inchoate signification. But they are so suspended, as I have already suggested, because in various more or less poignant ways, these posthumanist children resemble the first beings of a new world.[113] They are born to the world in ways that so many before them were not. That the world these children are poised to inherit is simultaneously figured in so many ways as coming to an end (ecologically, anthropocentrically, theologically) is just to say that these children have every right to be wild: our wilderness is where they will be most at home.

Bound up as they are with intimations of political, ontological, and climatological vulnerability, the narratives I will discuss allegorize the social and the ethical, relation and futurity, via portrayals of adults and children in scenarios of desperate or failed protection. These extreme situations, I will suggest, encode the ethical crisis occasioned by every reproductive decision and every attempt to bring another into relation. The posthumanist child is "born, never asked," to quote Laurie Anderson, and he or she or they bear the traces of a "monstrous" futurity that can always be figured (or misrecognized) as disaster.[114] But this posthumanist child also reminds us of the wildness of relational identity—of the self's constitutive dependence on an other with whom it can coincide only in the dangerously seductive utopia of the maternal (or parental) relationship. "The child does not know to what he/she attaches; yet the infant as well as the child must attach in order to persist in and of itself," writes Judith Butler in *The Psychic Life of Power*.[115] In this respect, American literature has, perhaps, already supplied us with a prototypical wild child, many years ago, in *The Scarlet Letter*'s Pearl. "Day after day," Hawthorne wrote, "[Hester] looked fearfully into the child's expanding nature; ever dreading to detect some dark and wild peculiarity, that should correspond with the guiltiness to which she owed her being."[116] But it is not Hester's guilt that Pearl seems to have inherited so much as the radical irresponsibility of her mother's desire ("[T]he mother's impassioned state had been the medium through which were transmitted to the unborn infant the rays of its moral life") and the revolutionary strain of her unconventionality:

"[Pearl's] nature appeared to possess depth, too, as well as variety; but—or else Hester's fears deceived her—it lacked reference and adaptation to the world into which she was born. The child could not be made amenable to rules."[117] Hester and Pearl anticipate the single-parent and child figures who populate much contemporary fiction, as well as all the many forms of parenthood that resist patriarchal and heteronormative models of the family and reproduction.[118] From our perspective, it is hard not to read the elements of Pearl's complex "wildness" as prophetic precisely insofar as they encode what will become our social normativity in the form of a "beautiful and brilliant . . . disorder; or . . . order peculiar to themselves."[119] It is Pearl, not Hester, after all, who threatens Puritan New England with its own inevitable undoing, even as she could be said to inherit her wildness from her mother's profound ambivalence ("the warfare of Hester's spirit").[120]

The posthumanist wild child belongs to the future—or, rather, to that conceptual space of the "to come" that Derrida suggests does not simply translate into a temporal distance. This child appears at the intersection of a crisis of reproductive decision (Who or what has the right and on what grounds to bring another into being?) and an equally critical deconstructive opening onto the irreducible relationality of being. "The other is prior to the subject," writes Jean Laplanche. "So you don't have to construct it, it first comes to you, as an enigma."[121] For Hawthorne's Pearl, the Laplanchean enigmatic parental message appears in the almost ludicrously tangible form of the letter (*A*) embroidered on her mother's clothing; "'Mother,' said she, 'what does the scarlet letter mean?'" To be fascinated by the material sign is, for Pearl, to be fascinated by the enigma of her own origin ("Pearl's inevitable tendency to hover about the enigma of the scarlet letter seemed an innate quality of her being").[122] But Pearl is also the novel's inscription of a future that emerges out of the quarantined space that her mother is forced to inhabit. Child of a failed and flawed patriarchy, child of the border between the town and the forest, child of allegory and enigma, rogue piece of signification ("It was the scarlet letter in another form; the scarlet letter endowed with life"),[123] Pearl anticipates some of the wild children one encounters in the pages of contemporary fiction.

The children that appear (and, in some cases, disappear) in the narratives under consideration here are surrounded by, if not submerged in, a climate of ethical uncertainty with respect to their very being and with respect to the future that they at once represent and are abandoned to. As an account of a child conceived in rape and raised in captivity, Emma Donoghue's *Room* (2010) depicts a mother–child relationship unfolding in a space of patriarchal violence that is also a space of precarious and terrifying maternal sovereignty. Donoghue's unforgettable child lives the first part of his life in an oddly utopian or prelapsarian space where social norms are suspended, his hair can grow long, and he and his mother are "sometimes naked and sometimes dressed, we never minded."[124] Part of Donoghue's literary achievement here is to have succeeded in depicting the wild side of maternal relation and in depicting the child not as the representative of a sanctified futurity but as a participant in a dangerous seduction. Jack's mother (Ma) protects him and teaches him the names of everything in his world. But this space of idealized relation is also the space of a violent imposition that Ma has to find a way to exit. The hyperbolic violence of Ma and Jack's male captor, Old Nick, conveys a sense of "realist" horror even as it allegorizes the always already perilous status of a full and present mother–child idyll. Jessica Benjamin's articulation of post-Oedipal dynamics and her invocation of a symbolic "thirdness" that does not simply emanate from the father helps us to read Donoghue's Old Nick not just as a figure for the terrifying psychopathological afterlife of patriarchy but also—and this is a necessarily risky procedure—as an allegorical representation of the extravolitional, traumatic, or "wild" aspects of the mother–child relation.

Cormac McCarthy's *The Road* (2006) has quickly become something of a locus classicus for contemporary forms of dystopian or postapocalyptic fiction, but its depiction of life after an unspecified catastrophe is inextricable at every stage from the event of a birth and the work of parenting. Disaster arrives with the child whose "wildness" takes the externalized or projected form of a world-destroying or world-remaking futurity. In the Schreber case, Freud famously theorized the relationship between the end of the world and intense cathexis, moving from Schreber's paranoia to Wagner's *Tristan and Isolde*: "An 'end of the world' based upon other motives is to be found at the climax of the ecstasy of love (cf. Wagner's *Tristan und Isolde*); in this case it is not the ego but the single love-object which absorbs all the cathexes directed upon the external world."[125] Parental love, as depicted in *The Road* (and other works in this study), has the capacity to be similarly world destroying. As I explain in chapter 2, *The Road* is also an intense depiction of a late-patriarchal father's confrontation with his own personal and ideological finitude and with the ethical implications of reproduction in the face of planetary and personal death. McCarthy's child is sometimes figured as the very opposite of wild; he is sanctified and pure in the midst of a terrifyingly wild, dystopian world. But he is "wild" in the posthumanist sense, I want to suggest, because the future that he is abandoned to, and that will be his "world," is also a postpatriarchal, postapocalyptic future.

Toni Morrison's *A Mercy* (2008) reminds us that in some sense, and for some people, apocalypse has already happened. *A Mercy* extends Morrison's complex engagement with the ethics of reproduction under chattel slavery and depicts a terrifying (and temporally disjointed or suspended) world in which a child's abandonment by her mother also figures the separation that haunts and determines every parental relation. Reading *A Mercy*, I suggest, means bringing its historical specificity (as an account of the beginnings of institutionalized American slavery) into dialogue with contemporary philosophical and psychoanalytic engagements with the ethics of reproduction and relation.[126] *A Mercy*'s ethical or wild space (*wild* is a significant word in Morrison's oeuvre) is Virginia in the seventeenth century, a space of "raw life" that is marked by lawlessness and by an almost universal state of orphanhood ("They were orphans, each and all").[127] But it is the institutionalization of slavery and slave law that produces the wildness that Florens is born into, and it is racist logic that enacts a fantasmatic separation of the wild space of maternal sovereignty from the "ordered" space of juridical white power.[128] Morrison's novel, once again, attempts to combine a narrative account of slavery's violent unfolding with an interrogation into the complex economy of parental responsibility and ethical relation. The traumatized "wild" child, apparently abandoned by her slave mother, is nevertheless exposed to structures of subject formation that remain invisible for, or disavowed by, a racist and hegemonically humanist orthodoxy.

If the fictional child in Lionel Shriver's *We Need to Talk about Kevin* (2003) is also a traumatized child, the novel suggests that his enigmatic condition might have something to do with his mother's struggle with the reproductive decision. Shriver's narrator is a woman who is almost undone by the freedom to choose and by the ethical impasses thrown up by that freedom. Her son's sociopathic violence marks him as a hyperbolically "wild" child, but, read allegorically, *We Need to Talk about Kevin* also addresses all parents' attempts to come to terms with the otherness of their children and dramatizes every child's struggle to come into relational being via a destructive relation to the other which he or she may or may not survive. Eva's original difficulty deciding whether or not to have a child anticipates (and, in this novel, parallels) all the ways in which she is challenged to make a relationship with and for her son and all the ways in which he calls on her to engage in the ongoing and never-guaranteed work of survival. Shriver's novel offers us a magnified account of the forms of violence and failure that haunt intersubjectivity and suggests that relation might be inseparable from a certain philosophical work. "I have had to go backward," Eva concludes in contemplating her responsibility for her son's violence, "to deconstruct," whereas, for Kevin, "progress was deconstruction. He would only begin to plumb his own depths by first finding himself unfathomable."[129]

Both Morrison's *A Mercy* and Donoghue's *Room*, in their own ways, describe a maternal refusal to play into a patriarchal game of sacrifice (the fantasy of an all-justifying and fully realizable paternal promise). There is something antisacrificial, in other words, about a maternal, posthumanist ethics of relation that combines a commitment to social reproduction with a refusal of the fantasy of absolute redemption or protection. The father in McCarthy's *The Road* registers the loss of this fantasy in alternately elegiac and dystopian registers, but Shriver's Kevin is less ambivalent. Kevin's uncertainty regarding the grounds for his being coincides with the collapse of a patriarchal sacrificial economy, and the result is an eruption of destructive nihilism. In Denis Villeneuve's *Prisoners*, however, this crisis in the logic of sacrifice takes a uniquely disturbing turn when a parent finds himself contemplating the sacrifice of one child for another.[130]

The parent who would kill his own child can, of course, be invoked as the figure of absolute power—the father, or *patria potestas*, of Roman law. Curiously, various mothers in this study experience this absolute power precisely because they are abjectly powerless (see *A Mercy* and *Room*).[131] The father in *The Road* cannot kill his son, despite the impending horror, both because he fears this death would be not sacrificial but nihilistic and, strangely, because to kill his son and to kill himself would be the only way for them *not* to be separated, the only way for the man *not* to desert his son. He says, essentially, "I need to desert you, even as I promised never to desert you." (Similarly, in *Room*, Ma will *not* be rolled up with Jack in Rug when he must "play" dead in order to escape their confinement: "'Will you be in Rug too?' I know the answer but I ask just in case.")[132] McCarthy's father cannot kill his son, even as he thinks it is the right thing to do and even as his son wants him to do it. The sacrifice-as-seduction imagined by the father in *The Road* is a sacrifice that would, through a certain violence, preserve the being that has been—the boy in his perfection saved from a life of appalling suffering and degradation. This kind of sacrifice calls to mind the philosopher David Benatar's apparent willingness to preserve humanity (an ethical humanity) by advocating its self-destruction via the choice not to reproduce (an argument I discuss in more detail in chapter 4). But the fiction I look at in this study participates in a widespread uncertainty about what might take the place of this sacrificial logic. In a crucial passage in *Room*, Ma is asked why she didn't sacrifice either Jack or her relationship to Jack by giving him up for adoption ("It would have been a sacrifice, of course," says the television interviewer, "the ultimate sacrifice").[133] And Morrison repeatedly explores the parental sacrifice that can never be read as such by the child ("Beloved" is, after all, the inscription on a tombstone—the title itself registers a materialization that marks the discursive incompletion of every human subject) and yet is preserved in a kind of suspense analogous to the unconscious.[134] This study reads examples of contemporary parents, or would-be parents, who find themselves contemplating the reproduction or sacrifice of life in the absence of any ethical certitude about what it means to choose to bring children into this world, in the wake of a humanist idealization of being that they can no longer rely on.

The plot of Denis Villeneuve's *Prisoners* (2013) revolves around the abduction of a child, but the film is full of lost children, adult children, and adults haunted by their childhoods. The intensity and desperation of the parental desire to protect in Villeneuve's film translates a broader cultural preoccupation with the ethics of reproduction and with a "gift of life" that is always and everywhere also a "gift of death." In *Prisoners*, this ethical crisis takes the hyperbolic form of a father's attempt to save his daughter. This American father would sacrifice anything for his child; he not only would give his own life but would go so far as to torture another human being—indeed, another "child." *Prisoners* (which appears to tell the father's story; it is the only text under consideration in this study in which the child is not really a character but merely a figure) concludes that such a sacrifice is sometimes necessary and that it can "work"—the family can be restored, even the torture victim can be saved from the worst, and the father's decision will turn out to have been the right one. *Prisoners*, on such a viewing, seeks to reassure us about the traumatic ethical ordeal it depicts, and if some sense of unease nevertheless pervades the mis-en-scène (if not the plot), any lingering ethical uncertainty is finally displaced, for the viewer, onto a monstrous maternal figure. Reading this complexly symptomatic post-9/11 narrative alongside a short story from an earlier moment, Alice Munro's "Miles City, Montana" (1985), reveals the extent to which the later text remains traumatized by the responsibilities of reproduction. The protagonists of *Prisoners*, on the one hand, are determined to protect their children (and the children they themselves once were) from their own finitude, but the attempt to do so turns these characters into monsters of one kind or another. Munro's story, on the other hand, opens with a recollection of a "wild" and "free" boy whose death by drowning is brought into relation with the near death of the narrator's own child many years later. The story tries to come to terms with the death of children and the responsibility of parents by revisiting the stages of the narrator's own struggle with autonomy and relation. With its deft telescoping of recent history (the narrator's autobiography coincides with the era of greater reproductive autonomy and marital equality for many women, an era that also introduced new encounters with maternal ambivalence and with the parental "failure" to protect), Munro's story reminds us that the twenty-first-century wild child is also heir to certain late twentieth-century transformations in the structure of the family and in the psychodynamics of parent–child relations.[135] How we continue to imagine the ethical ordeal of parenting—of bringing and being brought, sometimes kicking and screaming, into being and relation—is the subject of the narrative fiction and the critical posthumanist thought that I want to explore in the pages that follow.

1

Is There a Space of Maternal Ethics?

Emma Donoghue's *Room*

The world is in this room.

—Toni Morrison, *Beloved*

"I mean you as in anyone."
Why I am as in anyone?

—Ma and Jack in *Room*

Emma Donoghue's harrowing 2010 novel, *Room*, exposes us to an extended scene of intensive parenting in a world of isolation, terror, and deprivation. A young woman has been abducted and is imprisoned in a well-secured garden shed by a psychopath. She has had a child in captivity. At the beginning of the novel, "Ma" has been confined for seven years; her son, Jack, the novel's narrator, has just turned five. *Room* is a contemporary parent–child narrative that, like the other narratives discussed in *Wild Child*, also invokes a kind of pre- or extrapolitical reality, a space apart (a space, for example, in which a powerless figure might have the power of life and death in relationship to her own child). The world Ma makes for Jack, the world Ma and Jack make *together* away from the world, is also, however, a space of almost utopian richness. For Jack, it is all ("the world is in this room"), and Ma later says of Jack, "He's the world to me."[1] How do we account for this disjunction or, more disturbingly, for this relationship between the hyperbolic masculine violence that produces and the relational idealization that comes to be associated with this extreme isolation?

Genre might provide us with some clues. The academic reader, at the very least, will recognize Donoghue's deployment of motifs taken from the captivity narrative, the gothic novel, and domestic fiction, and indeed *Room* might be said to both use and pass beyond such forms and their gendered histories. Yet I'd argue that *Room* is less focused on the politics of masculine violence in real or generic form—surely everyone can think of a "real" story that Donoghue's narrative reminds them of—and more intimately concerned with questions of ethical relationality.[2] *Room* depicts, in great detail and with striking originality, the story of subjecthood as primarily and profoundly relational or "ethical." In this respect, *Room* deserves to be read in the context of a posthumanist (and, as we shall see, post-Platonic), Levinasian, and feminist philosophical engagement with the question of what it means to be responsible for what we cannot be said to have freely chosen. After introducing just such a context in the first part of this chapter, I will go on to argue that *Room*'s weaning narrative represents the difficult work of substitution and separation—the ongoing work that situates us as social beings and that is one of the central preoccupations of intersubjective psychoanalysis and the work of Jessica Benjamin. I will then turn to consider *Room*'s engagement with the ethics of maternal decision by making more explicit the novel's relation to aspects of the abortion debate (Ma says to Jack, "I'm your mother. . . . That means sometimes I have to choose for both of us" [115]). Whereas some recent writing on abortion has shifted away from the model of rights and personhood to a model of responsibility and relation, I want to consider *Room*'s posthumanist resistance to any version of a solution that might be said to "miss" the ethical. *Room*, this chapter argues, refuses the sacrifice of irreducible relationality, suggesting that the wild child—every child—must take a parent hostage in order for it to come into being. One leaves Donoghue's text, in other words, with an education in the dangerous and difficult proximity between care and violence. *Room* ultimately depicts a departure from Platonic allegory and from the cave of childhood via a maternal gift of death.

Mother as Hostage

It might seem strange to look for insights into ethical relation in a hostage scenario, but not for anyone who has read the work of Emmanuel Levinas. "The responsibility for another, an unlimited responsibility which the strict book-keeping of the free and non-free does not measure, requires subjectivity as an irreplaceable hostage," writes Levinas in *Otherwise Than Being*.[3] The ethical address, according to Levinas, has the force of a trauma precisely because here one encounters oneself as both substitutable (there is no *essential* reason that one is the addressee) and simultaneously irreplaceable. As Thomas Keenan usefully explains,

> Others address me (such as I am) with an appeal that takes me over, and the boundaries that would be those of identity, ego, subject are shattered in this experience: in responsibility, the hostage is first of all not "I" but "*me* that is to say, *here I am for the others* [moi, c'est-a-dire me voici pour les autres]." This "me," in the accusative case, marks first of all the place of the addressee, of the accused, and not of an originary agency, free or determined, or of any prior commitment.[4]

One can't be both "free" *and* responsible, we might say, because one would then be responsible as oneself and therefore, in a sense, only to oneself (to that which does not disrupt an economy of the same). The ethical, as opposed to what I'll call the contractual, relation (or the fantasy of contractual relation) profoundly disrupts selfhood ("boundaries are shattered") even as it might also be said to *give* selfhood in the first place. Indeed, this is what Maurice Blanchot emphasizes or "radicalizes" in his account of Levinas: "It is the other who exposes me to 'unity,' making me believe in an irreplaceable singularity, as if I must not fail him, all the while withdrawing me from what would make me unique: I am not indispensable, in me anyone at all is called by the other, anyone at all as the one who owes him aid. . . . The responsibility with which I am charged is not mine, and makes me no longer myself."[5]

What is being explicated here is not some terrifying and unusual event (although the concept of the event is also indispensable to an understanding of the ethical—ethics as performative) but rather the very conditions for being in relation with another. "We are all taken hostage in this way every day and every night," Keenan reminds us.[6] Similarly, if Levinas invokes the hostage, he also invokes the far more banal "After you" (when passing through a doorway) as an instance of the priority of the other.[7] And we might add our own everyday examples: the child cries, "Mommy," in the supermarket, and almost every woman turns to respond. Such scenes record an instance of the simultaneity of substitutability and irreplaceability; it is urgent that one respond to this call and this "name" that is at once less and more than a "proper" designation.

In fact, Levinas himself used not only a hostage scenario but also maternity as a privileged figure for ethical relation, and, not surprisingly, this gesture has provoked a range of responses from his feminist readers.[8] In "'Like a Maternal Body': Levinas and the Motherhood of Moses," Lisa Guenther does not shy away from certain obvious or difficult problems, even as she offers a particularly compelling feminist reading of Levinas and maternal ethics: "Levinas's own use of maternity as a figure for ethics in general threatens to appropriate one aspect of maternity—its generosity—without acknowledging women's very particular, historical and embodied experience as mothers. . . . How might a feminist reader of Levinas respond to his account of ethical maternity without either accepting this account as the truth about motherhood as such, or overlooking the feminist potential of his work?"[9] Much will turn on Guenther's careful reading of the textual allusion in *Otherwise Than Being,* in which the mother in question is the biblical Moses who cannot believe that he is to be held responsible for such a discontented people. Levinas cites Numbers 11:12 in accounting for the self's responsibility for the other: "In proximity, the absolutely other, the stranger whom I have 'neither conceived nor given birth to,' I already have in my arms, already bear, according to the Biblical formula, 'in my breast as the nurse bears the nurseling.'"[10] A reading of this passage and its corresponding Talmudic commentary allows Guenther to argue that a Levinasian ethics of maternity opens up a crucial gap between being and imitation and suggests that imitation comes first: "[O]ne becomes a mother by becoming *like* a mother; . . . one becomes responsible not by drawing on some innate female capacity, but by imitating in advance of any example the gestures of substitution by which I take the place of an Other who both faces me and exceeds my grasp."[11] Even in Levinas, Guenther argues, the ethical always requires a political supplement: "Given the exposure of the responsible self to violence and persecution—given the possibility of abusing the generosity of Others or being abused oneself—we need a politics of justice that protects both mothers and children from a reification of the ethical asymmetry between self and Other into a social asymmetry between those whose role it is to bear Others and those who enjoy the luxury of being borne, perhaps without even realizing it."[12] Something of the dizzying play of self and self-undoing in Levinasian ethical relation ("substitution") can also be seen at work in Donoghue's *Room*. Consider, for example, the following exchange between Ma and Jack. After their escape from "Room," Ma has to explain to Jack her difficult relationship with her own father, who is revolted by Jack's very existence. Ma says to Jack, "He thinks—he thought I'd be better off without you." Their conversation continues:

"Somewhere else?"
"No, if you'd never been born. Imagine."
I try but I can't [thinks Jack].
"Then would you still be Ma?" [he asks.]
"Well, no, I wouldn't, So it's a really dumb idea." (227)

Jack's demands on Ma are incalculable—almost unbearable—yet he has also given Ma the gift of self. There is, in other words, no return to "before" the moment of traumatic subject formation, and both Ma and Jack know this.[13]

But how are we to account for *Room*'s father/captor/rapist figure? As I suggested earlier, genre gives us some clues. "Old Nick" (Ma and Jack's not-incidental name for their captor) may be the conventional tormentor of gothic fiction, but he is also merely the male provider with a stay-at-home mom for a wife, even if the "home" is an eleven-by-eleven-foot cell. Old Nick is both Satan and Santa Claus, gothic tormentor and provider, bringing gifts ("Sundaytreat") as well as horror. The domestic novel is miniaturized and intensified in *Room*, and a reference to *The Stepford Wives* names this particular zone of indistinction between gothic and domestic fiction (233). *Room* foregrounds, in other words, the way older genres (gothic novel, domestic fiction, captivity narrative) can register, exploit, and protest patriarchal norms of gender construction and relation. Old Nick says to Ma, "Aboveground, natural light, central air, it's a cut above some places, I can tell you. Fresh fruit, toiletries, what have you, click your fingers and it's there. Plenty girls would thank their lucky stars for a setup like this, safe as houses. Specially with the kid—" (69); "You have no idea about the world of today. . . . Six months I've been laid off, and have you had to worry your pretty little head?" (72). Nick is delusional, of course, yet he simultaneously reads and performs what remains (for him at least) an available cultural script—the script of "patriarchal sex right" (or domesticity as "bride capture"). Nick, Ma explains to Jack, thinks that they are *things*, they are his property: "He thinks we're things that belong to him, because Room does" (81); "We're like people in a book, and he won't let anybody read it" (90).[14]

But *Room* also participates in another and perhaps less obvious genre: the postapocalyptic narrative. This aspect of the novel comes with its own account of violence and with the suggestion that Old Nick may himself be a victim. Not insignificantly, this postapocalyptic scenario first appears as Jack's private and perhaps merely half-registered thought. At the beginning of *Room*, Ma uses the word *crater* and explains its meaning to Jack, who narrates:

> "Look," I show her, "there's holes in my cake where the chocolates were till just now."
>
> "Like craters," she says. She puts her fingertip in one.
>
> "What's craters?"
>
> "Holes where something happened. Like a volcano or an explosion or something." (24)

At the very end of the novel, Jack returns to say good-bye to Room and finds that it is craterlike (321), but this figure is also used to account for (and not account for) the "evil" that is Old Nick. Ma explains to Jack that Old Nick looks human but has "nothing inside," no "feeling bit":

> . . . "You know your heart, Jack?"
>
> "*Bam bam.*" I show her on my chest.
>
> "No, but your feeling bit, where you're sad or scared or laughing or stuff?"
>
> That's lower down, I think it's in my tummy.
>
> "Well, he hasn't got one."
>
> "A tummy?"
>
> "A feeling bit," says Ma.
>
> I'm looking at my tummy. "What does he have instead?"
>
> She shrugs. "Just a gap."
>
> Like a crater? But that's a hole where something happened. What happened? (112)

Room's narrative unfolds, according to this reading, in the emptied space left by an event ("something happened") that, like the enigmatic apocalyptic disaster of McCarthy's *The Road* (as we shall see), coincides with the violence and the self-undoing of patriarchy.

Nevertheless, the question of who is holding whom hostage in *Room* is not as obvious as one might expect. For the captivity is not simply confined to Ma's relationship with "Old Nick." *Room* is also a profound meditation on motherhood itself as a hostage crisis. One thinks here of stories of extreme violence, of mothers who kill their children or who are tempted to kill their children out of their own experience of radical subjection and powerlessness (both Adrienne Rich and Sara Ruddick tell such stories).[15] In the more obviously "political" articulation of this nightmare, such mothers are isolated from other adults and lack the necessary supports for the rigorous work of parenting, and *Room* is surely haunted by the history of this patriarchal motherhood (a "history" that may or may not be past). That is to say, it is not only a certain patriarchal experience of motherhood that takes women hostage, because mothers can also be held hostage by the inevitable demands of small children, those wild "subjects-coming-into-being." "Would an 'individual,'" asks Carole Pateman in *The Sexual Contract,* "ever enter into a contract to be a parent?"[16] And with whom would such a contract ever be made? With a "little savage"? With a person "incapable of entering into a contract"? With the social or with humanity? These are some of the questions that contemporary parenthood exposes us to and that the present study pursues through the pages of contemporary fiction. While never losing track of the violence represented by Old Nick's patriarchal presence, *Room* succeeds in conveying something of the threat that motherhood itself poses to Ma's being. Although a certain formal logic dictates that "Ma" is only ever "Ma" (Jack is the narrator of *Room,* and there is only a very limited sense in which we are ever in Ma's head), this formal choice is clearly overdetermined: "Ma" certainly doesn't "choose" motherhood, and she is, as the novel powerfully reminds us, the victim of repeated rape.[17]

Hence, *Room* also asks us to think about the forced or violent aspect of any form of relation. One can choose to *formalize* entering into a relationship (and this is, of course, one reason why marriage ceremonies are significant), but relation is, by definition, extravolitional. And this is where we might begin to read *Room*'s two hostage crises together. The hyperbolic violence of Old Nick's psychopathology (what we might call the afterlife of patriarchy as well as the persistence of a certain generic fictional form) can also be read—and this is a necessarily risky procedure—to represent, or allegorize, the extravolitional and traumatic ("wild") quality of the novel's mother–child relation and of ethical relationality more generally.

Mother as Surviving Other

In *Beyond the Pleasure Principle,* Freud tells a story to explain the emergence of subjectivity and the entrance into the social that takes place when a child learns that he can tolerate his mother's absence. This is all possible because Freud's protosubject has become a subject of representation: he has given up omnipotence for language. The child plays the *fort-da* game and re-presents his mother's absence and her return: "The interpretation of the game then became obvious. It was related to the child's great cultural achievement— the instinctual renunciation (that is, the renunciation of instinctual satisfaction) which he had made in allowing his mother to go away without protesting. He compensated himself for this, as it were, by himself staging the disappearance and return of the objects within his reach."[18] Freud (who is observing a particular child, his own grandson) remarks that this child was intensely attached to his mother, "who had not only fed him herself but had also looked after him without any outside help."[19] Yet this child might also be said to remain inside a certain fantasy of omnipotence. To be inside this fantasy is precisely not to be able to tolerate the mother's absence, an absence that would also mark the child's own radical limitations as a subject. Perhaps the child is just practicing, preparing, playing—he hasn't crossed over from being the tyrannical, egoistic, dependent infant to being the subject of language (and who ever entirely completes this passage?). And, less remarked on, I believe, is how the little subject of the *fort-da* game also practices and represents his own death or absence (even as this must simultaneously evade his capacity as a representing subject). Freud's eighteen-month-old grandson, that is to say, comes up against the very limitations of representation and human being.

In its own way, *Beyond the Pleasure Principle* anticipates Donoghue's weaning narrative about a child, Jack, who comes into being as a social subject by learning to tolerate a degree of separation from his mother. Separate rooms are, in a sense, the telos of the novel, even as they were once Jack's version of hell, and the novel marks Jack's toleration of this separation as always only provisional. Ma has told Jack a very selective story about his origin, one that Jack likes to rehear and repeat:

> ". . . You were all sad until I happened in your tummy."
> "You said it." (3)

Room has been Jack's world, but now his mother begins to "unlie" to him, to teach him about the "outside" so that they can plan their escape. At the beginning of the novel, Jack regularly breastfeeds and talks about it, and at the end we hear him saying good-bye to his mother's breasts:

> "No," says Ma, putting her hand between, "I'm sorry. That's all done. Come here."
> We cuddle hard. Her chest goes *boom boom* in my ear, that's the heart of her.
> I lift up her T-shirt.
> "Jack—"
> I kiss the right and say, "Bye-bye." I kiss the left twice because it was always creamier. Ma holds my head so tight I say, "I can't breathe," and she lets go. (303)[20]

Clearly, weaning in *Room* is traumatic for *both* Jack and Ma, and, for both, as I have suggested, it involves an incalculable loss. Insofar as *Room* is a weaning narrative, it is the story of a child's linguistic, cognitive, psychological, and ethical development, but it is also the story of parenting, of primary caregiving. *Room*, in other words, is not a sentimental manipulation of the figure of a child, and it doesn't give us a version of Lee Edelman's ideological child of "reproductive futurism." In Edelman's provocative and well-known critique, this "reproductive" future is "no future"; instead it is a grandiose and heteropatriarchal repetition of the same.[21] But the relationship to the future in *Room* is very different. In *Room*, we might say, the mother wants a future that her child blocks. In *Room,* Jack wants to escape, but "not really":

> . . . "You said you were going to be my superhero."
> I don't remember saying that.
> "Don't you want to escape?"
> "Yeah. Only not really."
> "Jack!" (113)

And after their "adventure," he wants to go back to Room and to Bed:

> . . . I snuggle against her, I say, "Want to go to Bed."
> "They'll find us somewhere to sleep in a little while."

"No. *Bed.*"

"You mean in Room?" Ma's pulled back, she's staring in my eyes.

"Yeah. I've seen the world and I'm tired now." (155)

In wanting separation from Jack, Ma expresses a desire for a future—for herself and for Jack; but this separation is also a kind of loss and a death. Ma wants, one might say, to be a subject with rights (to depart from the state of nature where she must provide absolute care), but she also wants no separation from Jack and thus no future for anyone. This impossible crisis of desire is represented by the suspense or utopia of *Room*, the timeless time of relation that is its state of exception *and* a kind of call to death. The first section of *Room* is entitled "Presents," and although gifts are important here, surely we are also to hear the temporal significance of this title. Elizabeth Freeman writes of the impossibility of imagining "family" without any technological supplement; she is interested in how the supposedly natural family is produced by photography, video, and so on.[22] But crucially, in *Room* there are no cameras. In fact, Ma's (adoptive) mother says,

"It must be terrible to not have any" . . .

"Any what?" says Ma.

"Pictures of Jack when he was a baby and a toddler," she says. "I mean, just to remember him by."

Ma's face is all blank. "I don't forget a day of it." (299)

The relation between mother and child in its very presentness and fullness is undocumentable, or at least that is the experience or fantasy of this relation (it "will not be televised"). In Room, there are no substitutions, no supplements, no future, no rights. Part of *Room*'s literary achievement, then, is to be able to depict the wild side of maternal relation (what André Green calls "maternal madness")[23] and to depict the child not as the representative of a sanctified futurity in the sense discussed by Edelman, but rather as a participant in a dangerous seduction.[24]

The future will be work for Ma and Jack. Room will have been, for Jack, a kind of prelapsarian space ("In Room we were sometimes naked and sometimes dressed, we never minded" [283]), and for the world beyond Room, he and Ma have a list of things to try when they are braver. The future, as we have seen, means being able to survive separate rooms: as part of an attempt to convince Jack, Ma says, "I read a book at college that said everyone should have a room of their own" (304); but it also means being able to survive substitution and the chaotic promise of a world beyond one's illusory control: "In Room we knowed what everything was called but in the world there's so much, persons don't even know the names" (267). But with its depiction of Ma and Jack, *Room* also explores the set of philosophical and ethical principles that every subject must negotiate; Donoghue's novel is, in other words, a study of "ethics as first philosophy."[25]

To appreciate this aspect of Donoghue's achievement is to follow Jessica Benjamin's attempt to privilege a feminist theory of intersubjectivity as the necessary supplement to the classical Freudian intrapsychic model. The ethical burden of Benjamin's work is to move from thinking in terms of polarized power dynamics ("domination is an alienated form of differentiation")[26] to the possibilities of intersubjectivity ("[T]his focus allows us to grasp how difficult it is—developmentally, clinically and socially—to achieve that felt experience of the Other as a separate yet connected being with whom we are acting reciprocally").[27] Benjamin usefully argues that "splitting" (using a psychoanalytic vocabulary of subject versus object, active versus passive, masculine versus feminine, good versus bad) is characteristic not of the psyche but of one psychic *position*—the position that Melanie Klein referred to as the paranoid-schizoid position, as opposed to the depressive position, and that D. W. Winnicott understood as the omnipotence that must be given up for being-in-relation to emerge. An account of splitting is invaluable for understanding forms of anxiety and defensive organization and their manifestation as both personal and political forms of domination and abjection. But, thankfully, according to Benjamin, this splitting doesn't tell the whole story. Benjamin writes insightfully of Freud's partial vision: "Thus, his categorical oppositions between activity and passivity describe a psychic reality, that of splitting, in which the theory itself participates."[28]

Drawing on a particular aspect of Winnicott's work, Benjamin writes of the "good-enough mother" who orchestrates for an other (or others) the very developmental process that culminates in the possibility of ethical relation. The mother does this by gradually failing her child, gradually being less attuned to his every need and desire. By surviving his destructive—or "wild"—response, this mother figure, then, allows the child to discover that there really is an other beyond his omnipotent control. *"Any subject's primary responsibility to the other subject,"* Benjamin writes, *"is to be her intervening or surviving other.*"[29] "There is somebody, an Other, out there whom I might connect to," exclaims Benjamin's child. "In short," Benjamin goes on, "since the outside can be a source of goodness, it becomes safe and even desirable to go outside. Otherness is not, simply, inherently threatening."[30] I am for the other, in other words, in precisely the way that I *fail* to be for the other (and this is maternal work). Thinking intersubjectively, for Benjamin, also means thinking in terms of what she calls the "third"—the fragile thirdness of intersubjectivity that can, for example, break down and appear in "masquerade" or in "persecutory" form: "In the analytic situation, we are continually confronted with the fear and desire for submission rather than the surrender to the third. In social life, we see the collapse of the third into a simulacrum that demands compliance or offers merger, undifferentiated oneness, between people and leader, leader and ideals."[31]

Benjamin credits the emergence of a discourse of the third to Lacan ("In so far as we remain within the register of analysis," Lacan writes, "we will be obliged to admit an original intersubjectivity"),[32] yet there is a distinctiveness to her own account. First and most crucially, Benjamin's account is post-Oedipal (which is to say, not dependent on a specifically Oedipalized narrative) and is in fact highly motivated by the acknowledgment of non-Oedipal forms of familial configuration. Benjamin writes,

> Unfortunately Lacan's Oedipal view equated the third and the father, equated the difference between twoness and thirdness with the division between a maternal imaginary and a paternal symbolic or law. . . . I have tried to show how the notion of the father as creator of symbolic space denies the recognition and space already present in the dialogue between mother and child. In that notion it is as if the third, the symbolic representation of the father, were the cause rather than the result of symbolic processes, or what I am calling thirdness.[33]

Benjamin credits careful study of caregiver–infant interaction for knowledge concerning the crucial role of "affective accommodation," play, rhythm, and "lawfulness" in establishing a protorelation with thirdness:

> Precisely this early aspect of lawfulness was missed by Oedipal theory, which privileges law as boundary, prohibition, separation. It frequently misses the

element of symmetry or harmony in lawfulness—its musical aspect. Such theorizing fails to grasp the origins of the third in the nascent or primordial experience that has been referred to by such terms as oneness, union, resonance. . . . [T]he semiotics of two collaborating to create a third form the basis for our relation to larger thirds that we constitute as "the law."[34]

Room, I want to argue, helps us to understand mother–child relations in precisely these Benjaminian terms. There is always already a thirdness in the elaborate play that characterizes Ma and Jack's mother–child bond and makes their very survival possible. And this is play in a strong Winnicottian sense, play that occupies a transitional space that "has the paradoxical quality of being [both] invented [as if it came from the "inside"] and discovered [as if it were already there awaiting joint discovery]."[35] Winnicott writes, "The thing about playing is always the precariousness of the interplay of personal psychic reality and the experience of control of actual objects. This is the precariousness of magic itself, magic that arises in intimacy, in a relationship that is being found to be reliable."[36] One of the more compelling aspects of *Room* is the linguistically rich world that Ma makes for Jack, full of all sorts of cognitive, physical, and tactile play (from "word sandwiches" to "phys ed"). "We have thousands of things to do every morning," comments Jack (8). That Donoghue so successfully conveys this is both a narrative feat and a tribute to the creative power of a primary caregiver.[37] One is also struck by the fullness of *Room*, by its presentness, which is also to say (again), by the absence of substitutions. And this condition, while always illusory, effectively captures a certain psychical moment. Room is Room. Bed is Bed. Wardrobe is Wardrobe. Table is Table. Rug is Rug. Toothpaste is Toothpaste. And so on. Many a reader will also notice that this resonates with a certain world of children's television: *Dora* (a crucial intertext in *Room* and not to be confused with Freud's Dora!), *Blue's Clues*, and *Pee-wee's Playhouse* come to mind (as does Freud's *The Uncanny*, with its animation of things). Jack remarks, "I flat the chairs and put them beside Door against Clothes Horse. He always grumbles and says there's no room but there's plenty if he stands up really straight" (8).

It is also in the space of Room, therefore, that Jack begins his education (this is the weaning narrative as bildungsroman). He encounters the primal scene, sexual difference—

"You cutted the cord and I was free," I tell Ma. "Then I turned into a boy."
"Actually, you were a boy already" (4)

—the question of humanness (Jack thinks in relationship to what his mother tells him about Old Nick, "I thought humans were or weren't, I didn't know someone could be a bit human. Then what are his other bits?" [135]), and the distinction between inside and outside (Jack experiences his own interiority and the opacity of the other, and he experiments with secrecy when he decides not to tell his mother about a spider and its web, for fear that she will kill it and brush the web away: "It's weird to have something that's mine-not-Ma's. Everything else is both of ours" [10]). These are all preliminary lessons for Jack in substitution and separation. *Room*, in other words, is both allegorical and subtle, and as such it refuses to endorse an absolute distinction between what characterizes life in Room and life after Room. These spaces are clearly not identical, but neither can they be divided into a space before and after the arrival of a thirdness that, as Benjamin suggests, traditional Oedipal accounts tend to associate with "the law."

Hence, Jack *must* experience days when Ma is "gone," days when she doesn't create the world for him and with him but stays in bed. This, of course, indicates to us something significant about the psychic state of the character in the realist plot, but it also testifies to certain "failures" when it comes to mothering or giving primary care, failures that a child survives and maybe even needs (although, in Winnicott's account, the good-enough mother is always in charge of these failures, managing them). Ma's goneness functions for Jack as a *fort-da* episode or rehearsal for trauma, death, and the entry into a cultural field, and in such instances, *Room* conveys to us Jack's developing and resistant capacity for relationship and insight. He maintains a certain faith, for example, in maternal omniscience ("Ma knows everything except the things she doesn't remember right, or sometimes she says I'm too young for her to explain a thing" [9]), even if her power is indissociable from Jack's fantasy of her power and is linked to her inseparability from Jack. To plan to leave Room, to plan an escape from Room and Old Nick, is to reveal both Jack's and Ma's vulnerability (to Jack), and this, Jack says, is a "bad idea":

"I'm OK," she says, rubbing her cheek, "it's OK. I'm just—I'm a bit scared."
"You can't be scared." I'm nearly shouting. "Bad idea." (92)

While Ma and Jack are still in Room, she loses a painful bad tooth, and Jack claims this object, while also encountering it in all its strangeness: "He ['Tooth'] was part of her a minute ago but now he's not. Just a thing" (70). Jack insists on taking this part of Ma with him when he escapes from Room, and later, when he is separated from her, he sucks on it for comfort. Tooth is a version of Winnicott's transitional object, in that it is "between" Ma and Jack. Winnicott writes, "It is not the object, of course, that is transitional. The object represents the infant's transition from a state of being merged with the mother to a state of being in relation to the mother as something outside and separate. This is often referred to as the point at which the child grows up and out of a narcissistic type of object-relating, but I have refrained from using this language because I am not sure that it is what I mean."[38] Although Jack's object, *unlike* Winnicott's object, "goes inside"—Jack thinks that he has swallowed Tooth and that "maybe he's going to be hiding inside me in a corner forever" (307)—it shares with Winnicott's object the quality of being neither "forgotten" nor "mourned." Winnicott continues: "[Instead] it loses meaning, and this is because the transitional phenomena have become diffused, have become spread out over the whole intermediate territory between 'inner psychic reality' and 'the external world as perceived by two persons in common,' that is to say, over the whole cultural field."[39] It is in this sense that Ma gives Jack the world.[40]

Ma and Jack, as the novel makes clear, are vulnerable to the extent that they are separate and separable from one another and each subject to debilitating limitations. But *Room* also suggests that they are vulnerable to the extent that they are subjects of language; they are each a "somebody" and an "anybody," and Jack has to learn to negotiate the structure of pronouns and, more generally, of substitutability. Ma tells Jack as they plan the escape,

> . . . "You're the one who matters, though. Just you."
> I shake my head till its wobbling because there's no just me. (128)

And immediately upon his departure from Room, Jack thinks, "I'm not in Room. Am I still me?" (138). What we hear when we listen to Jack is not just his development, or his resistance to development, but his insights into the nature of being and relation. His questions, in other words, reveal certain ideological fractures that we all learn to ignore. "Am I meant to forget?" Jack asks when others are surprised later by his memories of Room (210).

While Jack and his mother are still in the hospital (transitioning to life in the outside), the well-intentioned Dr. Clay tries to teach Jack about the fundamental laws of property. A puppet that Jack is playing with belongs to Dr. Clay and so can only be borrowed:

> "Why?"
> "Well, everything in the world belongs to somebody."
> Like my six new toys and my five new books, and Tooth is mine I think because Ma didn't want him anymore." (209)

Dr. Clay presumably thinks better of what he has said and elaborates:

> "Except the things we all share," says Dr. Clay, "like the rivers and the moun-
>   tains."
> "The street?"
> "That's right, we all get to use the streets."
> "I ran on the street."
> "When you were escaping, right."
> "Because we didn't belong to him."
> "That's right." Dr. Clay's smiling. "You know who you belong to, Jack?"
> "Yeah."
> "Yourself."
> He's wrong actually, I belong to Ma. (209)

This brief and almost innocuous conversation, to which I will return, is extremely illuminating, for here Dr. Clay is teaching Jack the ABCs of (Lockean) liberal individualism. He teaches him about property and self-ownership. For this, Dr. Clay knows, is what it means to live in the "outside" or the social, even as Jack's questions and resistance tell another story.

For all that *Room* explores the richness of what Benjamin calls the "semiotics of two collaborating to create a third," the novel is also haunted by a hyperbolic version of the persecutory third, the evil "father." Jack, as we have seen, experiences profound anxiety about the fragility and the threat of "thirdness," as well as about what it means to survive in a state that is provisionally separate from his mother. He cannot, for example, bear the thought of moving the furniture in their little space; such movement is a concretization of the principle of substitution and thereby also endangers the materiality of his linguistic universe: Bed can't be moved to the place where TV is, because "That's TV Wall" (note that the capitals belong to Jack and not to Ma's recorded speech). "That's just what we call it," replies Ma (42). But Jack is not convinced. He also occasionally stutters (revealing fractures in his own experience of self-continuity) and counts in an effort to keep his world together. But the most immediate source of danger is, of course, Old Nick, and thus Jack's anxiety also signifies, on the realist level, as a less-than-conscious response to, or registration of, the trauma that he and his mother survive on a daily basis. Although Ma does her best to keep Jack sheltered from Old Nick, Nick regularly appears at night after Ma has put Jack to bed in Wardrobe. From this concealed space, Jack frequently gets to witness the repetition of the scene of his own origin, as primal scene and rape:

> When Old Nick creaks Bed, I listen and count fives on my fingers, tonight it's 217 creaks. I always have to count till he makes that gaspy sound and stops. I don't know what would happen if I didn't count, because I always do.
> What about the nights when I'm asleep?
> I don't know, maybe Ma does the counting. (37)

And in a quite extraordinary scene of interpretation, Jack registers his father/captor as a rival: "Then I have a terrible idea, what if he's having some [breastfeeding]? Would Ma let him have some or would she say, *No way Jose, that's only for Jack*?" (47). At such moments, the "realist" horror of patriarchal violence coincides powerfully with *Room*'s allegory of the always already perilous status of a full and present mother–child idyll.

Donoghue's novel is quite explicit about the idea that Jack's survival must involve a kind of death (indeed, it is both Jack and Ma who must pass through death—the five sections of the novel are entitled "Presents," "Unlying," "Dying," "After," and "Living"). But *Room* shows us how this death, this precarious process of separation, coincides with the possibility of a less anxious and more complex relationship to the world. And what, we might ask, would happen to the child who *failed* to separate? One is reminded here of the infamous literature on bad mothering, from Leo Kanner's and Bruno Bettelheim's "refrigerator mothers," who provide no love and produce autistic offspring, to Philip Wylie's "Mom," whose "smother love" emasculates her son.[41] What is interesting about these infamous accounts is not their misogyny, plain and simple, so much as the way that they symptomatically make the entire question of being and ethics a question of good and bad mothering. *Room*, on the other hand, takes up these questions (as do Toni Morrison in *A Mercy* and Jessica Benjamin throughout her work) in a more profoundly ethical register. Even so, I would suggest, Donoghue's novel prompts us to think of Old Nick as a kind of monstrous child: Nick is an example of what can go wrong when the child fails to separate!—"No way Jose, that's only for Jack!" Old Nick, or patriarchal masculinity as psychopathology (and that is the equation at work here), would constitute a kind of failure to work through the *fort-da* game that results in holding the mother/ woman/other hostage. Obviously, this has more than isolated psychological consequences. At the end of the novel, Jack addresses Ma:

> "Grandma says there's more of him."
> "What?"
> "Persons like him [Old Nick], in the world."
> "Ah," says Ma.
> "Is it true?"
> "Yeah. But the tricky thing is, there's far more people in the middle."
> "Where?"
> Ma's staring out the window but I don't know at what. "Somewhere between good and bad," she says. "Bits of both stuck together." (316–17)

Maternal Power and the State of Nature

Following Ma and Jack's escape from Room, Ma is interviewed by a TV journalist who tries various forms of provocation, culminating in a question that stops just short of invoking the possibility of infanticide: "When Jack was born—some of our viewers have been wondering whether it ever for a moment occurred to you to . . ." (237). The reporter interrupts herself and asks instead whether Ma ever considered giving Jack up for his own good: "[D]id you ever consider asking your captor to take Jack away? . . . To leave him outside a hospital, say, so he could be adopted. As you yourself were, very happily, I believe. . . . It would have been a sacrifice, of course—the ultimate sacrifice" (237). "The ultimate sacrifice." The only kind of maternal relationship that would not have been a failure, the journalist essentially suggests, would have been killing Jack or giving him up for his own good, precisely refusing the more difficult task of substitution and separation, the ongoing work of what it means to be both dependent and individuated, to belong only to each other *and* to the world.

The journalist's invocation of a certain maternal "sacrifice" recalls the Hobbesean mother's power of life and death—the original form of sovereign power—in the "state of nature": "If there is no contract, the dominion is in the mother. . . . [S]he may either nourish or expose it."[42] But it also, quite specifically, inserts *Room* into the fraught discourse on abortion. I want to approach this aspect of the novel by looking at two distinctive philosophical engagements with the abortion question that, I will argue, evade an encounter with the ethics of intersubjectivity that informs Donoghue's novel. In her classic essay "A Defense of Abortion," Judith Jarvis Thomson argued that a woman has no obligation to continue an unwanted pregnancy, precisely because it is analogous to being held hostage (it should be noted that Thomson deploys the hostage-taking scenario to very different ends from Levinas!). Thomson devises an imaginative scenario whereby you wake up and "find yourself back to back in bed with an unconscious violinist. He has been found to have a fatal kidney ailment and the Society Of Music Lovers has canvassed all the available medical records and found that you alone have the right blood type to help."[43] Thomson argues that, although it might be very nice of you to help out, you are certainly under no obligation: "If anything in the world is true, it is that you do not commit murder, you do not do what is impermissible, if you reach around to your back and unplug yourself from that violinist to save your life."[44] Thomson's case for abortion is based through and through on the notion of consent and on the cordoned-off concepts of "rights" and of individual personhood, concepts that need to be safely separated from any sense of what one "ought" to do: "[T]his," she writes, "is to obscure what we should keep distinct."[45] Thomson's essay concludes by clarifying that "the permissibility of abortion in some cases" is not an argument "to secure the death of an unborn child," since "the desire for the child's death is not one which anybody may gratify, should it turn out to be possible to detach the child alive."[46]

In a more recent engagement, "Abortion, Killing, and Maternal Moral Authority" (2008), Soran Reader makes a radical (and at the same time oddly conservative) case for abortion rights. For Reader, Thomson's liberal proabortion argument, with its particular respect for the rights of the autonomous individual, fails to adequately account for the unique aspects of the mother–child bond. Although prochoice arguments assert that women should not be morally or legally obligated to gestate a fetus (and Reader comments on many such arguments, ranging all the way from those that invoke fetal–maternal relationships experienced as the most intimate form of "dyad," to those which draw on the language of occupier and occupied), they do not show "how women can have a moral right to secure the death of the fetus once it is out of their body."[47] This is exactly Reader's (distressing) goal. Reader, in this sense, picks up immediately where Thomson left off, in order to make the opposing case. Thomson concludes her essay by reminding her reader that she is merely "pretending" that a fetus is a person for the sake of argument *and* by emphasizing that a right to an abortion is precisely *not* a right to the death of an other. But women who seek abortions don't merely want to give up the *fetus*, Reader explains, they want to give up the *relation* ("they want to ensure that there is no being at all in the world to whom they are related as mother to child" [134]), and hence this "moral right" is "vulnerable to developments in medical technology" (that is, improvements in neonatal care) (134). The crux of Reader's argument is that killing actually prevents a far more devastating outcome, for if a fetus might, in Thomson's words, be merely "detached" and yet survive, to be surrendered to the care of others, the mother, according to Reader, would never outlive her failure as a mother, and her child would live the rest of his or her life as unworthy and abandoned! "You can justifiably end your fetus's life," Reader explains, "but you cannot justifiably abandon it. That this seems an extraordinary conclusion underscores how unique motherhood is in human life, and how much we are likely to be misled if we assume moral categories that work between adults will capture the moral realities of person-creation adequately" (144). For Reader, abortion constitutes an early termination of one's responsibility.

There are odd contradictions in Reader's argument, however, that even a brief account should not leave unrecognized. For example, while Reader draws on the importance of technological change, on the one hand, she simultaneously invokes a kind of "normal motherhood" that would seem to be impervious to such developments, on the other: "In normal motherhood, the procreative mother becomes the gestating and birthing mother, who becomes the caring, socializing, and educating mother" (139). And while, on the one hand, Reader gestures toward the "social construction" of maternity, on the other hand, this "construction" is universalized and absolutized to such an extent that its "construction" appears almost irrelevant. Reader writes, "To be a mother in our culture is to be absolutely required to perform these works of person-creation. The power of maternal norms is without peer in our moral life. Immanuel Kant's categorical imperative has nothing on the normativity of the cry of your own needy child" (140). The critical reader (with a small *r*) will wonder whether this absolute responsibility extends to fathers (the answer is no) and whether the mother maintains her right of life and death in relationship to her child beyond the threshold of birth (the answer is, surprisingly, yes): "When circumstances are objectively terrible, when the mother is in a good position epistemically, and when she judges it would be best for the child's life to end, she alone has the authority to determine that this should happen." And, as if sensing that we need some reassurance, Reader adds, "But the moral dangers are not great because the standard for justification of infanticide set by our concept of motherhood is very high" (145).

Reader's extraordinary argument invokes a specifically maternal authority that culminates in what she refers to as "the final protection": "A mother who fails to extend the final protection to her child of killing arguably fails in the hardest of many hard but inalienable maternal duties" (146). Here, Reader (who explicitly invokes Toni Morrison's *Beloved* as well as Hobbes's *Leviathan*) might be said to theorize abortion and the maternal from the perspective of Morrison's Sethe—from the perspective, that is to say, of an enslaved woman, radically exposed and completely bereft of any form of legal protection, abandoned to "the state of nature."[48] And although it is hard not to be distracted by Reader's excessive or fantasmatic mode of identification (she reads every mother as the Hobbesean mother or as Morrison's Sethe, and *not* as the mother in *A Mercy*, who does, as we shall see, "abandon" her child), this is also, it must be said, Reader's *real* argument. This is both how "we" do think the maternal, she suggests (in this respect she is simply teasing out the implications of our conventional thought), and how we *should* think the maternal. The maternal is, in a crucial sense (to be distinguished from the liberal individualist humanist sense), *prior to the social*. The social emerges, in Reader's account, in the very process of birth:

> As soon as it is born, even while it is being born, a child forms relationships with others. These relationships, like motherhood, impose moral duties on the capable relata. . . . The extreme situation in which the mother's moral authority

over the life and death of the child is actualized, then, is by definition one in which no others known to be safe are available to protect the child when the mother cannot do so. . . . [Yet m]others, bearing the awesome responsibility they do, cannot be expected in an instant and under stress to trust their child to the protection of just any volunteer, or the impersonal state. Where there is no known, trusted, safe person available, a mother may well conscientiously judge it right to end her child's life, rather than abandon it to the mercies [see Morrison's *A Mercy*!] of unknown, untested and perhaps unsafe others. (146)

The mother's job, it would seem, is to police the border between the wilderness and the social and to decide whether to relinquish her child, before or after birth; one can kill one's child, in other words, and thereby save it from sociality—save it from the world. To fulfill one's maternal responsibility is to make certain "the fetus [or child] will never be abandoned to the unknown will of others" (143).

Reader explicitly addresses several objections to her argument, including the idea that another concept of motherhood might be "morally preferable" (147). Here, interestingly, the concept of reproductive technologies makes a brief (re)appearance. Reader refers to this as the normalization of "partial mothering": "Some of these possibilities [in vitro conception, surrogacy, adoption, paternal care] are actualized in other cultures, and some have been or will be actualized in our own. But it is far from clear that such changes represent moral progress" (148). Reader stands up instead for the norms of motherhood that have "stood the test of time." She can't imagine a replacement or alteration that would "ensure the protection of new people anywhere near as well as the passionate commitment of mothers has done. . . . It is part of motherhood to love your children and protect them no matter what" (148). Reader's extreme yet fascinating account crosses paths with many of the motifs and concerns that will emerge in subsequent chapters of this book (from the "ethics of abandonment" and the maternal gift of death to the discussion of philosopher David Benatar's *Better Never to Have Been*) and with the various accounts of intensive parenting that I will discuss in more detail; but, despite its definitive severance of mothers from fathers, Reader's account of the maternal sounds surprisingly like the fantasies of absolute *paternal* protection that I will return to in my discussions of McCarthy's *The Road* and Villeneuve's *Prisoners*.

To read Emma Donoghue's *Room* is to encounter a mother who finds herself in the very situation that Reader conjures up. The journalist, in the scene that I touched on at the beginning of this discussion, is unwilling to relinquish her quest for sensation. She says to Ma, "You must feel an almost pathological need—understandably—to stand between your son and the world," and Ma "nearly snarls" in reply: "Yeah, it's called being a mother" (236).[49] But Donoghue's allegory of parenting troubles Reader's approach. Reader imagines a kind of radical maternal responsibility and relation, but she also suggests that one has the right to say no to such relation, and, to this extent, Reader still separates out nonrelation from relation—as if it were a choice. At the same time, Reader imagines that it is possible *not* to abandon a child, a possibility that *Room*, and, indeed, all the narratives in this study, suggests would conflict with a specifically maternal ethics of abandonment. Indeed, insofar as she imagines that one might fulfill one's responsibility as a mother and *not* abandon the child, Reader participates in the fantasmatic invocation of what one can only call maternal omnipotence (or sovereignty). Yet, even as Reader's maternity presents itself as an awesome and truly terrifying responsibility, it nevertheless promises safe exits and solutions—even the possibility of successfully achieving "normal" motherhood and of avoiding having to abandon one's child. One grows out of dependency and relation, Reader finally suggests, and, hence, the relationship between mother and child can be absolutely set apart from any other form of relation.

Two distinct approaches to the abortion question are on display in Reader's and Thomson's essays. By appealing to the concept and language of individual rights, Thomson solves the abortion dilemma in what have become familiar terms, even if they are not without their own strangeness: "There may well be cases in which carrying the child to term requires only Minimally Decent Samaritanism of the mother, and this is a standard we must not fall below."[50] Reader instead privileges the notion of the absolutely vulnerable and dependent "child" and the corresponding figure of the absolutely responsible mother. Reader also suggests that this relationship of absolute vulnerability and responsibility has a temporal dimension: a point comes at which an individual is no longer dependent upon the mother, and thus the relationship comes to an end. Given this relational structure, to abort a fetus is to "complete" one's "responsibility early." "She fulfills her maternal responsibility for her fetus's life," explains Reader, "in such a way that the fetus will never be abandoned to the unknown will of others" (143), that is, never abandoned to the social. For all their differences, then, both Reader and Thomson demonstrate an ethical dependence on the classically humanist conception of the self-contained individual. Thomson's absolutely individuated rights-bearing mother and Reader's figure of the child who has outgrown either dependence on another or the absolutely powerful protecting mother with no relationship to the social, in other words, are fantasmatic figures of isolated self-responsibility and self-right. If abortion presents us with wild demands—with what I want to insist are the ethical demands of relation—then Thomson and Reader both posit isolated being as a (false, magical) solution. They suggest, implicitly, that the answer to the problem of relation is to say that we are not related—because our "rights" radically distinguish us from each other, or because we can choose to not choose relation, or because at a certain age we just stop being reliant on others for our survival. In *Room*, Ma's response to the interviewer's invocation of infanticide or abandonment takes the form of a suicide attempt (a very nonplayful *fort-da*). She is driven to this extreme, I would suggest, by the implication (emanating from the interviewer, who is, in this sense, the voice of the social) that the normative (Christian?) ethical model demands a sacrifice she is not willing or able to make—the sacrifice of being's irreducible relationality. "If we understand maternity in this way," Lisa Guenther writes, "not as a fixed biological or even social identity but as the response to an ethical imperative from the Other, then maternity might become disengaged from a strict biological interpretation without being thereby disincarnated."[51] *Room* stays with us precisely because, in accordance with an ethical itinerary that I want to claim is at once wild and posthumanist, it refuses to give up on this relationality, not for anything under the sun.

Room's Allegory of the Cave

One day, some time after he and Ma have been rescued, Jack catches a few moments of a TV discussion (a somewhat academic discussion, it should be added) on the subject of his own abduction:

> "I would have thought the more relevant archetype here is Perseus—born to a walled-up virgin, set adrift in a wooden box, the victim who returns as hero," says one of the men.

"Of course Kaspar Hauser famously claimed he'd been happy in his dungeon,
    but perhaps he really meant that nineteenth-century German society was
    just a bigger dungeon."
"At least Jack had TV."
Another man laughs. "Culture as a shadow on the wall of Plato's cave."
Grandma comes in and switches it right off, scowling.
"It was about me," I tell her.
"Those guys spent too much time at college." (294)

Despite Grandma's dismissal, those of us who have, perhaps, spent too much
time at college can't help receiving Donoghue's message here. In case we
missed it, *Room* is also a feminist and deconstructive retelling of Plato's
founding fable of Western metaphysics. In fact, it is such a careful and effective retelling that the comparison deserves a closer look.

"Next," writes Plato (speaking as Socrates) in *The Republic*, "think of our
nature in relation to education, and the lack of it, in terms of the following
image."[52] Socrates proceeds to tell Glaucon his allegory of the cave. "Imagine
human beings as if they were in a cave-like dwelling underground. . . . They
have been there since childhood. . . . [D]o you think people in that condition will have seen anything of themselves or of each other except for their
shadows, cast by the fire on to the surface of the cave in front of them?"
(514a, 515a). As one of the TV intellectuals remarks, *Room*'s cave has its own
"shadow on the wall of Plato's cave," in the form of TV, and Dr. Clay, who
oversees Jack's treatment after his release, articulates the standard version of
a modern understanding of enlightenment when he asks Jack about the bees
he has recently seen (and been stung by): "Is it exciting seeing them for real,"
the doctor asks, "not just on TV?" (274). The second half of Donoghue's
novel might, then, be read as an extended contemporary account of "what
will naturally follow," as Socrates puts it, "if the prisoners are released and
disabused of their error" (515c).

Socrates's allegory serves, primarily, to reinforce a fundamental Platonic
notion of the truth as that which escapes the play of representational distor-
tion and remains uncontaminated by iterability. A simple reading of *Room*
might hear only an echo of Plato's lesson. Donoghue would then be thought
to have given new force to Plato's condemnation of pre- or unphilosophi-
cal understanding by personifying its shadows and delusions in the form of

a terrifying kidnapper of women and children. According to this reading, Donoghue's subtle account of the difficulties experienced by Ma and Jack upon escaping Room would translate Plato's account of the "pain" experienced by the cave dwellers upon first confronting the "glare" of the truth. Even as the escapee approaches "closer to the truth of things" and his eye is turned "towards things that more truly are," Plato explains, he will "turn round and try to bolt back in the direction of the things he could see, thinking these really and truly clearer than what was being shown to him" (515d, 515e). Jack and Ma look out the hospital window and see cars and people outside and below them on the street. Jack asks,

> "Are they real for real?"
> "As real as you and me."
> I try to believe but it's hard work. (176)

This would be the Platonic irony of *Room*: that the imprisoned subjects of false appearance at first resist enlightenment and are tempted to want to return to the safety and familiar numbness of their captivity. "I've seen the world," says Jack, "and I'm tired now" (155).

But while *Room* does record the profound ambivalence experienced, particularly by Jack, in the wake of its protagonists' release (Ma's suicide attempt is also, of course, an expression of ambivalence), it nevertheless resists a Platonic ethical conclusion. As such, it helps us to see where Plato's allegory of enlightenment reaches an impasse and substitutes what we could call a patriarchal (or phallogocentric) violence for an ethical ordeal. Upon leaving his captivity, Plato says, the cave dweller first sees only more shadows and reflections:

> First of all, he'd find it easiest to see shadows; next it would be
> Reflections of human beings and everything else in water, then
> the things themselves; and from these he'd move on to the heavenly
> bodies and the heavens themselves, though he'd start by looking at them
> at night, gazing at the light of the stars and the moon, because that would
> be easier than looking at the sun and the sun's light by day. (516a–b)

In this almost negligible hesitation ("the sun and the sun's light by day"), we can begin to sense an impending aporia. Does the progress of enlightenment end with seeing what the sun shows or with seeing the sun? Is all seeing, even outside the cave, the seeing of a light show? Plato's allegory is a fiction of the possibility of growing up and out of the illusions and fictions of mediated seeing, but it is on a direct path into the sun.

"Then finally," says Socrates, "he'd be able to catch sight of the sun, not just reflected in water, or as it appears in any alien location, but the sun itself, by itself, in its own place, and observe it as it is" (516b). The disavowed impossibility (or blinding violence) of this Platonic apex (seeing the sun) could be read, against the grain of Plato's text, as a registration of and fantasmatic solution to the deep ambivalence that clings to Ma and Jack's escape from Room. Indeed, one might even suggest that the sun in Plato's allegory (and in accordance with a reading that one could find in Derrida's *Dissemination* and elsewhere) has a profound relationship to the (patriarchal) father of logos (and thus to *Room*'s Old Nick). The progress Plato describes from illusory imprisonment (in a world of shadows and echoes) toward a direct encounter with blinding sunlight might be reread to describe Ma's forced initial displacement from a world of representationality (or writing) to an order of power, with its absolute distinction between the single source of light and the blindness of its subjects: Ma is "blinded" by the all-commanding light of Old Nick's patriarchal violence. But *Room*, in deconstructive fashion, does not simply reverse the Platonic narrative (logos as imprisonment in darkness rather than emancipation into the light). It does not repeat the Platonic tendency to pit a space of shadow and illusion against a diametrically (temporally and spatially) opposed world of light and truth. Instead, and specifically with the arrival of Jack (the arrival of relation), *Room* depicts a world of play and fiction developing within the space opened up by the violence of patriarchal imprisonment. And this is also why Ma and Jack's "escape" cannot be experienced as a simple emancipatory triumph. In other words, Donoghue's account of the profound ambivalence that adheres to the postcaptivity world of Ma and Jack extends her deconstructive engagement with Platonic metaphysics and with a classically phallogocentric ethics. Hence, an alternative, and to some extent, parallel narrative for Ma and Jack sees them being forced to leave the world of *Room*'s constitutive relationality, a world of storytelling in which the sharp distinction between play and real cannot take hold, in order to enter a social "enclosure" characterized by insistently logocentric divisions and separations.[53] "Am I meant to forget?" asks Jack in response to what he has heard from the medical professionals.

"I don't know," replies Ma (210). One of the first lessons Jack receives from Dr. Clay, as we have already noted, concerns property relations in the "real" world: "[E]verything in the world belongs to somebody. . . ." the doctor tells Jack. "Except the things we all share." Even Jack, he adds, belongs to somebody. "You know who you belong to, Jack? . . ." he asks. "Yourself." But Jack is not convinced: "He's wrong, actually, I belong to Ma" (209). And Jack continues to struggle with this sense of propriety. "What's humankind? . . ." he asks. "Is that me too?" Then: "Me and Ma . . . what's the name for that that I belong to?" (274). The novel is sensitive to the fact that the "outside" world of "freedom" is still, to some extent, Old Nick's world, a world defined by patriarchal, logocentric, and appropriative logics of identity and posses-sion; hence, the novel also reminds us that the world Ma and Jack made for each other in Room *was* also a world, a version of an alternative world, and its loss remains a kind of disaster. "[W]hat I actually meant," says Jack, "was, maybe I'm a human but I'm a me-and-Ma as well. I don't know a word for us two. Roomers?" (274).

If, as I have suggested above, *Room*'s ethical challenge proceeds from its willingness to consider the allegorical possibilities of Old Nick (that is, that he is not just a patriarchal misogynist, that he may also function as a figure for the "wild" violence of the mother–child attachment, the "sov-ereign" wildness of the state of nature that structures every mother–child, or parent–child, relationship), then we also have to consider the possibility that the world of Plato's cave, with its shadows and echoes, but also with its chains and walls, is not a delimited space *in* the world but is itself a world. Plato's cave suggests a space of infantile quarantine, a kind of wild mother–child (or parent–child) zone that the fully human subject has to grow out of and leave behind in order to come into the light of the truth. But the spatializing and temporalizing rhetorical work of Plato's allegory (we can progress, over time, from the world of shadows and illusions into the space of the truth) effects its own kind of patriarchal violence. Its power to per-suade is dependent on our recognizing an absolute difference between the false worlds of play and imitation (whether those worlds take the form of caves, prisons, theaters, or all the rooms in which women have told stories to children from Plato's time to ours) and the real world of sunlit truth. This opposition, in turn, depends on our not registering the blinding violence of what it would mean to look directly into the sun. The rhetorical and meta-physical force of Platonic idealism finds allegorical representation, I suggest, in the brutal, patriarchal violence of Old Nick. Old Nick thinks he can master the world, his desire, and the desire of others by enforcing an absolute separation between the domestic space, the space of his power and property, and the outside world. He imagines that he can have relation and a certain patriarchal omnipotence without the risk of loss; he imagines, that is to say, that he can look into the sun. Ma and Jack pay the price for maintaining this illusion.

But as I have been trying to suggest throughout this chapter, *Room* proceeds along more than one allegorical path at the same time. The imprisonment Ma experiences is at once coded as patriarchal (and, as I have just been suggesting, Platonic) *and* coextensive with motherhood.[54] Survival, in *Room*, depends on relation; Jack saves Ma: "Actually I felt saved. . . . Jack was everything. I was alive again. I mattered," Ma tells the TV reporter, and we should hear "matter" in this formulation with all its maternal/material/ discursive weight (233). But the mother–child relation is also a kind of tyrannizing madness for Ma. Ma is in danger of losing herself, of having no relation with herself, as long as her world consists of her and Jack in Room. The parent–child relationship here describes an imprisonment that the child (here uncannily recalling Old Nick) needs in order to develop a self. In this sense, Old Nick's horror also proceeds from the way in which he functions as a child who has never grown up; he needs a (motherlike) captive woman to shore up his being and protect it from loss.[55] A captured and imprisoned woman is an adult man's version of a mother. This dynamic also helps to account for the disturbing edge introduced by Jack's desire to return to Room at the end of the novel.[56] Jack's request to stay in or return to Room hints, for Ma and the reader, of the uncomfortable relationship between this child (any child) and Old Nick: every child is a version of a dangerous man; every child is an excessive demand on the other, a demand for relationality in order to come into being. Every child is *this* "wild child," too: no child can survive without at some point holding someone (a parent, a guardian) hostage in order for it to come into being. (The child's desire is insatiable, Freud suggested, because the child wants "all.") Hence, Ma is held hostage by both Jack and Old Nick, even as she also loves Jack and, in her own way, might not have survived without him. This is the case for every parent and, indeed, for every adult: we need children, and we need them like a hostage taker. This is the wilderness of the social. We take each other hostage in order to come into being and to survive—to continue to reproduce (our) being. This irreducible violence of relation, this taking hostage, this absolute demand, is also condensed in the horror of Old Nick. It is the novel's incredible achievement that it is not afraid to suggest, albeit very subtly, that there's a relationship (could we even call this an ethical relationship?) between Jack and Old Nick—even as it includes the idea that Old Nick is insistently not Jack's father in the biopatriarchal sense: "Jack's nobody's son," Ma insists, "but mine" (234).

The dangerous and difficult proximity of care and violence that is woven throughout *Room* is in play and at work in all the narratives I examine in this book. Moreover, significant transformations in the politics, culture, and technology of reproduction (post-heteronormative, postpatriarchal, deconstructed reproduction) have taken away some of the ideological and material layers that once helped to shield us from this ethical ordeal of reproduction and parenting. Particular historical forms of violence and particular inequalities have served, paradoxically, to conceal the intimacy of the relationship between the affection that defines a parent–child relationship and the violence of need that all being requires to get going and to keep going. My use of the word *wild* throughout this study names this violence, but it is also meant to name the ethical challenge of the intimacy between this violence and what we call care and love. It is this irreducible contamination or mutuality that is "wild" and, hence, the locus of the ethical.

Plato's allegory of the cave in book 7 of *The Republic* includes this odd finale: the philosopher contemplates a scenario in which his subject returns to the cave, only now, dazzled by and accustomed to the sunlight, the enlightened one is like a blind person, and the cave dwellers pity him and conclude that it would be a terrible mistake to try to leave the cave or to lead anyone else out of the cave. Socrates hereby allegorizes the way in which the true philosopher is mistakenly taken for a blind fool in the land of illusions. But, of course, the scene might just as easily be read to suggest that sight (and hence sanity or health) is profoundly contextual (sociohistorically and geographically, not to say geopolitically, determined). If this is not the lesson we take from *The Republic*, it is because we remain hostages in Socrates's cave: he has told us which light is real light (the sun) and which is not (fire, the play of which produces the shadows on the wall of the cave). But on what basis is fire a lesser form of (an imitation or echo of) the sun, unless it be as the result of a declaratory imposition—the force of law? Henceforth, such a declaration would insist, all fire will be, will have been, artificial sun.

In the allegory of the cave, it is Socrates who announces, as if it were merely a constative assertion, the distinction between mere fire and the fire that we call the sun. This naming of the real and the imitation has to be done in the dark (in the dark of rhetorical concealment; the dark in which Plato hides behind Socrates), because it is this naming that produces the very distinction between light and dark (between enlightenment and ignorance) on which metaphysics depends for its epistemological authority. This is Plato's fiat lux: let there be light, says Plato, and there was light, and he saw that it was good.

The allegory of the cave participates in Plato's attempt throughout *The Republic* to describe the kind of (childhood) education required in order to produce "able ministers of State" and to maintain an ideal political community. But, as such, it also works strenuously to disguise power as knowledge (to disguise the performative as the constative) and hence to conceal the state's and the citizen's constitutive wildness (or roguery, to recall Derrida's term).[57] The wildness of the ethical is concealed behind the illusory science of enlightenment. This is how a Platonic logocentrism takes the world hostage. But if every child, as I have suggested, takes the other hostage in order to come into being, then every child also has to learn to let go of what Platonism desperately tries to hold on to. *Room* narrates a giving up and a letting go that might be understood according to the terms of a decidedly post-Platonic (and posthumanist) maternal gift of death.

Ma and Jack's escape plan requires Jack to know about play and imitation in a very particular way: in order to save his and Ma's life, Jack must be able to play dead. To learn to live is to learn about fiction, representation, and play, and it is to learn how to play *fort-da* with one's own death ("I'm dead dead dead" [137]). Insofar as this lesson coincides with Jack's escape from Room, the novel suggests that this is a kind of last lesson or a rite of passage. Jack doesn't want to learn this lesson—he doesn't want to play dead (understandably), but Ma forces him to do it. This scene, too, gives us an intriguing reimagining or figuration of the maternal gift of death and of a certain child sacrifice. Jack asks Ma, "'Will you be in Rug, too?' I know the answer but I ask just in case" (125). Part of the preparation for this escape will have been Ma and Jack's reading (or retelling) of *The Count of Monte Cristo, Romeo and Juliet,* and the story of Jesus's resurrection (this section of the novel is entitled "Dying").[58] "But you said you wanted to be the hero," says Ma. Yes, says Jack, "but only pretend . . . not for real" (113). By insisting on Jack's need to follow through with their escape plan, Ma tells Jack that despite what she may have suggested, or he may have thought, in the end, the safe distinction between real and pretend cannot hold. You must pretend for real, Ma says.

> "I don't want to get buried and gooey with the worms crawling."
> Ma strokes my head. "It's just a trick, remember?"
> "Like a game."
> "But no laughing. A serious game." (124–25)

But Ma is also, on the story's allegorical level, telling her son that he is mortal and that the world (of Room, of their intimacy, of everything) will come to an end. And, of course, Ma will also have to pretend, for Old Nick, that her son is dead. Jack leaves Plato's cave, in other words, at the site of a performance (by Jack and Ma) of Jack's death.[59]

The possibility that a death can be feigned, and that Old Nick will not be able to tell, is the possibility that allows for Ma and Jack to have a future at all. Fiction, and the possibility that the real and the fictional can be confused, saves them and brings them out of the cave. This would be a counter-Platonic lesson about the relationship between representation and emancipation. Plato, as we know from elsewhere in *The Republic*, is obsessed with policing women's control over the storytelling that, nevertheless, remains essential to a child's education: "[T]he first thing we must do is to supervise our story-tellers, approving any story they put together that has the required quality and rejecting any that doesn't. We'll induce nurses and mothers to tell children the ones we've approved" (377c). They must not tell children just any stories, says Socrates. Why? Because, in addition to any particular problematic content in such stories (disrespectful, unmanly, anarchic behavior), there is also the problem, for phallogocentric culture, of the danger of the fictional and the mimetic in and of itself. Teaching just "any" stories also means teaching stories as stories first. There is a power to fiction and imitation that is not reducible to, and hence manageable as, content. Fiction propagates the appeal of imitation per se, of substitutability, of representationality, of language as productive of being and meaning in a manner that undoes the manageable opposition between performative and constative. Plato is clearly worried that one might become what one imitates. We must therefore insist, he continues, that "good men" never "imitate a woman, whether young or old, whether ranting at a man, setting herself up in competition with gods, boasting because of her supposed good fortune, or gripped by misfortune, grief, lamentation and the like; still less will we permit imitation of a sick woman, a woman in love, or a woman in labour" (395e). Men might become (be like?) mothers![60] This is the "wild" aspect of fiction and storytelling—the wildness of an imitative contagion and of the suggestion that imitation is its own generative and communicable source of pleasure and power. Donoghue's *Room* allegorizes an alternative pedagogical trajectory whereby the passage out of something figured as the cave of childhood (a frighteningly constraining space for mother and child even as it can be the site of a powerful happiness—a wild space) coincides with a maternal gift of death that is itself indissociable from a lesson about loss and play. To survive, Ma teaches Jack and herself, is not to leave Plato's cave but to leave (if we can, once and for all) Plato's allegory of the cave. For a posthumanist ethics, that is to say, one should read not Plato's cave but Donoghue's *Room*.

2

Postapocalyptic Responsibility

Patriarchy at the End of the World in Cormac McCarthy's *The Road*

So to finally answer your question, no, *I never learned-to-live*. In fact not at all! Learning to live should mean learning to die, learning to take into account, so as to accept absolute mortality (that is, without salvation, resurrection, or redemption—neither for oneself nor for the other). . . . I remain uneducable when it comes to any kind of wisdom about knowing-how-to-die, or if you prefer, knowing-how-to-live. I still have not learned or picked up anything on this subject.

—Jacques Derrida, *Learning to Live Finally*

Can I ask you something?
Yes. Of course you can.
What would you do if I died?
If you died I would want to die too.
So you could be with me?
Yes. So I could be with you.
Okay.

—Cormac McCarthy, *The Road*

How does Cormac McCarthy's *The Road* think about death? More particularly, how does *The Road* depict a singular subject contemplating his own death, a death figured as the end of the world? *The Road* is the story of the death of the father in a specific sense; McCarthy's central figure represents a recognizable moment—the passing of Cold War–era masculinity and American hegemony. But it is also a story about responsibility to the other, and, notably, to one's own child. Does the question of one's own death, the novel implicitly asks, open out onto or close down on the question of the other, of relationality? Is one's own death one's property? In addressing these questions, I want to pay particular attention in what follows to the figure of the child ("the son") and to the related figure of the future. The future, in this bleak text about personal mortality, parental responsibility, and the "end of everything," can be read as an example of paranoid post-9/11 fantasy: a father strives to protect his son at the end of the world; there are bad guys out there in the wild—protect your own! (Chapter 5 of this book will return to another version of precisely this fantasy in a reading of Denis Villeneuve's *Prisoners*.) As such, *The Road* gives us an unforgettable portrait of the contemporary family as the smallest unit of the security state. But the novel's vision of the future also takes the form of a remarkably "primitive" or regressive fantasy (complete with cannibals!), reminding us that McCarthy's insistent externalizations still demand to be read.[1] Is this novel's dystopian future simply signature McCarthy? Or is it perhaps an instance of a more general literary impulse to externalize—to turn structures or conflicts into events or narrative? *The Road*, this is to say, is a text in which it is extremely hard to untangle symptom from self-consciousness. We can never be sure what *The Road* "knows" and what it simply participates in.

Although in the reading that follows I do not want to privilege the end of McCarthy's novel (the counterreading emerges most clearly, I think, as a response to *The Road*'s affectual climate and not to its closural logic), I do want to consider the father's decision, finally, not to kill his son. In one of the novel's endings, the father dies, and the son takes on his tasks and is immediately and magically (as if part of a grandiose patriarchal econ-omy) discovered by an intact nuclear family—"good guys"—complete with a daughter who inevitably serves as a token of reproductive futurity. The relationship between the man and his son is consequently entirely spiritual-ized: "He tried to talk to God but the best thing was to talk to his father and he did talk to him and he didnt forget. The woman said that was all right. She said that the breath of God was his breath yet though it pass from man to man through all of time."[2] But is McCarthy's novel merely a rather indul-gent late-patriarchal text featuring a failing virile subject? Is it an example of traditional patriarchy posing as an elegy for patriarchal tradition?[3] Or might there be something new under the sun, after all? Might *The Road*, against all the odds, also give us a depiction of patriarchy narrating its own end?[4]

The psychopolitical terrain of *The Road* is characterized by what one could only call a primitive and insistent opposition between the good and the bad: "Goodness will find the little boy," we read. "It always has. It will again" (281). As such, McCarthy's postapocalyptic milieu recalls *Room*'s state of captivity and the stark contrast between good and bad that structures Donoghue's mother–child idyll. But while Ma eventually teaches Jack that most people are not like Old Nick but rather "somewhere between good and bad. . . . Bits of both stuck together,"[5] McCarthy's father promises his son that the good and the bad will not become mixed up; he assures his son that the two of them are the good guys and that they always will be. "There's not a lot of good guys in *Blood Meridian*," McCarthy told an interviewer, "whereas good guys is what *The Road* is about. That's the subject at hand."[6] Both novels evoke Melanie Klein's paranoid/schizoid *and* depressive/reparative modes, but while *Room*'s maternal ethics finally comes to favor a depressive position, *The Road* returns repeatedly to a psychic space organized around Klein's charting of a good/bad, paranoid/schizoid kind of splitting. Indeed, Klein's trajectory from the paranoid/schizoid to the depressive position (and beyond) offers a particularly persuasive account of the developmental movement—insofar as there is any!—in McCarthy's novel. Klein writes,

> There are thus two sets of fears, feelings and defences, which, however varied in themselves and however intimately linked together, can in my view, for purposes of theoretical clearness, be isolated from each other. The first set of feelings and phantasies are the persecutory ones. . . . The defences against these fears are predominantly the destruction of the persecutors by violent or secretive and cunning methods. . . . The second set of feelings which go to make up the depressive position I formerly described without suggesting a term for them. I now propose to use for these feelings of sorrow and concern for the loved objects . . . a simple word derived from everyday language—namely the "pining" for the loved object.[7]

It is worth emphasizing that for Klein, these two positions, while roughly sequential, are also implicated in one another and therefore not *simply* sequential; psychical crises can produce a return to these earlier "positions."

Moreover, both positions need to be worked through to produce a subject with the capacity for mourning and thus a relationship to the other. This is why Jessica Benjamin asserts that "the alternative to a defensive fantasy of omnipotence is the labor of mourning."[8] *The Road*, I would argue, partakes of precisely this psychic quality, with its rigid, "schizoid," good-versus-bad opposition, tempered by encounters with loss ("He thought each memory recalled must do some violence to its origins" [131]), but it is also not without its larger political implications.

Judith Butler gestures toward these political implications in her "decidedly un-Kleinian" reading of Klein. While "moral sadism" passes itself off as virtue, Butler argues, "responsibility" must "own" its own aggression:

> Even if aggression is coextensive with being human (and implicitly undoes the anthropocentric understanding of the human animal), the way that destructiveness is lived and directed varies enormously. Indeed, it can become the basis of a "non-moralized" sense of responsibility, one that seeks to protect the other against destruction. This is precisely the alternative to moral sadism, a violence that righteously grounds itself in an ethics of purity wrought from the disavowal of violence.[9]

Although *The Road* might never quite reach the point of "owning" its own aggression, it could be said, at various moments, to witness its own undoing. In a small yet characteristic moment, for example, McCarthy rewrites Lacan's mirror stage. Instead of an infant jubilantly misrecognizing his own autonomy (even as he is supported by his mother), McCarthy's son saves his father from an act of fantastic paranoid obliteration: "They came upon themselves in a mirror and he almost raised the pistol. It's us, Papa, the boy whispered. It's us" (132). Here, the son might be said to enact a reversal and to take upon himself the role of the supportive parent in a mundane yet miraculous scene ("Look! Look! It's *you!* [or] It's *us!* There in the mirror. See?"). Or perhaps the father and son might be said to split the mirroring function between them. More crucially, however, this scene condenses the father's hardened oppositional logic (us versus them) and the son's resistance to such structures (the other *as* us). Although the son's resistance can be read as a kind of idealization (the saintly child), and both McCarthy and his novel certainly participate in this idealization, it also, I would argue, constitutes a kind of depressive/reparative possibility, a glimpse of futurity characteristic of the posthumanist wild child. McCarthy's text, I would suggest, exhibits a doubled relationship to the depressive or reparative poetics of remains (as the possibility of mourning) *and* to more grandiose and paranoid fantasies of transcendence: "The name of things slowly following those things into oblivion. Colors. The names of birds. Things to eat. Finally the names of things one believed to be true. More fragile than he would have thought. How much was gone already? The sacred idiom shorn of its referents and so of its reality. Drawing down like something trying to preserve heat. In time to wink out forever" (88–89). As such, the novel inscribes a distinctive ethics of abandonment and self-mourning linked via the child—the postapocalyptic wild child—to the relinquishment of patriarchal grandiosity.

The Trauma of Birth

In a 2009 interview with the *Wall Street Journal's* John Jurgensen, Cormac McCarthy was pressed on what causes the disaster that precipitates the events of his Pulitzer Prize–winning novel, *The Road:* "A lot of people ask me. I don't have an opinion. At the Santa Fe Institute I'm with scientists of all disciplines, and some of them in geology said it looked like a meteor to them. But it could be anything—volcanic activity or it could be nuclear war. It is not really important."[10] McCarthy's dismissal ("It is not really important"), far from signaling that not much is at stake, suggests instead that "all" is at stake (where "all" means all of those differential systems and their material supports that produce and sustain human life). The cause is irrelevant because what *The Road* actually presents us with is a profound encounter with the Traumatic Real, with what happens when the Symbolic is blown away, is reduced to ashes, and then very tenuously seeks to reassert itself or merely to hold on. Indeed, *The Road* might be said to belong to a post-9/11 moment of profound crisis for the protective powers of an omniscient patriarchy: "Do you think that your fathers are watching? That they weigh you in their ledgerbook? Against what? There is no book and your fathers are dead in the ground" (196).[11]

One thing we do know about the disaster, however, is that it nearly coincides with a birth: "The clocks stopped at 1:17. A long shear of light and then a series of low concussions. He got up and went to the window. What is it? . . . What is it? she said. What is happening?" (52–53). "A few nights later she gave birth" (59). The man then crucially delivers his own son and cuts the cord: "*Her cries meant nothing to him.* Behind the window just the gathering cold, the fires on the horizon. He held *aloft* the scrawny red body so raw and naked and cut the cord with kitchen shears and wrapped *his son* in a towel" (59 [emphases added]). The almost negligible reference to "his son" in this passage announces the beginning of a relationship that, in some sense, could be called utopian. There is little or no room in *The Road* for father–son conflict *or for the mother*.[12] Instead we are given a father doing his best, his good and vulnerable son, and their life together. It is as if all that might be experienced as negative and aggressive and internal to a (father–son) relationship is projected, in McCarthy's novel, onto an apocalyptic outside that, in turn, produces an idealized space of goodness in which the father and son can reside together. Patriarchy, it would appear, loves the apocalypse! Despite all its extravagant acts of violence, *The Road* also tells the story of a father's love for his son at the end of the world and even of his escorting his son toward what looks surprisingly like safety and a new life. The father dies at the end of the narrative, but not before immortalizing and spiritualizing their filial bond: "You have to carry the fire [he says to his young son]. . . . It's inside you. It was always there. I can see it. . . . You have my whole heart. You always did. You're the best guy. You always were. If I'm not here you can still talk to me. You can talk to me and I'll talk to you. . . . Okay?" (278–79). Does this father's love for his son, his wild and terrifying, world-creating, world-destroying love, *produce* this end-of-the-world scenario? And doesn't this suggest that (the fantasy of) radical destruction makes (the fantasy of) full presence possible? Is this patriarchy stripped bare or is it perhaps a glimpse of a new reproductive and ontological regime? Might the war of all against all that defines the postapocalyptic world produce the very possibility for the relationship of absolute care and responsibility that defines the father and son's new state of nature? And who or what is a man at the beginning of the twenty-first century? This most pressing contemporary question certainly haunts McCarthy's text, as it does postindustrial America, and there are a couple of striking moments in *The Road*, both moving and pathetic, when the man refers to his "job"—his job at the end of the world—as if the world ends precisely so that he can know who he is and what he must do.[13] Yet one might add that it is surely not the end of the world as long as you know what your "job" is. This knowledge is profoundly reassuring. The father says to his son, "You wanted to know what the bad guys looked like. Now you know. It may happen again. My job is to take care of you. I was appointed to do that by God. I will kill anyone who touches you. Do you understand?" (77). Or again: "This is my child, he said. I wash a dead man's brains out of his hair. That is my job. Then he wrapped him in the blanket and carried him to the fire" (74).

The son's birth in *The Road* is identical with the novel's end-of-the-world disaster, and, as a trauma for the man who encounters his own finitude *and* immortality with his son's birth, it could be read as a familiar version of patriarchy's traditional story. But I would like to consider the possibility that this birth is simultaneously a call to responsibility: a traumatic call with an ego-shattering force beyond calculation. In other words, if the apocalypse might be said to externalize the ambivalence of Oedipus, thereby producing a kind of utopian/dystopian or paranoid/schizoid (good versus bad) space, it also precipitates a loss of all the mediating social formations that might protect the man from experiencing relationship in its most simple and even primal form.[14] *The Road* thus throws into question whether, or in what sense, this man and this boy are a father and a son. (Indeed, the terms *father* and *son* are used quite sparingly in the novel. The narrative voice refers to the man as "the man" or "he," and the boy is, for the most part, simply "the boy"; he refers to his father as "Papa," but the man rarely uses any explicit form of address in return, as if he does not quite know how to name this new [wild] child.) Can there be fathers and sons when there are no longer any symbolic and meaningful structures? How could there possibly be one father and one son? Or are we to experience this father and son as the very essence of the paternal–filial relation, and hence this text's fantasy as the fantasy of a Symbolic relationship purified of contingency?[15]

Clearly, the father–son relationship in *The Road* is sanctified: "The boy didnt stir. He sat beside him and stroked his pale and tangled hair. Golden chalice, good to house a god. Please dont tell me how the story ends" (75). And the novel (almost) begins with the father's *word*, not just his thought: "He said: if he [referring to his son] is not the word of God God never spoke" (5). God's existence and that of the child are interdependent, and the familial and the divine also collapse in the novel's implicit identification of its fictional "son" with the Son and its father with the Father. The father and the novel's omniscient narrator are, in turn, closely related, if not entirely identified, and this indeterminacy, taken together with the novel's fragmentary form, poses difficult questions for *The Road*'s reader: What or who holds it all together? Is it the man's consciousness, the narrator's voice, the author's implied consciousness? Or might it be nothing at all? Indeed,

The Road hovers in its very sanctification between a kind of biblical/theological paradigm (note its repeated references to gods, tabernacles, anointing, and so on, not to mention the story's intense relationship to Abraham and Isaac, the Exodus, the story of Job, and the Gospels) and the discourse of American masculinity in the second half of the twentieth century.[16] In a move familiar to students of American literature, moreover, this still-legible form of masculinity fantastically appropriates a version of Native American spirituality. The "good guys" of McCarthy's text, those who "carry the fire," are not only biblical patriarchs and prophets but also cowboys and Indians. But while McCarthy's novel, with what I would call its poetics of transcendence, crucially disavows violence and mortality, it also offers us an insistent and materialized poetics of remains. The apocalyptic fantasy in *The Road* works, as I have been suggesting, to destroy everything that might interrupt or spoil a perfectly nonviolent relationship between father and son, but the text's representation of mourning also complicates this account. Mourning must negotiate between accepting death (and even accepting one's implication in the other's death) and a certain resistance to mortality that, in turn, hovers between hallucination and representation. While this negotiation might look different at different moments (this is indeed the "work" of mourning), the doubleness never entirely disappears; mourning is always a resistance to mourning, and hence any absolute opposition between mourning and melancholia will not hold. *The Road*, I would argue, achieves its figurative effects and generates its pathos as it vacillates between a grand denial of mortality (in the form of a poetics of transcendence) and a more partial acceptance-in-process (the poetics of remains).

There is much to be gained, therefore, by reading McCarthy's text alongside the pioneering account offered by Freud in "Mourning and Melancholia." When one mourns, Freud argues, one hypercathects all the bits and pieces (the remains), and this intense investment precedes the ability to relinquish the object: "Normally, respect for reality gains the day. Nevertheless its orders cannot be obeyed at once. They are carried out bit by bit, at great expense of time and cathectic energy, and in the meantime the existence of the lost object is psychically prolonged."[17] Freud also reminds us that mourning is not necessarily undertaken for an individual loved person but can be for the loss "of some abstraction which has taken the place of one, such as one's country, liberty, an ideal, and so on."[18] Perhaps the missing observation here, and one that is crucial for understanding *The Road*, is that one can also mourn for oneself, and that, in a certain sense, all mourning is self-mourning. Numerous objects and cultural artifacts (valuables? detritus?) take on an intense importance in *The Road*, located as they are amid utter devastation. There is, for example, a crucially minimal reference to an arrowhead and to a Spanish coin. The man picks up the arrowhead and hands it on to his son: "He spat on it and wiped away the dirt on the seam of his trousers and gave it to the boy. It was white, quartz, perfect as the day it was made" (203); but then, somewhat enigmatically, he does not pass on the coin (204).[19] *The Road* also includes references to stories, both in the sense of children's books as actual material artifacts ("You can read me a story, the boy said. Cant you, Papa? Yes, he said. I can" [7]) and in the sense of a less materializable cultural inheritance. What kind of stories can be told, what kind of stories can one still tell? When do stories become mere words that don't seem to refer to anything at all? What kind of story is *The Road*? The father tells his son "[o]ld stories of courage and justice as he remembered them" (41), but the boy later shows an impatience with these tales. "Those stories are not true," he says to his father (268). *The Road* also includes various minimal yet telling references to toys and games as "culture" and as examples of that which a father might hand on to his son (for example, a yellow truck, a deck of cards). In one particularly telling passage, the man and the boy come across an ash-covered train:

> They pushed into the cab and he blew away the ash from the engineer's seat and put the boy at the controls. The controls were very simple. Little to do but push the throttle lever forward. He made train noises and diesel horn noises but he wasnt sure what these might mean to the boy. After a while they just looked out through the silted glass to where the track curved away in the waste of weeds. If they saw different worlds what they knew was the same. That the train would sit there slowly decomposing for all eternity and that no train would ever run again.
> Can we go, Papa?
> Yes. Of course we can. (180)

Such moments resonate beyond the confines of this narrative world, and while registering the son's status as a child of a different "culture" or even another world they suggest, I think, what remains and what does not remain of the author's "classic" boyhood. Some things refuse to go.

Hence, mourning almost always requires a set of decisions regarding things. Should one keep them, give them away, throw them away, destroy them, sell them? In McCarthy's novel, the man lays out the contents of his wallet (money, credit cards, driver's license, a photo of his wife) on the black-top "like gambling cards." He throws the billfold itself into the woods and holds the photo of his wife for an indefinite period of time before laying it down again beside the other pieces and heading on his way. So the apocalypse has come and a man leaves his money and credit cards behind; why not? On the one hand, these cards, documents, and bits of legal tender are the mere symbolic trappings of a world blown away, signifiers that only ever signified other signifiers. Yet, of course, they are also the only pieces that allow one to live the fiction of subjecthood and symbolic legitimation: what is a man without his wallet? In such passages, in other words, we encounter two of this novel's crucial recurring questions: What is the relationship between "social death" and "my death"? Does mortality mean the loss and relinquishment of oneself piece by piece, or can a certain sacrifice produce transcendence and the revelation of essential being?

And what about the picture of the man's wife? In *No Future*, Lee Edelman considers the way the death drive is "recurrently projected onto those who occupy the position of the queer: those abjected as nonreproductive, anti-social, opposed to viability, and so as threats to the Child who assures and embodies collective survival."[20] In *The Road*, as I have been arguing, the death drive is projected onto an entire world, an entire landscape that is not of the father and son's making (and, it goes without saying, onto its child murderers and cannibals). This projection might be said to begin with the novel's profound investment in getting rid of the mother. Although this might seem to mark a distinct departure from Edelman's account—wouldn't one expect the female reproductive body to be affirmed by the hegemonic social order that Edelman posits?—McCarthy clearly casts a wider net. And indeed, *The Road* betrays a profound ambivalence in relationship to the maternal. Notably, pregnant women accompany both the good guys and the bad guys. The pregnant body therefore becomes the very sign of the text's self-undoing idealization.

An indefinite number of years after the apocalyptic event, the mother decides to leave the man and the boy and to take her own life (58). If she could, she would take the boy with her: "You have two bullets and then what? [She confronts the father.] You cant protect us. You say you would die for us but what good is that? I'd take him with me if it werent for you. You know I would. It's the right thing to do. . . . Sooner or later they will catch us and they will kill us. They will rape me. They'll rape him. They are going to rape us and kill us and eat us and you wont face it. You'd rather wait for it to happen. But I cant. I cant" (56). And then, as if that weren't enough: "You can think of me as a faithless slut if you like. I've taken a new lover. . . . I am done with my own whorish heart and I have been for a long time. . . . [M]y only hope is for eternal nothingness and I hope it with all my heart" (57). The son later expresses a desire to be with his mother, which the father misreads (who is to say?) as a desire to be dead:

You musnt say that.
But I do.
Dont say it. It's a bad thing to say. (55)

And the mother, who is long gone by the time the novel begins, returns in the father's dreams as a corpse bride: "Her nipples pipeclayed and her rib bones painted white . . ." (18, 21). There is not much to unpack here! The woman is she who would call "you" seductively to your death, to traumatic dissolution (*jouissance*) and eternal nothingness. Woman is a dream that calls the man to "languor and . . . death. . . . [H]e was learning how to wake himself from just such siren worlds" (18).

McCarthy's father and son represent the Symbolic fighting to hang on, to reestablish itself in a more general field of traumatic *jouissance*: a field populated by women, apocalypse, cannibals. This equation (women = death) is a familiar one, as old as the hills; yet this project of getting rid of the mother, I would contend, both partakes of the desire to produce a kind of eternal logocentric-transcendent-present time of masculine relation (for which reproduction is both required and disavowed) and at the same time betrays an identification with—of all things!—mothering. The rewarding surprise of *The Road*, for many readers, seems to be the record of intimate care provided by the father for his son as he washes his hair, gives him swimming lessons, feeds him, and more generally reassures him: "He washed his dirty matted hair and bathed him with the soap and sponges. He drained away the filthy water he sat in and laved fresh warm water over him from the pan and wrapped him shivering in a towel and wrapped him again in a blanket. He combed his hair and looked at him. Steam was coming off of him like smoke. Are you okay? he said" (147). This is a portrait of a father who must manage, in the most charged of circumstances (the end of the world!), the work of orchestrating separation and individuation:

> I've got to go for more wood, he said. I'll be in the neighbourhood. Okay?
> Where's the neighbourhood?
> It just means I won't be far.
> Okay. (95)

Certainly, *The Road* is a text for our time as we encounter the triumphant rugged masculinization of child care! Here, one might recall Sara Ruddick's nontraditional definition of motherhood: "A mother is a person who takes on responsibility for children's lives. . . . [A]lthough most mothers have been women, mothering is potentially work for men and women."[21] To read *The Road* is surely to encounter a historical shift in parental roles, and McCarthy's biography would bear this out (his first son was born in the 1960s, his second in 1999). But I would suggest that *The Road* also asks us to contemplate the reinvention—with a difference?—of patriarchal fantasy via new technologies that make it possible to imagine, yet again, a child of one's own.[22] *The Road* is indeed symptomatically split between its investment in the father's "own" child and the idea of the wild child, who might be said to belong only to himself and to the social.

The Future: Nobody's Home

It's hard to ignore the possibility that *The Road* was generated out of a profound intimation of paternal mortality. McCarthy was seventy-four when the novel was published and was the father of a nine-year-old boy, John Francis McCarthy, to whom *The Road* is dedicated. "I am going to die," says the fictional father. "Tell me how I am to do that" (175). But the novel can also be read as a rigorous defense against any such experience and perhaps even as a fantasy of escape from the Traumatic Real, a fantasmatic escape that Lee Edelman designates "the Child."

Edelman's notorious and provocative association of queerness and the death drive argues "that *queerness* names the side of those *not* 'fighting for the children,' the side outside the consensus by which all politics confirms the absolute value of reproductive futurism."[23] Although this may go without saying, it is crucial for Edelman that "queerness" not be thought of as a substantializable identity but rather as a radically antiessentialist concept: "Queerness as name may well reinforce the Symbolic order of naming, but it names what resists, as signifier, absorption into the Imaginary identity of the name. Empty, excessive, and irreducible, it designates the letter, the formal element, the lifeless machinery responsible for animating the 'spirit' of futurity."[24] To put this a little more simply, Edelman sees a certain critical potential in queerness as a resistance to being and makes the case for this sheer resistance (as opposed to promoting something as banal as an "alternative lifestyle"). Queerness is the force that, like it or not (and part of what is going on here is the oddness of making the case for what is also inevitable), disrupts Imaginary totalization. And the "pervasive" figure of the child is precisely this fetishistic, totalizing, imaginary figure: the child is "the prop of the secular theology on which our social reality rests: the secular theology that shapes at once the meaning of our collective narratives and our collective narratives of meaning."[25] "Fighting for the children," then, is shorthand for a coherent political, sociosymbolic order that renders certain subjects abject.[26]

Can we read *The Road* as a raging instance of the kind of fantasy Edelman outlines? Yes. But this is not simply pejorative; such a reading, after all, would place *The Road* in the company of *Hamlet*: "*Hamlet*," Edelman argues, "no less than the Oedipus complex itself, belongs to the universe in which the Child has become the guarantor of futurity: a fantasy figure produced as the promise of secular temporal closure intended to restore an imaginary past in a future endlessly deferred."[27] Edelman's reading of *Hamlet* dwells on the figure of Hamlet's brain as a book that contains and preserves his father's words:

Remember thee?
Yea, from the table of my memory
I'll wipe away all trivial fond records,
All saws of books, all forms, all pressures past,
That youth and observation copied there,
And thy commandment all alone shall live
Within the book and volume of my brain
Unmixed with baser matter.[28]

This fantasy of a "living book," argues Edelman, profoundly cheats Hamlet of a future—he can be only his father's child—and renders him a kind of "monster of normativity":[29] "Futurism in this sense might be understood as a sort of proleptic behindsight: the father's penetration from behind, from the back of what he thereby conceives as the future in an act of self-affirmation by which the Child, like Hamlet, gets screwed."[30] The fantasy of the living book, in other words, is the fantasy of logocentrism, or writing that is not writing (material and perishable) but instead a set of magic signs that would transcend materiality and preserve the father's legacy in and as the figure of the child.

The Road is similarly concerned with the father's book and also quite specifically with the destruction of the Western cultural tradition as archive (it is, in fact, the very nature of this "destruction" that we must interrogate). In a crucial passage, the unnamed central character recalls a visit to a ruined library and contemplates the sheer and sodden materiality of writing without a future: "He picked up one of the books and thumbed through the heavy bloated pages. He'd not have thought the value of the smallest thing predicated on a world to come. It surprised him. That the space which these things occupied was itself an expectation" (187).[31] Later, he contemplates "[t]he names of things slowly following those things into oblivion. . . . More fragile than he would have thought. How much was gone already? The sacred idiom shorn of its referents and so of its reality" (88). But to follow Edelman's line of thought here is to ask if The Road's child, as being, meaning, and goodness successfully commingled, is the one sign that transcends such ruin. As such, this child belongs to a narrative that vacillates between a world of remains and an idealized future for the world. The Road seems to contemplate a kind of absolute mortality (the true end of "education," the last lesson), but this apparent confrontation, as we shall see, might also be said to enable fantasies of otherworldliness.[32] Is the boy in The Road the "priceless" child? The heteropatriarchal child? Or might he be just a little bit wild?

In Archive Fever, Derrida unravels a semantic cluster (starting with arkhe) that reminds us of the importance of "housing" an archive. He argues, in fact, that there is no "archic" or "patriarchic" function without such a scene of domicile: "The meaning of 'archive,' its only meaning, comes to it from the Greek arkheion, initially a house, a domicile, an address, the residence of the superior magistrates, the archons, those who commanded. . . . [I]t is at their home, in that place which is their house . . . that official documents are filed. The archons are first of all the documents' guardians. . . . They are also accorded the hermeneutic right and competence."³³ These archons make an appearance in *The Road*, not surprisingly, as McCarthy's "fathers" with their "ledgerbooks." This novel forces us to contemplate the end of patriarchy and the end of writing, but it achieves some of its most haunting effects with its depictions of placelessness. In *The Road*, haunted spaces or places give way to the terrifying spectralization of place itself. In a telling moment, the man makes a phone call to *his* father's house from the remains of a roadside gas station: "The pumps standing with their hoses oddly still in place. The windows intact. The door to the service bay was open and he went in. . . . Dust and ash everywhere. . . . He crossed to the desk and stood there. Then he picked up the phone and dialed the number of his father's house in that long ago. The boy watched him. What are you doing? he said" (6–7). Crucially, no one is home; no one could be home.³⁴ The father is dialing up his past. One hears here the scriptural allusion: "My father's house has many rooms" (John 14:2). For why, after all, is it the *father's* house (at once *the* place and the place that transcends spatiotemporality)? It is because, according to the terms of this secular theology, this patriarchal ideology, nobody at home means no father, no patriarch, no God. *The Road*, in such moments, attempts to begin to mourn the (patriarchal) self and the whole world of that self, to bear witness to the passing of a cultural moment with its books and stories. So, it is about the end of *this* subject but it is also about the end of his archive, which is *the* archive insofar as it is the patriarchal archive. And yet, as Edelman's work might suggest, *The Road* is also profoundly invested in this "death" precisely as it is tied to the self's immortality in the child. Phallogocentrism (and indeed every "ineducable" self) clings to that death which is not death. Hence, we can begin to think about the ways in which the child and the father's relationship to the child in *The Road* represents not merely a patriarchal fantasy of omnipotence but also the fragile possibility of a move beyond patriarchy. ([T]his is also the fragile possibility that marks this novel's child as another example of what I am calling the posthumanist wild child: "The boy watched him. What are you doing? he said.") [I]t is this possibility, moreover, that I believe Derridean thought and post-Freudian psychoanalysis might allow us to articulate. *The Road*, in other words, may harbor the postpatriarchal traces of some other future.

Derrida's account of the future, with its distinction between the messianic and messianism (a call to the wholly other to come, as opposed to the closed future anticipated by religions of the Messiah), differs, not surprisingly, from the critique of futurism offered by Edelman. "It is a question of this performative to come," writes Derrida, "whose archive no longer has any relation to the record of what is, to the record of the presence of what is or will have been actually present. I call this the messianic, and I distinguish it radically from all messianism."[35] What this means for Derrida—who, like McCarthy, can be said to have witnessed the "end" of his cultural moment and to have written about it—is not that the archive is filled with the decaying work of dead white men but rather that it poses the very question of the future: "[T]he question of the future itself, the question of a response, of a promise and of a responsibility for tomorrow . . . a spectral messianicity is at work in the concept of the archive and ties it, like religion, like history, like science itself to a very singular experience of the promise."[36] But such formulations do not simply locate Derrida on the side of the future, precisely because deconstruction tends to take sides apart. There is no future without (also) repetition, no archive without the death drive: "If repetition is thus inscribed at the heart of the future to come, one must also import there, *in the same stroke*, the death drive, the violence of forgetting, *superrepression* (suppression and repression), the anarchive, in short the possibility of putting to death the very thing, whatever its name, which *carries the law in its tradition*: the archon of the archive, the table, *what* carries the table and *who* carries the table, the subjectile, the substrate, and the subject of the law."[37] Death (and this will come as no surprise to any reader of Derrida) always already haunts the archive, and this haunting significantly distinguishes Derrida's philosophy from McCarthy's fictional vision of death as a cataclysmic occurrence that comes from the outside.[38]

Edelman, however, wants no part of the future, even in Derridean terms. In "Against Survival," he writes in surprisingly critical terms of Derrida's affirmation of the future to come: "This fantasmatic future, even when adduced without explicit belief in its possible realization, even when understood as performatively instantiating the openness for which it calls, imposes on messianicity a form that is already our own, reflecting in this the rigor mortis of our attachment to the Symbolic order and to the name of the father that Derrida, like Hamlet, construes as 'life.'"[39] For Edelman, in other words, Derrida's future-to-come, his future "if there is any" is still filled in. Edelman turns to the interview given shortly after 9/11 in which Derrida designated what was "unacceptable" in the "'strategy' . . . of the 'bin Laden effect'": "not only the cruelty, the disregard for human life, the disrespect for law, for women, the use of what is worst in technocapitalist modernity for the purposes of religious fanaticism. No, it is, above all the fact that such actions and such discourses *open onto no future, and, in my view, have no future.* . . . [T]here is, it seems to me, *nothing good* to be hoped for from that quarter."[40] Edelman objects to Derrida's attempt to have bin Laden stand for a kind of sheer negativity (incorrectly, in Edelman's assessment), which in turn is what makes the future as Imaginary projection (as opposed to the Traumatic Real) possible. "How," Edelman asks, "could an event take place *for us* if the event itself, as the radically unknown, would revoke the ways of knowing by which we understand ourselves and thereby understand our world? How can we survive the event that ruptures the order of survival itself?"[41] Although he is certainly willing to endorse Derrida's complication of the opposition between life and death and his affinity for the specter, Edelman cannot read Derrida's "messianic" as anything but symptomatic.[42] Derrida, despite his critique of phallogocentrism, is tainted, Edelman argues, by normative secular theology: he complicates the opposition between life and death but then chooses "life." This, for Edelman, means choosing the "death" of a heteroimperative reproductive futurism. Edelman, by contrast, chooses "death," which for him means choosing "life" (the radical refusal of any recuperative, conservative, repetitive gesture that leaves the way open to the new, to the event). But these reversals seem to turn us around in circles and bring us back again to the very binaristic terrain that Derrida began by problematizing. Edelman's absolute "no" to the future, in other words, emerges from a reification of precisely that Symbolic that his work would claim to undermine.[43]

But where is McCarthy in this picture? How does he see the future? Some readers have suggested that *The Road* distinguishes itself from other examples of the postapocalyptic genre precisely by *not* depicting a rebuilding of the world and instead attempting to depict the time and place of no future.[44] But I would suggest that *The Road* (for all the ways in which McCarthy's work might resist deconstruction) shares with Derrida a sense of faith in the future precisely *as* performative. Consider, for example, McCarthy's profound depiction of the performative force of familial bonds.[45] One of the man's responses to this erasure of the past, with its implication of no future (he hasn't "kept a calendar in years"), is precisely to ignore it, to disavow it, as a gift to his son; this is what it means to make a "world" for his son, since each is to the other the "world entire" (6). Hence, the father acts as if there is a future; they have a goal, and it is very important that they reach the coast: "He said that everything depended on reaching the coast, yet waking in the night he knew that all of this was empty and no substance to it" (29). The son later returns his father's message when he inquires after their "long term goals":

> He looked at his father. What are our long term goals? he said.
> What?
> Our long term goals.
> Where did you hear that?
> I dont know. (160)

The father's production of a future that he doesn't believe in functions as an act of faith (and this is very much a novel of faith: the father's faith in his son and the son's faith in his father), and we don't know, finally, quite how to distinguish this faith from a lie:

> Do you think I lie to you?
> No.
> But you think I might lie to you about dying.
> Yes.
> Okay. I might. But we're not dying.
> Okay. (101)

For in an insightful way, the odd temporal space (if one can say that) generated by the future / no future moment, the moment of what I'm calling the father's disavowal, is a kind of radical present. This making of a world in a utopian suspense is, in this respect, very similar to the world Ma makes for Jack in Room (Room's "Presents" as The Road's "presence"; McCarthy's "I'm right here" as Donoghue's "I think what babies want is mostly to have their mothers right there").[46] This, I would suggest, also constitutes an encounter with the groundlessness of reproduction. What the (secular) parent gives, or struggles to give or to say in this experience of groundlessness, is the very act of the saying. It is when this saying is exposed as "saying"—and, of course, the reference here is Levinas—that one encounters a posthumanist ethics. Lisa Guenther writes, explicating Levinas, "The distinction between saying and said is articulated on an ethical-temporal level. Anarchically prior to the said, the saying embodies my proximity to the Other; even while I speak about the weather or dairy farming or philosophy."[47] Not surprisingly, McCarthy's language repeatedly allegorizes this "moment" in theological terms, but it is also a crucial part of what I would insist on calling the utopian dimension of *The Road*: "No lists of things to be done. The day providential to itself. The hour. There is no later. This is later. . . . So, he whispered to the sleeping boy. I have you" (54). This future / no future moment also describes the time of the bond or relation, and this space of timelessness functions in several registers in McCarthy's novel. It functions developmentally insofar as it suggests the illusory, hypnotic space of infancy, the timeless space the parent must produce for the entirely dependent infant; but it also functions repetitively and structurally, paired with its own overcoming or crisis (in the psychoanalytic accounts I favor, the developmental narrative never arrives at its telos; rather, it is repeated in the very structures and events of subjectivity and relation). Yet such a "timeless space" also conveys, I would suggest, a certain historical specificity that is, in turn, doubled: if McCarthy's novel (and our moment) recognizes the vigilant, intensive parent who would protect the child in his sanctity from any event of futurity, it also gestures toward the parent as he (in this case) who affirms relation and continuity in the face of the child's wildness and the groundlessness of being.[48]

Indeed, the novel also conveys this fragility and affirmation by way of certain repeated utterances between the man and the boy. A crucial word in almost all of their exchanges is "okay":

> Okay.
> Okay what?
> Nothing. Just okay.
> Go to sleep.
> Okay.
> I'm going to blow out the lamp. Is that okay?
> Yes. That's okay. (10)

The very spareness of the language foregrounds the function of this minimal and repeated word. Its function, as Roman Jakobson would tell us, is "phatic"—it works to ensure that the "channel of communication" is open and that there is indeed a connection between these two beings.[49] And this even as "okay" in the McCarthy dialogues tends to signal the end of a particular verbal exchange: "okay" says, "Okay. We will keep on going. We will keep on being in relation. Okay." The text foregrounds a similar function with its play on the constative and the performative. Recall, for example, two of the novel's crucial, though minimal, sentences: "There's a little boy" and "There are people" (84, 244). The peculiarity of these sentences is all the more apparent when they are heard out of context: they are nothing if not constative utterances, mere declarations or statements of fact; yet it is as statements of fact that they must be asserted with a kind of blind and performative insistence. The vulnerability of human being-in-relation is effectively conveyed by such sentences, as it is by McCarthy's persistent play on *world* and *word*: "the world a lie every word" (75).[50] *The Road* inscribes its own fictionality, in other words, and its author's identification with a waning tradition of aggressively minimalist, masculine prose on the surface of an apocalyptic encounter with the near impossibility of being and relation.

An Ethics of Abandonment

In one of *The Road*'s most disturbing incidents, father and son encounter a house in which a group of captives is being held in a basement and gradually cannibalized: "Huddled against the back wall were naked people, male and female, all trying to hide, shielding their faces with their hands. On the mattress lay a man with his legs gone to the hip and the stumps of them blackened and burnt. The smell was hideous. . . . Then one by one they turned and blinked in the pitiful light. Help us, they whispered. Please help us" (110). With its reference to chattel slavery ("Chattel slaves had once trod those boards bearing food and drink on silver trays" [106]), this episode resonates as at once psychologically primitive and historically American (this is one of the few moments in the text that readers can use to establish location in this borderless world of ruin). The boy is profoundly troubled not only by the scene he and his father witness but also, and more crucially, by their failure to respond to the call for help. This is something that he must revisit and work through in a characteristic conversation with his father:

> And we couldnt help them because then they'd eat us too.
> Yes.
> And that's why we couldnt help them.
> Yes.
> Okay. (127)

And again:

> We wouldnt ever eat anybody, would we?
> No. Of course not. . . .
> But we wouldnt.
> No. We wouldnt.
> No matter what.
> No. No matter what.
> Because we're the good guys.
> Yes.
> And we're carrying the fire.
> And we're carrying the fire. Yes.
> Okay. (128)

The boy, as these lines make clear, is principally characterized by his profound anxiety about goodness and about the potential harm done to others.
He represents something of a miracle (or a god) to his father in his very wish
both to give to and to forgive those whom they encounter along the road;
the father wants only to give to his son, and in so doing expresses a repeated
desire for forgiveness for himself. The boy gives Ely food; Ely speaks with
the father—

> People give you things. . . .
> No they dont.
> You did.
> No I didnt. The boy did (170)

—and begs for the life of the thief. This is in stark contrast to the father's
constant perception of his fellow man as dangerous and monstrous: "[T]his
was the first human being other than the boy that he'd spoken to in more
than a year. My brother at last. The reptilian calculations in those cold and
shifting eyes. The gray and rotting teeth. Claggy with human flesh. Who has
made the world a lie every word" (75). The boy's anxious care extends even
to a possibly hallucinatory other boy, a dog, a dead baby ("[I]f we had that
little baby it could go with us" [200]), and other "good" others who would
be just like himself and his father. The father regularly protects his son from
anxious dissolution by recognizing his fear ("I know") and apologizing ("I'm

sorry"), and, in a particularly interesting protective moment, the father also participates in his son's capacity for imagining good others. In the face of "Nothing," the boy posits, "There must be something [on the other side of the water]." Here again, the novel stages a kind of mirror-stage scene that the boy takes over and rewrites according to a potentially postpatriarchal, posthumanist sociality. His father enters into the fantasy:

> Maybe there's a father and his little boy and they're sitting on the beach.
> That would be okay.
> Yes. That would be okay.
> And they could be carrying the fire too?
> They could be. Yes.
> But we dont know.
> We dont know.
> So we have to be vigilant. (216)

Although I hardly want to dispute that this child at the end of the world is "good," I do want to supplement this (apparently banal) observation by remarking again on the stark Kleinian schizoid opposition between good and bad and the way in which it is both opposed to and negotiates with what one could call depressive possibility. From the perspective of a Kleinian allegory, the son, precisely in his radical vulnerability and with his language of the vulnerability of the other, represents the emergence of a depressive position in a paranoid/schizoid world: "The drive to make reparation . . . shows a more realistic response to the feeling of grief, guilt and fear of loss resulting from the aggression against the love object."[51] This is worth bearing in mind when we consider that to read *The Road* is to experience the good child as at once the man's projection and a "real" separate character or person (a reality we experience particularly in the novel's dialogue). This duality speaks, of course, to the mundane reality of our relationship to otherness: the other is all our projection, yet there is also an other. The same structure describes the father's relationship to the future: he is torn between the appeal to an eternal present, the utopian space of idealized relation between father and son (this is also, as I have suggested, the appeal of apocalyptic destruction as logocentric fantasy), and the appeal of a future for his son (hence a future per se) that is inseparable from his own death and, thus, from his own abandonment of the child; both the future and the son, in other words, become marked with

a wildness that requires or coincides with the father's death. These two irrec-
oncilable investments are also both haunted by a third investment in his (the
father's) own immortality. It is this third dimension that Edelman effectively
analyzes in his account of the hegemonic fantasy of the child and the future:
"The affirmation of such a survival, which extends the living being's identity,
at its preference, into the future, enacts a resistance to the radical event as
which the future is also invoked."[52] But, insofar as this patriarchal desire for
immortality does not tell us the whole story, perhaps we need to turn (again)
to a Derridean account and witness a father faced with an ethical demand
that he performatively produce a future for his child by demonstrating faith
in a tomorrow about which he knows nothing except that it would contain
his own nonbeing: "Slumping along. Filthy, ragged, hopeless. He'd stop and
lean on the cart and the boy would go on and then stop and look back and
he would raise his weeping eyes and see him standing there in the road looking back at him from some unimaginable future, glowing in that waste like
a tabernacle" (273).

We read literary texts, in part, because we want to encounter representations and experiences of profound psychic conflict, and, in this respect,
The Road surely does not disappoint. As I have been suggesting, McCarthy's
novel is characterized by a conflict between mourning, with its acceptance
of the need to relinquish so that there can be a future (and its characteristic disruptive moments of resistance along the way), and a more grandiose
economy divided between fantasies of radical destruction (no meaning)
and transcendent meaning, God's meaning, or destruction as holocaust: the
absolute gift. *The Road*, we might say, gives us mourning as a "secular theology," complete with all the internal tension that this phrase harbors.

As we have seen in the preceding chapters, D. W. Winnicott offers a portrait of the "good-enough" parent whose "job" (and here I invoke McCarthy's use of this term [75, 77]) is, perversely enough, to fail the child, and this
failure is a question of timing. "Time is kept going by the mother, and this
is one aspect of her auxiliary ego-functioning," writes Winnicott, "but the
infant comes to have a personal time-sense, one that lasts at first only over
a short span."[53] In contemporary extreme-parenting scenarios (patriarchy at
the end of the world, motherhood in captivity), however, "timing" presents
itself not as a simple task or a creative art but rather as a nearly unmanageable violence. To note the extraordinarily charged question of separation in
The Road's apocalyptic landscape is, perhaps, to come to the recognition

that love is always the end of the world. "You're the king," says Carol to Max in Jonze's *Where the Wild Things Are*. "And look at me. I'm big. How could guys like us worry about a tiny little thing like the sun?"[54] When McCarthy's father faces what he believes will be his son's last illness, he also faces what he thinks of, quite simply, as "the last day on earth" (250). Although one might offer a general account of how all parents make a world for and with their children, in the contemporary moment of environmental crisis, economic vulnerability, and postpatriarchal sociality, this world making is all the more exposed in its fragility. All there is, indeed, in *The Road* is the end of the world and parental love, and the boy, as posthumanist wild child, might be said to figure their coincidence.

If, as I have suggested, two distinct allegories of parent–child relations characterize contemporary fiction, McCarthy's story surely partakes more of "late-patriarchal terror" than of "maternal ethics." Yet *The Road* is not without its own complexity, both because patriarchy has come to borrow something from the maternal (even if this is in the counterintuitive form, as I have suggested, of a heightened masculinity) and because it seems fair to say that *The Road* understands very well the affective complex that would resist development and the relinquishment of fantasied omnipotence: indeed, it figures this resistance as a fantasy scenario *of* the end of the world. The father's first words to his son are "I'm right here"; the son's reply, "I know." But the novel also includes traces or glimpses of another world and of what we might call ethical abandonment.

An ethical burden realizes itself, for McCarthy's father figure, in the form of an almost unbearable question. *The Road* is full of conversations about the father and son's radical interdependency: "each the other's world entire." But, in addition, the father considers more privately (this is the father's interiority) whether or not he could kill his son were this the only remaining option: "Can you do it? When the time comes? When the time comes there will be no time. Now is the time. Curse God and die. What if it doesnt fire? It has to fire. What if it doesnt fire? Could you crush that beloved skull with a rock? Is there such a being within you of which you know nothing? Can there be? Hold him in your arms. Just so. The soul is quick. Pull him toward you. Kiss him. Quickly" (114). To suspend the narrative premise of *The Road* is to be reminded of how peculiar it is to be reading a narrative that concerns a parent's sovereign power over his child's life or death and, at the same time, it is not so peculiar if one considers the contemporary intensification around questions of sexual and social reproduction: "The only thing that you actually know for one hundred percent certain about a baby that you are bringing into the world is that it will die. It's the only given. Everything else, there is a lot of wild chance involved."[55] But what does it mean that the father's ultimate answer to his own question here is no: I could not kill my son even if it were the "right" or best thing to do; I cannot make this sacrifice? Should we conclude that McCarthy's father is not Abraham—and not God? Or should we simply note that this contemplated paternal violence constitutes the return of what has previously been banished from the landscape, the ambivalence internal to the father–son relation? And, finally, how do we come to terms with the possibility that in the scenario McCarthy depicts, killing the child would also represent keeping a certain parental promise to the child and refusing to tolerate any separation?[56]

Indeed, another related component of the father's ethical burden accounts for a formally very disquieting passage in The Road, a moment when the narrative voice markedly shifts, calling attention to itself in a way that is unique in the novel. The man speaks in the first person and invokes a time back before the mother's departure when he attempted to capture and kill a dog but ultimately promised his crying and begging son that he would not hurt the animal. The passage concludes, "The next day it was gone. That is the dog he remembers. He doesnt remember any little boys" (87). A single paragraph would seem to use the memory of the dog to smuggle in and simultaneously dismiss the reference to a little boy who is in some sense extraneous to the passage in question. So there never were any little boys at the end of the world other than his son, we are told. The man's assertion that there were not any other little boys to be remembered underlines, once again, his very tenuous hold on being and relation while simultaneously, and even more acutely, performing the work of insisting (but to whom?) that he would not have deserted any child. This moment justifies, both provisionally and symptomatically, precisely that which can never be justified: the man's commitment to his own son as his own son.[57] It is as if the father's failure (he will not keep his promise to his son) seeks a kind of compensation in the idea that he would not have abandoned any child. At the very end of the novel, the son asks his father, "Just take me with you. Please." The father responds:

I cant.
Please, Papa.

I cant. I cant hold my son dead in my arms. I thought I could but I cant.
You said you wouldnt ever leave me. (279)

Not only does this father not save all children, all little boys, or even specifically that "other little boy," but he also deserts this very intimate and
vulnerable one. It is perhaps this "other little boy" or "other child" who, by
disrupting the opposition between one's own child and Children, figures
(posthumanist) wildness and haunts the specificity of any ethical commitment.

The Road, in other words, does not completely remain inside what Edelman characterizes as a desire to protect the other who is really only ourselves. Edelman takes on, with unmatchable wit and vitriol, the extent to
which we succumb to this false desire and thus misrecognize Oedipal urges
as ethical goals in taking up the side of the children. But I want to suggest
that "maybe"—and just maybe—McCarthy's father is also able to contemplate his own irrelevance to the son and to the future. I have suggested, and
will continue to argue in the chapters that follow, that the very intensity of
the parenting scenario (parenting in a state of emergency) testifies to the
emergence of the wild child as a critical signifier of posthumanist futurity.
And again, I think, Winnicott proves helpful in grasping some elements of
this child and this parent–child relation. Winnicott depicts a clinical scene
in which a subject glimpses externality, "the world," through a destruction
of the beloved object while the analyst's intimacy and identification with
the patient allows him to grasp this process: "Should the philosopher come
out of his chair," writes Winnicott, "and sit on the floor with his patient . . .
he will find that there is an intermediate position. In other words, he will
find that after 'subject relates to object' comes 'subject destroys object' [as
it becomes external]; and then may come 'object survives destruction by
the subject.' But there may or may not be survival."[58] And here is the crucial
twist: if, in Winnicott's developmental scheme, it is the child who must come
to destroy, tolerate, and survive the other's otherness, in McCarthy's novel
it is also the father. The father, in other words, is the subject who relates to
the object (the son, in the economy of patriarchy) and the subject who then
destroys the object—insofar as the father fails in his promise to his son, fails
to protect him. In this instance, "destroying" refers to relinquishing the son
as a projection, an idealization, or the subject of absolute protection; and
the object (the son) may or may not survive. The father takes on such a

primal developmental process both because, for Winnicott, such a trajectory gets replayed—"*playing has a place* and a time. . . . *[I]t is play that is the universal*"—and never surmounted, and, more crucially for this analysis, because the contemporary moment, with its attendant and specific anxieties, suggests that the world may not survive our destructive capacities.[59]

What does "world" mean? It is surely not identical with the earth, although it is not entirely separable either. Is "world" (merely) akin to a symbolic structure? Are there many worlds? Who shares a world or worlds? The very signifier "world" echoes back to us in its strangeness. Although I hesitate to compare the world to a mother (*the* mother?) for numerous reasons, the Winnicottian paradigm does suggest a compelling way to approach this line of thought: for the subject of humanism, that is to say, the world might have functioned like a (good-enough) mother, but a certain "failure" may provide us with new ways to think and practice care. And, indeed, McCarthy's paternal and decidedly allegorical figure does seem to minimally register that the future, if there is one, is not his, and that for him this future is, by definition, wildly unimaginable. Waking from a dream of "creatures of a kind he'd never seen before . . . crouching by the side of his cot," the father "turned and looked at the boy. Maybe he understood for the first time that to the boy he was himself an alien. A being from a planet that no longer existed. The tales of which were suspect" (153).

3

Maternal Love / Maternal Violence

Inventing Ethics in Toni Morrison's *A Mercy*

I always think of the sacrifice from the Bible. If God came to Sarah and told her, "Give me your only son, your only one, your beloved Isaac," she will tell him, "Give me a break," not to say "Fuck off." She will not collaborate with it, not a chance in the world. And Abraham immediately collaborated.

—David Grossman

There is nothing foreordained about maternal response.

—Sara Ruddick, *Maternal Thinking*

Many critics have written about the failure of psychoanalytic theory to address maternal subjectivity adequately, even as it relies on the person of the mother as the ground for the emergence of every figure (a kind of ground zero). Barbara Johnson, for example, in an account of the work of D. W. Winnicott, has deftly analyzed how the very attempt to move away from extolling maternity repeats, rather than departs from, the violence of idealization. Winnicott tells us that what every child needs is a good-enough mother, who is usually, although not necessarily, the child's biological mother: "Naturally, the infant's own mother is more likely to be good enough than some other person, since this active adaptation demands an easy and unresented preoccupation with the one infant; in fact, success in infant care depends on the fact of devotion, not on cleverness or intellectual enlightenment."[1] As we have seen, this devoted mother, in Winnicott's account, strategically fails her growing infant, relieving this subject-coming-into-being of the very delusion of her omnipotence. In a complex play of

101

relation and the possibility of relation, the child comes to realize that it does not control the other and thus that there is an other. She is ushered into a vulnerable yet survivable state of subjecthood. *Too* good, argues Winnicott, would be no good at all. "The 'good-enough mother,'" Johnson writes in response, "is the new 'good mother'; the former 'good mother' has now become 'bad.'"[2]

Johnson, at once attuned to the possibilities of Winnicott's account and to the tyranny and endurance of a particular fantasy of the maternal, explores the way in which every perceived failure of any particular mother merely does the work of sustaining an uninhabitable ideal: "The child thus gets to believe in the possibility that deprivation is not necessary but contingent, a function of the sins of this particular mother and not of the process of becoming human itself."[3] But if psychoanalytic theory sometimes appears to fall symptomatically short—perhaps participating in the very fantasy it would also analyze (the mother as the child's perfectly adequate other)—an abundance of literary texts *do* contemplate this nexus of concerns. In this regard, literature seems to be a necessary supplement to any psychoanalytic theory of the parent–child bond.

Toni Morrison, as is well known, offers her readers numerous provocative and complex accounts of the mother–child bond. One need only recall the rather stark example of Eva Peace in *Sula* (1973), who kills her adult son, setting him on fire in his bed after he loses himself in drug addiction. In words few readers will forget, she asks her daughter, "Is? My baby? Burning?"[4] But Morrison's accounts of maternal psychopathology, affect, and conflict, or the lack thereof, also engage crucially with ethical discourse. Eva, for example, is able to kill her son precisely because she accepts absolute or sovereign responsibility for his life. Here, Derek Attridge's provisional distinction between "responsibility to" and "responsibility for" may prove helpful. To respond *to* the other, on the one hand, is to recognize the other as a different and complete subject, a fellow sovereign center of consciousness. To take responsibility *for* the other, on the other hand, is to risk a kind of (ethical) violence, both to the other and to the self: "Responsibility for the other involves assuming the other's needs, being willing to be called to account for the other, surrendering one's goals and desires in deference to the other's. (Exactly *to* whom we are responsible or answerable in this situation is one of the questions I shall have to leave unaddressed.)"[5] How presumptuous, one might conclude! Certainly, one cannot presume more than when one takes another's life. The reader may conclude that Eva makes a "mistake" in taking responsibility for and killing her adult son and that part of this mistake is her presumption that he is an infant ("[m]y baby") and thus less than a subject or less than an other. And what of the fact that her particular goal is to kill her son before he regresses too profoundly? He wants, as she says, to climb back into her womb—which would kill her and would certainly not constitute a dignified place for him to be. The world of *Sula* comprises curious and uncanny reversals (as well as some unforgettably wild children) and is suffused with a psychological logic that evades rational accounting, but might Eva's presumption and fiery authority be considered ethical nevertheless?

Temporarily leaving aside these speculations, this chapter calls attention to two distinctive factors in Morrison's maternal ethics. First, it accentuates Morrison's repeated preoccupation with subjects on the threshold of being—emerging, protolinguistic, or "wild" subjects. What does it mean to take responsibility for such beings—or to be such a being? Is there any other kind of responsibility? Perhaps ethics is always already a kind of violence? Second, this chapter emphasizes some of the ways in which Morrison's fiction recurrently explores the decisions of women who have little or no legal protection, characters who are always already located in the space of "wilderness" (a term I'm taking from Morrison) or in the space of "ethics." This somewhat unlikely pair of terms, *wilderness* and *ethics*, are almost interchangeable, because ethics emerges, as many thinkers have reminded us, precisely when and where established legal and moral codes fail to comprehend and protect. Morrison has said of Sethe's act of infanticide in *Beloved* (1987), "It was absolutely the right thing to do . . . but it's also the thing you have no right to do."[6] It is this repetition with a difference (the difference between the first "right" and the second "right") that I want to explore in what follows.

In Morrison's 2008 novel, *A Mercy*, this wild or ethical space has become generalized. It is not just here or there, markedly localized; it is almost everywhere. This is a significant part of what draws Morrison to early America. She writes of Bacon's Rebellion (1676), "Half a dozen years ago an army of blacks, natives, whites, mulattoes—freedmen, slaves and indentured—had waged war against local gentry led by members of that very class. When that 'people's war' lost its hopes to the hangman, the work it had done—which included the slaughter of opposing tribes and running the Carolinas off their land—spawned a thicket of new laws authorizing chaos in defense of order."[7] To be drawn backward is to be drawn toward historical source material, to the moment when race and slavery emerge as ways to "organize" ethical wilderness for white subjects; but it is also to be drawn toward yet another way of figuring those questions of subjecthood, ethics, and black life in America that have always arrested Morrison's attention. Valerie Babb argues that *A Mercy* "is an American origins narrative that re-places the racial, gender, and class complexities lost in the creation of a canonical narrative that sought to privilege the few over the many."[8] Babb, responding to John Updike's far more limited assessment of Morrison's novel as a "noble and necessary fictional project of exposing the infamies of slavery and the hardships of being African American,"[9] suggests that *A Mercy* is "not meant to characterize one racial history." Rather, she asserts, the novel succeeds insofar as it is "illustrative of the workings of a larger social and cultural system that creates 'infamies' and 'hardships' for any not part of the dominant classes."[10]

In this chapter, I would like to supplement Babb's more historical emphasis (on Morrison's account of the complex prehistory of "[the] development of a culture based on marketplace values")[11] with an account of *A Mercy*'s wrenching mother–daughter relationship, the enigmatic wild child that chattel slavery produces, and the novel's distinctly allegorical articulation of an original space for ethics. This articulation of precise historical formations with larger and more abstract structures of philosophical, psychoanalytic, and political import gives Morrison's oeuvre its distinctive force. But I also want to read Morrison in relationship to Jean Laplanche's account of the parent–child bond, an intergenerational "gift" or inheritance constituted by enigmatic messages, and in relationship to Derrida's writing on the "gift of death." In Morrison, this doubled "gift" is reimagined as decisively maternal and even as the foundation for what I have been calling a maternal ethics.[12]

The closest theoretical articulation of Morrison's literary treatment of parental signs can be found in Laplanche's psychoanalytic writings. Laplanche's return to and rereading of Freud's seduction theory (which Freud putatively abandoned in 1897 with the very foundation of psychoanalysis) allows him to articulate the primacy of the other for the structural development and sustenance of the subject. Laplanche argues that all children are "seduced" by the enigmatic messages of their parents, messages that remain opaque to the parents as well: "The primal scene conveys messages. It is traumatizing only because it proffers, indeed imposes its enigmas, which compromise the spectacle addressed to the child. I certainly have no wish to make an inventory of these messages. . . . A message of exclusion is virtually inherent in the situation itself."[13] All subjects, Laplanche insists, will continue to orbit around this encrypted and traumatic bit of signification, simultaneously misreading themselves as self-centered. We are, then, according to Laplanche, possessed by the material signifier—"the letter"—or, more accurately, by the (m)other's address.

At such moments, Laplanche's work clearly resonates with a deconstructive articulation of signification and inheritance: the fundamental uncertainty about whether or not a letter ever reaches its destination. Laplanche makes a case for what he calls the "reality of the message," crucially to be distinguished from both psychical reality (the reality of a single subject) and material reality (that which could be said to be objectively "there," an event insofar as it is free of the distortions of human desire and investment). "So we have the reality of the message," writes Laplanche, "and the irreducibility of the fact of communication. What psychoanalysis adds is a fact of its experience, namely that this message is frequently compromised, that it both fails and succeeds at one and the same time" (169).[14]

Both Laplanche and Derrida can be usefully juxtaposed with Morrison for their shared and profound sense of the elusive yet decisive way that signification and, more specifically, acts of address both make and undo us as subjects. Derrida writes, "If the readability of a legacy were given, natural, transparent, univocal, if it did not call for and at the same time defy interpretation, we would never have anything to inherit from it. We would be affected by it as by a cause—natural or genetic. One always inherits from a secret—which says 'read me, will you ever be able to do so?'"[15] Morrison echoes this question with her tale of a particular and violent history and its ghostly afterlife.

In the early American world of A Mercy, Jacob Vaark, an Anglo–Dutch trader and farmer who is not yet involved in the slave, sugar, and rum trades—"Flesh was not his commodity" (22)—goes south to Maryland and Virginia to collect a debt from a cash-poor Portuguese nobleman, who will pay what he owes with a slave. This is part of the account of Vaark's experience: "Breathing the air of a world so new, almost alarming in rawness and temptation, never failed to invigorate him. Once beyond the warm gold of the bay, he saw forests untouched since Noah. . . . Now here he was, a ratty orphan become landowner, making a place out of no place, a temperate living from raw life" (12). *A Mercy*'s ethical or wild space, the space of "raw life," is marked by lawlessness and an almost universal state of orphanhood: "They were orphans, each and all" (59). To put this more accurately, it is not that there are no laws or that everyone is an orphan in this colonial outpost but rather that the terrain is extremely precarious: it is unclear where a space ends and where another begins. Morrison's Virginia resonates with the New World as described in Jonathan Elmer's discerning study of race and sovereignty in early America: a "liminal space in which sovereign power and 'bare life' square off."[16] Where is law in this space, and whose law is it? This one here has legal protection, and that one there does not; this one here seems to have a claim to be mothered—a right to be mothered—yet she is abandoned. Or (and this is to jump ahead) this child is given the gift of her singularity, which is also the gift of (her) death.

Vaark meditates on the "cruelty" of "lawless laws": "In short, 1682 and Virginia was still a mess. Who could keep up with the pitched battles for God, king and land?" (11). In contrast, the narrator offers a more pointed account of the origin of a legal and ideological system that "separated and protected all whites from all others forever" (10). One pauses at the word *forever,* which seems to speak to a contemporary reader (when does "forever" begin?) and confronts and forcefully resists any characterization of the present moment as "postracial."[17] This "forever" might seem to proceed from an omniscient narrative voice, but it also invokes the timeless time of trauma that we might be familiar with from elsewhere in Morrison's work: "All of it is now it is always now."[18] This timeless time pervades *A Mercy,* suggesting that the novel is somehow suspended in its entirety, complicating what it means for us to call it a work of historical fiction in the usual sense of the term.[19]

The last decades of the seventeenth century were tumultuous for the Chesapeake colonies. The Navigation Acts (1651–96) and the ongoing Anglo–Dutch Wars (1652–54, 1665–67, 1672–74) for control of the tobacco trade forced Virginia planters to ship their tobacco to England in English ships. The result was a decline in the price of Virginia tobacco and an escalation of economic and political uncertainty. In the meantime, land hoarding by the eastern elite contributed to a growing sense of frustration among poorer colonial farmers unable to withstand the high rents they had to pay for their land and the low prices they were receiving for their tobacco. "[A] great many of us came in servants to others," declared one petition, "but wee adventured owr lives for it, and got owr poore living with hard labour out of the ground in a terrible Willdernis."[20] Conditions forced poorer farmers farther west into Indian territory, and tensions eventually erupted over the issue of who had the authority to wage war against the Susquehannock people dwelling north of the Potomac. Bacon's Rebellion thus brought class and race warfare to the colonies at a time when European empires (Dutch, French, Spanish, and English) were also fighting over who would control the economic resources of North America.

It was in this precarious context that a dramatic shift in the labor force of the Chesapeake colonies took place. The supply of (white) servants relative to landowners declined rapidly in the 1680s, and the following decade saw the beginning of an enormous rise in the number of enslaved Africans. "Between 1674 and 1679, there were nearly four servants for every slave found in inventories," writes Russell Menard in a discussion of probate inventories from the lower western shore of Maryland. "[By] the early 1690s," he continues, "there were nearly four slaves for every servant."[21] The decades before and after 1700 thus witnessed a transformation of Chesapeake society, Menard concludes, as the Tobacco Coast "moved from a labor system that promised poor men eventual integration into the society they served to one that kept a majority of its laborers in perpetual bondage and offered most of the others a choice between poverty and emigration" (115).

The rise of slave labor was accompanied by the gradual institutionalization and legal entrenchment of slavery in Virginia, beginning with a 1662 law passed in response to doubts about the status of "children got by any Englishman upon a Negro woman." The law declared, "[A]ll children born in this country shall be held bond or free only according to the condition of the mother."[22] In 1669, Virginia's Grand Assembly clarified the absolute right of the slave owner over his "estate": "[B]e it enacted and declared . . . if any slave resists his master . . . and by the extremity of his correction should chance to die, that his death shall not be accounted a felony . . . since it cannot be presumed that premeditated malice (which alone makes murder a felony) should induce any man to destroy his own estate."[23] In his account of late seventeenth-century Virginia, Alan Taylor writes, "As skin colour became the key marker of identity, race obscured the persistent power of class distinctions between the common planters and the great planters. . . . Chesapeake whites *felt* more equal despite the growing inequality of their economic circumstances."[24] The institutionalized racism of the slave system, in other words, helped to save white Virginians from the terrors of a social, economic, and geographical "willdernis" by producing what William Byrd called "a rank of poor creatures below them."[25]

This volatile late seventeenth-century colonial world is the setting of *A Mercy*. What does it mean, Morrison asks, to inhabit this space, this wilderness, this emerging ideological configuration, both as an abandoned "wild" child left to read signs ("Other signs need more time to understand. Often there are too many signs. . . . I sort them and try to recall, yet I know I am missing much" [4]) and as a mother whose responsibility would seem to be absolute? In fact, Morrison's black protagonists often seem to occupy the political space that Thomas Hobbes referred to as a "state of nature," in which the mother plays a decisive role:

> If there be no contract, the dominion is in the mother. For in the condition of mere nature, where there are no matrimonial laws, it cannot be known who is the father unless it be declared by the mother; and therefore the right of dominion over the child dependeth on her will, and is consequently hers. Again, seeing the infant is first in the power of the mother, so as she may either nourish or expose it; if she nourish it, it oweth its life to the mother, and is therefore obliged to obey her rather than any other; and by consequence the dominion over it is hers.[26]

As the institutional contours of slavery came into focus, Virginia's black population found itself increasingly isolated in a legally demarcated "state of nature" within the colonial space.

Not only does the mother in *A Mercy* not know who her daughter's father is—"I don't know who is your father. It was too dark to see any of them. . . . There is no protection" (163)—but she, and she alone, must decide whether to let her child escape slavery through death. Like many an enslaved woman, Florens's mother might have chosen "exposure" as the more merciful option. The mother's and daughter's situations remind us that the law forcing children to follow the condition of the mother ensures that all enslaved persons are excluded from participation in the symbolic (social and juridical) structures that constitute civil status. Slavery thus serves to generate and quarantine a "wilderness" of rightlessness ("laws authorizing chaos in defense of order" [10]) that, in turn, produces a domain of absolute rights for others: the same legal system that gives enslaved Africans no standing also allows white male rapists of black women to take advantage of a strategic legal invisibility in order to augment their wealth and power. The state in which the mother has dominion, the precontractual "state of nature," is, as Hobbes famously insisted, a state of terrible vulnerability. If *A Mercy*'s slave mother and child invoke a Hobbesean sense of prepolitical rightlessness, they also remind us that every mother–child relationship inhabits a kind of noncontractual "state of nature." "If there be no contract," writes Hobbes, "the dominion is in the mother."[27] Morrison, in other words, by depicting the plight of the powerless sovereign, the slave mother who makes a decision concerning life and death, at the same time explores the complex realm of maternal ethics. The challenge for Morrison's characters and readers is to disentangle the difficult experience of mothering and being mothered from the violence of racialized subjection.

While on the face of it Morrison's historical fiction would seem to have little to do with contemporary reproductive politics and its (apparent) choices, I suggest that this is indeed, and quite crucially, part of the context for her work. It has become commonplace to refer to the quasi-regulated state of reproductive technologies as a "Wild West."[28] The recent work of sociologist and legal scholar Dorothy E. Roberts is helpful here when it comes to decoding this figure. Although Roberts clearly accounts for the stratified system of reproduction in the United States, with its long and foundational history, she also argues that neoliberal policies and ideology unite all women, ironically, in the very act of isolating them from one another: "The women at opposite ends of the reproductive hierarchy are part of an interlocking system of privatization and punishment. . . . The most privileged women's increasing reliance on high-tech reproductive remedies for socially-caused problems thus obscures the role they share with the most disadvantaged women in the neo-liberal shift from social welfare to privatization and capital accumulation."[29] In addition, it is apparent that beyond the United States, forms of global inequality continue to abandon women to the so-called law of the market. In *Life as Surplus: Biotechnology and Capitalism in the Neoliberal Era*, Melinda Cooper writes of the "sourcing of human eggs" that is "increasingly drawing on the underpaid, unregulated labor of various female underclasses." Reminding us precisely of the border that would purport to separate the humanist subject from the animal and the free white person from the slave, Cooper adds, "the differences between human reproductive medicine and the brute commodification of labor and tissues that prevails in the agricultural industry becomes difficult to maintain."[30] There is, in other words, a certain correlation, as attention to the contemporary context of Morrison's novel makes clear, between the "neoliberal" and the "premodern" or "the state of nature." Morrison's novel would thus ask us to distinguish responsibility as an ideologically charged neoliberal term from a more complex (and historically informed) ethical account.[31]

A Mercy is a story of precarious relations in a place of minimal legal and political structure: "There had always been tangled strings among them. Now they were cut" (133). It tells its story by privileging several focalizing figures: not only Vaark but also his wife, Rebekkah, who comes from England to be his bride ("America. Whatever the danger, how could it possibly be worse?" [78]); his workers, Lina and Sorrow; his slave, Florens; and two indentured servants from a neighboring farm, Willard and Scully. The last few pages of the novel are a first-person address offered by Florens's mother to her daughter. But it is the consciousness of the novel's wild child, Florens, that is privileged or set apart in *A Mercy*; whereas most of the novel, with the exception of the last few pages, is written in the third person, Florens's sections, which punctuate the text, are written in the first person and in the present tense. Confessing or "tell[ing]" her story to her estranged lover, Florens scratches her narrative onto the walls of a room until "[t]here is no more room in this room. These words cover the floor" (160). This is a house that nobody will ever enter and that will probably be burned to the ground. What is more, her lover cannot read, or at least he cannot read this kind of writing: "You read the world but not the letters of talk. You don't know how to" (160). This motif of failed address becomes, in Morrison's work, an allegory for subjecthood and relation: "One question is who is responsible? Another is can you read?" (3).

Morrison imagines an insistent signifying force, an address, a claim, that never becomes transparent communication but nevertheless has disruptive effects. Ultimately, the reader is unable to decide whether Florens's signifying is pointless, going nowhere—"These careful words . . . will talk to themselves" (161)—or whether her words will be radically disseminated, in an almost Whitmanesque mode: "Perhaps these words need the air that is out in the world. Need to fly up then fall, fall like ash over acres of primrose and mallow . . . flavor the soil" (161). Florens's writing is the writing of a subject—the "slave"—presumed to be simultaneously inside and outside the world of language and law. To be enslaved is to be treated, repeatedly, as if one is and is not a signifying subject and as if one could and could not read the signifiers that produce a world. If, as we shall see, Laplanchean psychoanalytic theory emphasizes the constitutive function of miscommunication for the subject, Morrison's work, with its distinctive dovetailing of psychic and sociohistorical forces, takes the risk of exposing some of the ways in which the violence of slavery (as with the somewhat more figurative language of captivity in Donoghue's *Room*) merges with the violence of becoming a speaking, writing being.

Vaark first brings eight-year-old Florens home to his wife as a kind of offering, as they have recently lost a child. This is not a gift that Rebekkah is willing to receive, but Lina (his Native American servant) forms a close maternal bond with young Florens. Childlessness, whether the loss of a child (in the case of the women) or the lack of an heir (in Vaark's case), is a crucial element of this text. It is because Vaark lacks an heir that he is tempted and falls. Here, Morrison gestures toward a differently centered narrative focused on the need, greed, and fear that produce slavery (recall Vaark's own self-described trajectory from "ratty orphan to landowner"). This would be, of course, a story of generation and male hereditary power: "Now he fondled the idea of an even more satisfying enterprise. And the plan was as sweet as the sugar on which it was based. And there was a profound difference between the intimacy of slave bodies at Jublio and a remote labor force in Barbados. Right? Right, he thought, looking at a sky vulgar with stars. Clear and right. . . . [That night] he slept well enough. Probably because his dreams were of a grand house of many rooms rising on a hill above the fog" (35).[32] Vaark is seduced by the decadent Portuguese aristocrat's privilege even as he is repulsed by him. This leads to his involvement in the slave trade, which in turn finances the building of an impressive and thoroughly unnecessary home, "a profane monument to himself" (44), complete with magnificent iron gates crafted by a free black man, the unnamed blacksmith.

But Vaark contracts smallpox and only just survives to be carried into his palatial home, where he expires on the floor. His wife, Rebekkah, is then taken ill with the same disease, and Florens is sent on a journey to retrieve the blacksmith, who has proved himself to be skilled as a healer. Florens, about sixteen at this time, is eager to go, because she is madly in love with the blacksmith. But the passion that prevails in *A Mercy* is not what it appears to be. It is instead what Morrison calls "mother-hunger—to be one or have one" (63). Florens's love for the blacksmith is no exception. He is a substitute for that original maternal object. One will recall Freud's famous comment: "There are thus good reasons why a child sucking at his mother's breast has become the prototype of every relation of love. The finding of an object is in fact the refinding of it."[33] It is traumatic object loss, separation from this object, and perceived betrayal by this object—the failed parental promise—that form the crux of *A Mercy*. Indeed, the present-tense narrative of Florens's journey to find the blacksmith performs a displacement and repetition of a return to the mother. Psychic need, or we might say trauma, generates the narrative.

It is important to understand that this replayed traumatic separation is also, crucially for Morrison, the very primal scene of slavery: the separation of mother and child.[34] In other words, Morrison chooses to privilege the maternal story over a tale of fathers, property, and the patriarchal name even as she also shows us their profound interrelation: civil society produces the "state of nature" that it then appears to unearth.[35] Ethical dilemmas often— perhaps always—involve a reading of the difficult border between signification (what is meaningful, human, and alive) and what is designated "animal" or even sheer materiality. The institution of slavery supposedly solves this problem for those in power by performing a violently simple claim: we, white subjects, are meaningful, human, and alive; and you, black slaves, are materiality. Slavery says that black mothers and children can be separated because "we" have decided that they are closer to the merely material or "natural." Here, one might recall Schoolteacher's lesson in *Beloved*: his attempt to teach his students to separate out the human and animal characteristics of slaves is precisely what Sethe cannot allow her children to reexperience. Sethe reports hearing Schoolteacher with his pupils: "No, no. That's not the way. I told you to put her human characteristics on the left; her animal ones on the right. And don't forget to line them up."[36] Similarly, Lina tells Florens that Sir (Vaark) has "a clever way of getting [some*thing*] without giving [any*thing*]"; Florens remarks, "I know it is true because I see it forever and ever" (7). What she sees, of course, is her scene of traumatic separation from her mother, a scene that reduces the child to the status of a commodity. In *A Mercy*, the enslaved woman's child is purchased to be given to a white woman. When this woman chooses not to accept this gift, the child will be depersonified and desacralized as she is reduced to the status of a laboring body.[37] Morrison's characters are then left to read the excess of being designated mere materiality, and their acts of reading, acts most poignantly figured in the character of Florens, might then be understood as vital forms of resistance.[38]

Florens's mother gives her daughter away to Vaark, who, insofar as he returns to this moment at all, recalls only the mother "throwing away" (34) a child for whom she had "no use" (96). But, of course, Florens is not her mother's to give, and in reality she begs Vaark to accept Florens as payment for her master's debt. He should take Florens rather than herself. This, as we eventually learn, represents an attempt on the mother's part to protect her daughter from sexual violence. Florens certainly experiences this as an act of abandonment and as evidence of her own replaceability by her mother's male child, recalling Julia Kristeva's account of the child's fundamental query: What does my mother want? "At any rate, not I."[39] Florens also struggles throughout the text to hear and read her mother's message: "[M]others nursing greedy babies scare me. I know how their eyes go when they choose. How they raise them to look at me hard, saying something I cannot hear. Saying something important to me, but holding the little boy's hand" (8).

There are profound echoes of *Beloved* here and, in complex ways, throughout the text, but what I want to emphasize is the formative effect of the mother's unreadable message: it is not only that Florens tries to read a message from which she is cut off (both on the level of realist plot and on the level of the narrative structure) but also that this message constitutes her as a subject. It is important to think here in terms of a far less instrumental model of language, one that is crucial for understanding Morrison's goal and for engaging in psychoanalytic thinking. As I have already indicated, we hear the direct address that Florens herself can never quite hear ("Oh Florens. My love. Hear a tua mãe" [167]), whereas Florens is left to read the enigma of the maternal gift or wound. She cannot stop reading her mother's decision to give her away to Vaark, yet she cannot read this apparent failure to protect as love. Freud's infamous "What does a woman want?"[40] gives way here to Kristeva's and Lacan's revisions: What does my mother want? *"Chè vuoi?"*[41] The parental address that sustains this wild child simultaneously eludes her, because she is barred from receiving its full import (the signified). Morrison's wild child is precisely a bit of unmoored material-discursive signifying force. Although the distinctive nature of this scene is clear (the primal scene of slavery as separation of mother and child), it also resonates with every scene of intensive parenting under discussion in this study (with Ma's allegory of the cave in *Room*, for example, and with the ethics of abandonment in *The Road*). Morrison's fictional account of enslavement and the origins of race is a portrait of vulnerable being and maternal responsibility and, as such, it also anticipates a set of contemporary questions about the ethics of sexual and social reproduction.

A Mercy, like other Morrison novels, engages with parental gifts and encourages us to read these narratives as allegories of relationality and responsibility between generations and members of any community. But always there remains the insistent specificity of slavery. Slavery, one might argue, proffers at once a forced suspension of, and solution to, the ethical dilemmas of the "gifts" of life and death, and an engagement with those dilemmas as they continue to affect and produce the lives of both enslaved and freed African Americans. Parents always give children the violent gift of death (a "gift" of sustenance and poison), and parents also always give children the gift (again mixed) of an unconscious. The first is the gift of one's individuality and mortality, the second of unreadable, perpetual dependence—the enigma of indebtedness. However, under the specific historical conditions of slavery, as Morrison depicts them, these gifts are usurped.

One might ask, then, whether *A Mercy* is a novel with any kind of therapeutic trajectory (and here, again, my point of comparison is *Beloved*) or whether, as I contend, the text only tentatively inscribes the possibility of the future as a partial and belated reception of the other's enigmatic message. Florens, after all, not only gets the wrong or incomplete message, and this is what keeps her reading; her very being is sustained by the feeling that her mother wants to tell her something. Even if the mother is in an impossible and suspended position (on her knees), she too keeps signifying: "I stayed on my knees. In the dust where my heart will remain each night and every day until you understand what I know and long to tell you" (167). One almost has the sense that the mother and daughter's mutual energy has generated the text we are reading, a text that begins with Florens's words and ends with her mother's. Yet this is hardly a story with any promise of a future for Florens or any sense that ideal communication between mother and daughter will be achieved.[42] Morrison's novels collectively challenge us to think about the problem of the future—something else they share with that form of therapeutic endeavor we call psychoanalysis.

Morrison's representation of Laplanchean enigmatic signification (the gift of the unconscious) echoes a crucial precursor text: William Faulkner's *Absalom, Absalom!* In the first place, Vaark's ambitions borrow from those of Thomas Sutpen. Vaark realizes after he has gone "head to head" with the "rich gentry . . . that only things, not bloodlines or character separated them" (27). Recall, too, in that tortured text, the plight of Charles Bon, who wants a sign from his father, a sign that would indicate that his father is indeed his father.[43] For Bon, such a sign would constitute the most minimal form of bond and address. If Bon originally imagines receiving a letter, he eventually dreams of acquiring even the vaguest bit of perilously signifying or nonsignifying materiality: a hair, a fingernail paring.[44] Morrison picks up on this relation in *Jazz* (1992) and rewrites it in the context of Joe Trace's relationship with not his father but his mother, Wild. Trace pleads with the woman who may or may not be his mother: "'Give me a sign, then. You don't have to say nothing. Let me see your hand. Just stick it out someplace and I'll go; I promise. A sign.' He begged, pleaded for her hand until the light grew even smaller. 'You my mother?' Yes. No. Both. Either. But not this nothing."[45] This is to say that children in the work of Faulkner and Morrison can be constituted by a parental address, an unreadable message, even a lack of message (as one is left to decide what kind of absence an absence is).[46] According to Derrida, this gesture is integral to Western philosophy: "This essential drift bearing on writing as an iterative structure, cut off from all absolute responsibility, from *consciousness* as the ultimate authority, orphaned and separated at birth from the assistance of its father, is precisely what Plato condemns in the *Phaedrus.* If Plato's gesture is, as I believe, the philosophical movement par excellence, one can measure what is at stake here."[47] Orphaned children in this philosophical-fictional tradition are thus also inscriptions of "writing"; while she tends to shift the focus onto the figure of the mother, Morrison, like Faulkner, explores a particular traumatic severing of this writing from its fantastic point of origin. Thus, although both Faulkner and Morrison could be said to participate in a Western philosophical fascination with the anxiety of parental separation, they also complicate that tradition: Faulkner with his portraits of characters attempting to construct themselves as their own point of origin, and Morrison with her turn to the space of what I have been calling a maternal ethics.

Morrison presents us with a particularly dense account of the subject cut free of authority and protection when Florens is deprived of the letter of authorization and permission that her mistress has given her to carry on her journey to find the blacksmith:

> *The signatory of this letter, Mistress Rebekka Vaark of Milton vouches for the female person into whose hands it has been placed. She is owned by me and can be knowne by a burne mark in the palm of her left hand. Allow her the courtesie of safe passage and witherall she may need to complete her errand. Our life, my life, on this earthe depends on her speedy return.*
>
> > *Signed Rebekka Vaark, Mistress, Milton*
> > *18 May 1690* (112)

In other words, Florens is a wild piece of signification in need of a letter like this to locate her, to authorize her, in the semiotic chaos of late seventeenth-century Virginia. She is to be identified "*by a burne mark in the palm of her left hand,*" which oddly doubles her own being. What does a dark-skinned person signify at this moment and in this place? Upon whom will she stumble?

Florens is taken in and provided with sustenance by the Widow Ealing and her daughter Jane. The community currently suspects Jane of being a demon or a witch (another kind of "wild child"), but those with communal authority are temporarily distracted from the current target of the witch hunt by Florens's presence: "One woman speaks saying I have never seen any human this black. I have says another, this one is as black as others I have seen. She is Afric. Afric and much more, says another. . . . It is true then says another. The Black Man is among us. This is his minion" (111). Meanwhile, Florens attempts to show them her letter, which they are at first afraid to touch: "I shout, wait. I shout, please sir. I think they have shock that I can talk. Let me show you my letter I say quieter. It proves I am nobody's minion but my Mistress" (111). They then subject Florens to a dehumanizing bodily search—the very antithesis of intersubjective recognition—that has the effect of performatively constituting her as a thing. Despite their investigations, however, they are left uncertain; for Satan, it seems, is adept at deploying the unreliable materiality of the "orphan" signifier severed from its (divine, patriarchal, or authorial) origin. In fact, this would seem to be precisely his game: "A woman's voice asks would Satan write a letter. Lucifer is all deceit and trickery says another" (113).

The interrogators leave to "consult" and "pray," and Florens, with Jane's help, escapes bereft of the written supplement that lends her a very fragile claim to legitimacy: "With the letter I belong and am lawful. Without it I am a weak calf abandoned by the herd, a turtle without shell, a minion with no telltale signs but a darkness I am born with, outside, yes, but inside as well and the inside dark is small, feathered and toothy. Is that what my mother knows? Why she chooses me to live without? Not the outside dark we share, a minha mãe and me, but the inside one we don't" (115). Without the authorizing and protective "speech" of her owner, Florens is absolutely vulnerable (the turtle without the shell, the calf abandoned by the herd), deprived of any "encircling outside thing" (58), Lina's phrase for the minimal community necessary for survival. To be so vulnerable, it would seem, is to be minimally inscribed or blank, not to be spoken for or authorized.

The only sign she is left with, says Florens, is "a darkness," although this articulation is itself unstable, precisely because one can't tell whether "darkness" is or is not a kind of sign: "no telltale signs but [with the exception of] a darkness." Of course, this darkness is not only an "outside" darkness but also, quite crucially, an "inside" one; the "inside darkness" is simultaneously interiority itself, subjecthood, *and* racialization. Here, Morrison gestures toward the origins of "race" as a psychological reality and toward "race," not only slavery, as the experience of (maternal) abandonment. To be a racialized subject, then, is to be other to the subject of recognition, the entitled subject with rights, and this is a form of traumatically inflected racial subject formation that Morrison has explored throughout her work.[48] In *A Mercy*, this subjectivity is very much in process, both historically and for this particular individual; thus, rather than the violent simplicity of decisiveness, what we hear is Florens's haunting question: "Is that what my mother knows?" The figuration of this passage is even more complex because that "inside" darkness is also "small, feathered, and toothy." It is this "inside" that attacks and defies the blacksmith when he "repeats" the traumatic maternal abandonment: "No. Not again. Not ever. Feathers lifting, I unfold. The claws scratch and scratch until the hammer is in my hand" (142). It also echoes the various stories included in *A Mercy* of mother birds whose radical acts of protection fail, leaving their babies to survive on their own (61–63). Lina tells Florens the story of a fierce mother bird that attacks "the traveller," is attacked in turn, and is left "falling forever." Florens asks of the eggs and the new baby birds: "Do they live?" "We have," says Lina (63).[49]

I have argued here that *A Mercy* concerns "the reality of the message," in the Laplanchean sense, and that it is informed, as well, by a deconstructive account of the materiality of writing. But in *A Mercy,* one also encounters different kinds of signs and different kinds of reading. The blacksmith and Lina, for example, both teach Florens to read signs that often occur in the natural world and will predict the future: "Two hares freeze before bounding away. I don't know how to read that" (41).[50] Even as *A Mercy* is very conducive to a psychoanalytic reading, then, it is always on the threshold of articulating something extrapsychical or extrapsychoanalytic. But so are certain kinds of psychoanalysis that might be of most value to us as literary readers precisely when they depart from the rigorously or exclusively psychoanalytic. On the topic of clinical transference (or "the relation to the enigma of the other"), for example, Laplanche writes,

> [P]erhaps we are looking for something which has already been found. Or perhaps we are looking the wrong way round: we wish to transpose the model of clinical transference onto what lies beyond it (psychoanalysis "outside the clinical"), but maybe transference is already, "in itself," outside the clinic. . . . [P]erhaps the principal site of transference, "ordinary" transference, before, beyond or after analysis, would be the multiple relation to the cultural, to creation or, more precisely to the cultural message.[51]

One of the useful things about Laplanche's account, as I have suggested, is that it breaks away from the Oedipal structure and instead posits a simpler and more irreducible relationship between an adult—or adults—and a child. In Laplanche's account, a child is inevitably seduced and traumatized by an adult world of unmasterable signifiers. These signifiers are unmasterable because they are also inaccessible to the adult who signifies enigmatically, or "has" an unconscious. Language, we might then say, is the third term. The child is seduced by the very force of the enigma. Moreover, the child is even constituted performatively by the parental address with its enigmatic excess. One's very name, for example, is a parental message; we spend our lives reading and becoming our names. This account of the formation of a subject overlaps considerably with what Morrison offers us in her fiction: a traumatic articulation of the universal Laplanchean structure. Just as Laplanche offers us a theory of inheritance, of what is passed on, so too does Morrison. As a case in point, consider the crucial modulation at the end of *Beloved*: "It was not a story to pass on. . . . This is not a story to pass on" (275).

Beyond the more familiar reading, we might hear the "[i]t" and the "[t]his" in these formulations as corresponding with the two different versions of Beloved: Beloved the character, and *Beloved* the text. "It," "This," "Beloved," and *Beloved* all name the force of a kind of materialized enigmatic significa- tion, the desperate sliver of an act of address, an attempt at restoration:

> I will call them my people,
> which were not my people;
> and her beloved,
> which was not beloved. (Romans 9:25)[52]

In *A Mercy*, at the very end of her portion of the narrative, Florens writes, "I will keep one sadness. That all this time I cannot know what my mother is telling me" (161). I will keep one sadness. If Laplanche reads the established subject as an instance of misreading—one reads or misreads oneself as cen- tered, not as orbiting around the other's message—Morrison shows us how this centering or misreading might not ever successfully take place. And this, I think, gives us a different account of inheritance. Oddly enough, we might be led by Morrison's characterization to consider the possibility that traumatized subjects access a certain truth of subject formation. It is non- traumatized or less traumatized subjects who, for example, succeed in dis- placing the enigma of signification by way of a racialized othering and who enjoy the privilege of living a certain enabling pathology.

A Mercy, like *Beloved*, is a ghost story. It is concerned, as Derrida would say, with "hauntology"[53]—but not simply because we are presented with the figure of a ghost. A compelling moment in the novel occurs when the inden- tured servants Willard and Scully *believe* that they see Vaark's ghost in his never-to-be-inhabited mansion. The reader encounters the following unre- liable sentence: "Jacob Vaark climbed out of his grave to visit his beautiful house" (143). We are then offered a realistic explanation that eludes the char- acters; what Willard and Scully are really seeing is Florens in the deserted house, at night, writing her story: "I am holding light in one hand and carv- ing letters with the other" (160). It is as if at this moment, the ghost, so cru- cial in *Beloved*, is banished, even as something of Beloved's force is main- tained through the traumatic insistence of the message. In other words, it is address itself that comes across as spectral in *A Mercy*. Like Laplanche, Morrison reminds us that reading materiality into meaning is necessary for human survival—indeed, for the very constitution of the human—even as such reading is also always at risk of being merely delusional or symptomatic. We are "tricked" or seduced into being and relation (see, in this regard, the readings that follow of Lionel Shriver's *We Need to Talk about Kevin* and Kenneth Oppel's *Half Brother*). Reading and writing are potentially reparative gestures that can also be abandoned or suspended in (or out of?) time.

A Mercy is the story of a mother's choice and of a sacrifice that her daughter will never adequately read—unlike the reader who reads the whole text and then overhears the mother's address.[54] This is the "mercy" of the title, even as the mother attributes the gift of mercy to Vaark, and it recalls Derrida's analysis of the gift in *Given Time*. A gift, Derrida writes, is not a gift if either the giver or the receiver recognizes it as such: "*At the limit, the gift as gift ought not appear as gift: either to the donee or the donor.* It cannot be gift as gift except by not being present as gift. Neither to the 'one' nor to the 'other.' If the other perceives or receives it, if he or she keeps it as gift, the gift is annulled. But the one who gives it must not see it or know it either; otherwise he begins . . . to give back to himself symbolically the value of what he thinks he has given or what he is preparing to give."[55] The mother in *A Mercy* gives a gift that can't be recognized as such, and that is what constitutes it as a gift. In giving her daughter the "gift" of giving her away, the mother is crucially recognizing her daughter as a singular individual who can and must go on being in her very separateness from her mother.

Florens's mother gives, we might say, a gift of death that recalls the gift that the father gives to his son in McCarthy's *The Road*, and that Ma gives to Jack in Donoghue's *Room*, as well as a crucial Heideggerian claim as glossed by Derrida: "Death is very much that which nobody else can undergo or confront in my place. My irreplaceability is therefore conferred, delivered, 'given,' one can say by death."[56] Florens asks, "Is this dying mine alone?" (115). *A Mercy* dramatizes a situation in which a maternal gift of death (a giving of life or individual subjectivity) coincides with an effort to save the child from the dehumanization of slavery. Slavery exacerbates the element of abandonment that is at work in all subject formation and thus renders it impossible for Florens to distinguish its violence from the violence of becoming a person. Florens misreads the gift of her irreplaceability precisely as a registration of her commodified replaceability. Slavery thus leaves both mother and daughter in a state of almost unbearable suspense in relation to the mother's gift.

Florens's mother's message is that of her love for her daughter, yet she also has a lesson that she wants to pass on. This condensed philosophical discourse on the nature of sovereignty and selfhood will also remain in suspense:

> [T]o be given dominion over another is a hard thing; to wrest dominion over another is a wrong thing; to give dominion of yourself to another is a wicked thing.
>
> Oh Florens. My love. Hear a tua mãe. (167)

The first clause, "to be given dominion over another is a hard thing," would seem to refer to maternal responsibility (this is a posthumanist "absolute responsibility" and crucially *not* the neoliberal "responsibility" associated with a "society of ownership"). The second and third clauses would seem to speak to different forms of enslavement: it is wrong to take away another's right to contract or to contract away your own right to contract, through love or passion. Florens's mother, in other words, is trying to teach her daughter a lesson about the dangerous proximity of tyrannical and ethical violence. This, perhaps, is also what Morrison had in mind when she assessed Sethe's action in *Beloved*: "It was absolutely the right thing to do . . . but it's also the thing you have no right to do." The first "right" is the right that precedes civil society—the natural or divine right that does not need to wait for the law. The invocation of "no right" belongs, instead, to the civil state of constituted laws and the violation of a social contract. The slippage between these two senses of "right" opens up a space of wild indeterminacy that is the space of the ethical. This is the historical and philosophical space to which Morrison introduces us in *A Mercy*. What kind of right, *A Mercy* asks, can one seize in the wilderness of rightlessness? Morrison's novel is consumed with the relationship between wildness, or wilderness, and dominion (to have dominion or to be a minion). Florens's mother first fears for her because she is "wild" (4); the blacksmith repeats this assessment as a decidedly negative judgment (141). But ultimately, Florens claims ethical wildness for herself, a wildness that is intriguingly aligned, for her, with sheer being, survival, and persistence: "I am wilderness. I am"; "Slave. Free. I last" (157, 161).[57]

What threatens the ordinary nonenslaved child is the possibility of becoming detached from the mother too soon, too late, too little, or too much. As we have seen, this is the art of separation that must be so carefully orchestrated by Winnicott's "good-enough" mother: "The good-enough mother, as I have stated, starts off with an almost complete adaptation to her infant's needs, and as time proceeds she adapts less and less completely, gradually, according to the infant's growing ability to deal with her failure."[58] In *A Mercy*, the overwhelming threat is instead that of becoming the master's thing. In order to counter this threat, the mother must give her daughter a self, which is too much, too little, or too soon for the vulnerable Florens. This also ironically involves the mother treating her child as if she were a thing to be given: "Take the girl, she says, my daughter, she says. Me. Me. Sir agrees and changes the balance due" (7). Thus, Florens's commitment to reading and her inability (or refusal) to relinquish her mother's enigmatic message are inseparable from her struggle to tease apart the violence of slavery from the violence at work in the maternal gift of death.

There is only one "character" in Derrida's *The Gift of Death*: Søren Kierkegaard's Abraham. He experiences a terrible isolation, because he cannot explain his action to his son or wife or community (although, of course, it all does work out for Abraham in the end!). Morrison's mothers also make traumatically isolating choices that they will never be able to explain to their daughters. These mothers will never be recognized by their daughters for their profound acts of love. Such acts constitute "gifts" that are far from being unambiguously "good." And whereas Abraham and Antigone (to invoke another figure who stands for the difficulties of the ethical) each make a choice—Abraham chooses God over his love for his family, Antigone chooses family over the state—Morrison's mothers choose when there are no clear options. They forge a choice out of no option or choose between choice and no choice.[59] Morrison's mothers claim the paramount value of a familial bond when they have no rights as mothers or as any other kind of subject; they manage to give to their daughters the gift of entitled subjecthood even as it comes in the form of literal or figurative death: "It was absolutely the right thing to do . . . but it's also the thing you have no right to do." Morrison's mothers, then, might be said to bring an ethical realm into being, because they must performatively invent the right to mother as absolute responsibility: "'Yeah, it's called being a mother.' Ma nearly snarls it."[60] Florens's mother counters slavery's attempt to completely usurp the mother's role by wresting from slavery the right to give her child the gift of death. She founds a new "state" for herself and for her child in this wilderness of rightlessness. This extremely precarious maternal gesture about which Morrison seems to have no illusions resists, even as it must constitute, the psychic violence of slavery.

4

"Monstrous Decision"

Destruction and Relation in Lionel Shriver's *We Need to Talk about Kevin*

Having a baby is like leaving the back door unlocked.
Anyone could walk in.

—Lionel Shriver, "Be Here Now Means Be Gone Later"

The alternative to loving was disaster.

—Alice Munro, "My Mother's Dream"

"Believing in the Whole Human Thing"

Political and economic transformations in many of the world's wealthier countries have contributed to a cultural climate in which *not* having children feels, for more women and men, like a real and desirable option.[1] For many reasons, and for many people, procreation appears to be more of a choice than it has ever been, and the rapidly declining birth rate in those contexts in which women have the best access to education and health care certainly seems to support this claim.[2] But this apparent expansion of the power to choose has been accompanied by various manifestations of one or another form of ethical crisis: If I have a right *not* to be a parent, do I also have a right to be one? On what basis? And how do the rights of parents relate to the rights of children? Am I newly and more absolutely responsible for any life I produce, now that the decision could be said to be more authentically mine (now that the reproduction is less likely to take the form of an accident, a response to God's decree, or the practically unavoidable imposition of a patriarchal or heteronormative hegemony)? How, too, is the subject of this reproductive autonomy to think of his or her "personal" decision to have a child in relationship to questions of global overpopulation and environmental crisis? How is the decision to reproduce affected by ideological drives toward the privatization of desire and responsibility? And what, finally, is the relationship between any rationalization of procreation and the mere desire to reproduce?

To foreground this new context for "choice" is not to forget that myriad forms of reproductive compulsion and limitation continue to operate alongside, or in a relationship of dependency with, the right to choose whether or not to have a child. Expanded international adoption and more or less visible economies of surrogate pregnancy also participate in a moment of intensified concern over the ethics of reproductive decision making. Whereas some may have access to relatively reliable contraception or assisted reproductive technology, others may be politically or economically prevented from taking advantage of these same services or products.[3] And even those men and women whom we might tend to think of as "enjoying" the greatest degree of determinative choice in relationship to reproduction may themselves be subject to ubiquitous political discourses and practices that tie reproductive responsibility to anticommunal structures of economic independence. The illusory autonomous subject of choice, in other words, reveals herself to be deeply embedded in, and dependent on, a social and economic context that helps to shape her relationship to the ethics of reproduction.

These developments provoke numerous encounters (or reencounters) with the ethical demands of reproduction and hence with the child as a figure for and central component of such ethical struggle. If human reproduction is increasingly exposed to the political and ethical vicissitudes of "individual choice," we oughtn't to be surprised if fictional texts record traces of this realignment of childbearing and cultural anxiety. A new relationship between reproduction and choice might be expected to generate new confrontations with conventional philosophical, religious, and political accounts of the meaning and value of human life. It might also, as I hope to show, force a confrontation with reproduction itself as a concept and a practice that, in many contexts, goes unnoticed because it is thought to obey a biological or religious imperative so powerful as to preclude any investigation. What happens, then, when we are forced to articulate the relationship between biological reproduction and ethical relation? Does the political and technological defamiliarization of the decision to reproduce—

a new rendering of the "wildness" of reproduction—solicit deconstructive encounters with privileged metaphysical concepts? Does the radicalization of reproductive choice activate what is sometimes called a posthumanist reinvention of metaphysical and ethical ideals?

By focusing on the crisis of reproductive choice in Lionel Shriver's *We Need to Talk about Kevin* (2003), I want to think about some of the ways in which discussions of reproductive autonomy draw on and reconfigure conventional accounts of what it means to make or wrestle with an ethical decision and how certain models of responsible subjectivity might be thrown into doubt by transformations in the discourse and practice of reproduction.[4] Shriver's novel offers its readers a captivating literary representation of the newly weighty status of the decision to bring a child into the world, but it is also a dystopian account of the nearly impossible work of bringing a self and another (self) into relation. For Shriver's narrator (Kevin's mother), every day brings a new encounter with a marked resistance to being.

We Need to Talk about Kevin consists of a series of letters that Eva Khatchadourian writes to her husband, Franklin, letters that take us back before the birth of her son, Kevin, and track the events that lead up to "*Thursday*," Eva's name for the insurmountable and unforgivable day when her son becomes responsible for an act of mass murder.[5] But the letters also give us snapshots of Eva's life after the massacre and particularly of her visits with her son in the juvenile detention center. These are stripped-away moments of bare communication or noncommunication that allegorize what it means for relationship to happen or fail to happen. Kevin, in the last of these scenes, is notably about to turn eighteen (at which point he will be transferred to "a real prison"), and while this is of plot-level significance, it also functions to frame Eva's story between the time of her son's conception and the moment of his arrival at legal adult status. We eventually learn that Kevin killed not only seven of his classmates, a teacher who had taken a particular liking to him, and a cafeteria worker ("collateral damage") but also his own father and sister. Eva thus writes not to her estranged husband, as we are led to believe for the first 388 pages of the novel, but to her dead husband: the "volume of this correspondence," she suggests at one point, is "more of a *respondence*, isn't it?" (328). The motif of the dead addressee, Eva's husband, underscores the impossibility that affects the novel's title: the "need" to talk about Kevin may never be met by this, or perhaps any other, "we."

Although Eva ultimately admits to wanting to be held responsible and punished for the novel's tragic violence, she is also not sure who deserves what kind of blame, and she goes on to articulate an important distinction between what it means to be or feel responsible and the pressure to offer a transparent and rational account in which one serves as the cause or (maternal) point of origin: "Why, after all I have borne, am I held accountable for ordering their chaos? Isn't it enough that I suffer the brunt of the facts without shouldering this unreasonable responsibility for what they mean?" (165).[6] This crisis of responsibility begins, arguably, before Kevin is born. Shriver's novel includes an extended consideration of the decision about reproduction and an effort, on Eva's part, to come to terms with her powerful ambivalence. In a dispute with her husband over the various possible reasons for having a child, Eva suggests that having a child is part of "believing in the whole human *thing.*" He responds with a jeer:

> "Get out. Nobody has kids to perpetuate the species."
> "Maybe not consciously," [Eva replies.] "But it's only been since about 1960 that we've been able to decide without joining a nunnery." (24)

These passages of the novel pick up on Shriver's autobiographical relationship to pregnancy and recall something of the difficulty of her own reproductive decision. At age forty-two, in an emotionally and economically stable relationship, Shriver contemplated whether or not to have a child. "My partner," she writes, was "nightmarishly accommodating on this issue," abandoning her, in other words, to the mad zone of decision. But Shriver also suggests that the question of reproduction arrived, for her, in tandem with a very particular form of public violence. Out in the world, as she struggled with the decision, news reports recounted several instances in which armed teenage boys killed their teachers and classmates. "Like most Americans," Shriver explains, "I was appalled." But unlike most Americans, Shriver turned her terror and her indecision into fiction: "From this intersection of private and public angst I crafted *Kevin* in great trepidation."[7]

In what follows, I want to explore the intersection Shriver refers to between extravagant public violence and intimate reproductive choice, but I also want to suggest that two difficult ethicophilosophical lines of approach are at once called for and complicated by Shriver's novel: on the one hand, *We Need to Talk about Kevin* prompts us to think about what Derrida calls the "madness" that pertains to all forms of responsible decision making. From this perspective, the novel's hyperbolic violence itself figures the ethical ordeal of decision. On the other hand, the violence that defines the parent–child relationship in the novel also recalls Winnicott's account of the "destruction" that participates in every attempt to bring another into (relational) being. Eva's original difficulty deciding whether to have a child anticipates (and, in this novel, parallels) all the ways in which she will be challenged to make a relationship with and for her son and all the ways in which he will call on her to engage in the ongoing and never-guaranteed work of survival. The second part of this chapter will then draw on feminist-psychoanalytic and poststructuralist accounts of destruction, recognition, and language to argue that Shriver's novel offers us a magnified account of the forms of violence and failure that haunt intersubjectivity. Relation, the novel suggests, might be inseparable from a certain philosophical work. "I have had to go backward," Eva concludes in contemplating her responsibility for her son's violence, "to deconstruct" (400), whereas for Kevin, "progress was deconstruction. He would only begin to plumb his own depths by first finding himself unfathomable" (397).

We Need to Talk about Kevin situates itself self-consciously both in relationship to *Bad Seed* kinds of horror stories (nature, not nurture, is to blame for a child's capacity to inflict misery on others) and in relationship to the legacy of blame-the-mother accounts that suggest that "cold" mothers, "just happening to [have] defrost[ed] enough to produce a child," produce damaged children. "To put it differently," writes Bruno Bettelheim in a widely influential version of this approach, "feral children seem to be produced not when wolves behave like mothers, but when mothers behave like non-humans. The conclusion tentatively forced on us is that while there are no feral children, there are some very rare examples of feral mothers, of human beings who become feral towards one of their children."[8] Notably, *We Need to Talk about Kevin* refuses to be reduced to either of these categories as it undertakes to articulate a more complex account of reproductive choices, motherhood, and responsibility. If the novel is an allegory of the madness of decision, it is also, in other words, an account of the madness of relation. Relation is "mad," the novel suggests, both because it grapples with the constitution of self and other (as theorized by certain psychoanalytic writers) and because it simultaneously dreams of a kind of impossible "liberal" transcendence where two selves might "authentically" meet.

I want to begin, however, by looking at how two contemporary philosophers engage with the decision to have a child and that decision's newly vexed place in our everyday encounters with reason and responsibility. David Benatar's *Better Never to Have Been: The Harm of Coming into Existence* and Christine Overall's *Why Have Children? The Ethical Debate* suggest, in their otherwise quite disparate accounts, that reproduction can no longer simply be the default option; instead, in Overall's words, "the choice to have children calls for more careful justification and reasoning than the choice not to have children simply because in the former case a new and vulnerable human being is brought into existence whose future may be at risk."[9] Who "calls" us to this work, and how does philosophy help us to ensure that the "risk" of reproduction is met with what Overall calls "careful justification"?

"Coming into Existence Is Never Worth Its Costs"

The most attractive and appalling aspect of David Benatar's *Better Never to Have Been* is its unequivocal answer to the ethical conundrum of reproduction. "I shall argue," Benatar writes, "that not only is there no duty to procreate but there is a (moral) duty not to procreate" (14). Not only is the child— any child—deprived of consent at its very origin, he argues, but the decisions others make to produce a new being can never be said to be in the best interests of that being-who-will-come-into being: "Creating new people, by having babies, is so much a part of human life that it is rarely thought even to require a justification. . . . Those who *decide* to have a child might do so for any number of reasons, but among these reasons cannot be the interests of the potential child. One can never have a child for that child's sake. . . . My argument applies not only to humans but also to all other sentient beings" (2). Hence, the only way to effectively protect children, according to Benatar, is not to have them in the first place; human life is never worth it: "On my view there is no net benefit to coming into existence and thus coming into existence is never worth its costs. . . . Sound though I believe my argument to be, I cannot but hope that I am wrong. . . . I shall argue that it would be better, all things being equal, if human extinction happened earlier rather than later" (13).[10]

Benatar's approach to the ethics of reproduction depends on the recognition of a crucial asymmetry between the bad and the good, between pleasure and pain, and a very particular calculation of the value of nonevents:

the failure of bad things to take place, explains Benatar, is a good; but the failure of good things to take place is not "bad." Moreover, Benatar suggests, "human lives contain much more bad than is ordinarily recognized," and the simple conclusion we should draw is that we have a moral duty not to procreate. Having children, he suggests, may be analogous to attempting to increase your own value by taking hostages (12), or, in an even more violent figuration, to playing "Russian roulette with a *fully* loaded gun" aimed not at one's own head but at the heads of one's "future offspring" (92). "It is curious," he continues, "that while good people go to great lengths to spare their children from suffering, few of them seem to notice that the one (and only) guaranteed way to prevent all the suffering of these children is not to bring those children into existence in the first place" (6).

Benatar unabashedly offers what it is hard not to think of as a "phobic" or "grandiose" account of relation by idealizing the subject who would do the other no harm. The conceptual space of nonviolence, or nonresponsibility, the space in which a subject might do no injury to another, however, would also be the space of a curiously omnipotent transcendence of the ethical. Is it any surprise, then, that this dream of noninjury ends up calling for the end of all human life? The death drive makes an unrecognized return in Benatar's philosophy in the form of an absolute no to all violence that proceeds by saying no to all relation and thus no to life. But Benatar's suggestion that the world-destroying violence of self-extinction would rid the world of more evil than good, more suffering than joy, also reproduces a theological narrative of absolute divine intervention (absolute redemption through annihilation). In this respect, Benatar's is ultimately a narrative of salvation that looks toward a future cleansed of violence and suffering even if it is also emptied of life. Extinction is Benatar's figuration of an ethically uncompromised decision—an escape from the wilderness (and wildness) of being. The violence he imagines thus offers a solution to the crisis of decision (a solution, that is, to the ethical). This is related to the good/bad splitting characteristic of *The Road,* with its own fantasy of destruction/transcendence. For all its distracting and provocative novelty, then, Benatar's book calls for and imagines a perfectly ethical act of violence (on the part of the "good guys") that, by bringing about an entirely other future for the living, performs its own fantastic form of (anti)reproduction and solves, once and for all, the problematic contamination of relation and violence.[11]

If David Benatar makes (or, at least, performs making) a spectacular decision, Christine Overall, in what constitutes, in part, a response to Benatar—"I think he is mistaken" (16)—explores something much more like the terrain of the undecidable (even if she does not quite put it this way). Overall (who is far more attentive than Benatar to the range of socioeconomic differences affecting the decision to reproduce) insists on confronting the ethical challenge posed by a decision that binds us (and the life we engender) to an absolutely unpredictable future. It is now incumbent upon everyone, she argues, to justify why they choose to reproduce, not why they don't. Yet, at the same time, Overall insists, this is not a decision one can arrive at via calculation and reason:

> [I]f you wait to have children until you are absolutely sure that it is the right decision, then you may wait forever . . . [for] you cannot know ahead of time what it will be like to become a parent or what sort of child you will have. You cannot know what is good and what is hard about the process of creating and rearing until well after you have the child. . . . [T]he decision to have a child is a decision to change your life forever. It is irreversible and for that reason more significant than most other life decisions. (1–2)[12]

Thus, one must be responsible for such a decision, Overall argues, even as one cannot master it: "[Y]ou may wait forever. . . . You cannot know. . . . It is irreversible" and will "change your life forever." This, she suggests, raises questions about the decision's very ethical status. "Given the unknowability of the outcomes of a decision to have a child or not to have a child, it may seem unfair," she writes, "to elevate the decision to the level of ethics" (5).

Of course, it is precisely a decision's unmasterability by reason and calculation that makes it a *decision* in the first place and constitutes it as an ethical demand. "The indeterminate results of human freedom," writes Overall, "do not relieve us of the responsibility to consider carefully the moral aspects of our decisions" (5). In fact, we might add, responsibility begins precisely where predictability ends, and that is why decision making can seem monstrous or like a kind of madness. Overall's analysis risks exposing (while simultaneously warding off) the possibility that every decision is troubled by a "madness" that cannot be distinguished from the arrival of a new being (even if it is "only" the new being of our transformed self). These philosophical discussions of the decision to have a child thus confirm, no doubt unintentionally, much of Derrida's account of the "madness" that haunts every attempt to render a "responsible decision":

> Saying that a responsible decision must be taken on the basis of knowledge seems to define the condition of possibility of responsibility (one can't make a responsible decision without science or conscience, without knowing what one is doing, for what reasons, in view of what and under what conditions), at the same time as it defines the condition of impossibility of this same responsibility (if decision-making is relegated to a knowledge that it is content to follow or to develop, then it is no more a responsible decision, it is the technical deployment of a cognitive apparatus, the simple mechanistic deployment of a theorem).[13]

Any decision that strives to be "just" or "responsible," Derrida writes, must simultaneously draw on one's knowledge (on reason, law, and calculation) and suspend this same knowledge in the very effort to render a "fresh" or autonomous judgment; the decision could be said to be both "of the other" *and* "autonomous" precisely in the way in which it is not predetermined by calculation and reason.[14] Another way of approaching this impossibility or madness of decision is to note that every decision of consequence will always have been rendered too soon, no matter how apparently and painfully prolonged the period of consideration. "We even set ourselves a deadline," writes Shriver's narrator, recounting her back-and-forth with her husband on the question of childbearing: "my thirty-seventh birthday" (12–13). "[H]owever late it came," Derrida writes, the decision would be a "decision of urgency and precipitation, acting in the night of non-knowledge and non-rule."[15] Hence, Derrida refers to the "ordeal of the undecidable" that must be both experienced and "interrupted" in order to render a decision, and the interruption is hardly clean cut; instead, any decision leaves behind traces in the form of a certain insurmountable ghostliness that will not be "sublated": "The undecidable remains caught, lodged, at least as a ghost—but an essential ghost—in every decision, in every event of a decision."[16]

For philosopher L. A. Paul, the outcome of the ordeal of the undecidable is not (in the case of procreation) an instance of justice (a more or less successfully "fresh" and "autonomous" judgment) but a more or less successfully "autonomous" and "fresh" *being*. "In the past," Paul writes, in "What You Can't Expect When You're Expecting," "non-subjective facts and circumstances played a much larger role in the causal process leading up to parenthood."[17] Increasingly, Paul suggests, parents are left struggling with "phenomenal preferences" that find no security in "rational" deliberation, because the repercussions of this decision are, by definition, radically unpredictable and "epistemically transformative" for the deciders. But in Shriver's novel, the "essential ghost" of a decision on reproduction haunts those involved in the form of a profoundly unsettling violence, which is also to say, in the form of Kevin himself. What Derrida calls the "ghost of the undecidable" remains caught or lodged in this child insofar as he (inevitably) fails to simply and wholly confirm the freedom and responsibility (never mind the rationality) of the original decision. As such a "ghost," it is worth emphasizing, Kevin is not simply an allegorical figure; rather, his figuration reminds us of the very odd status of every child and every*one* as both singular other, "new event," and as parental message or address. Every child is, in this sense, an allegorical child (a wild child)—a figuration of the ghost of undecidability that haunts the event of its own coming into being.[18]

Christine Overall's study is primarily committed to unfolding the complexities of reproductive choice, and it goes a long way toward countering the masculinist bias of apparently gender-neutral accounts (like Benatar's). She, for example, opposes the minimizing of such decisions as "private" and "personal," arguing that they are ultimately of global significance. If in some settings women were (and are) called on to reproduce for the sake of their nation or cultural group, is there now an obligation, Overall asks, *not to reproduce* for the sake of humanity and environmental sustainability? And if the individual's decision is unmasterable, what would constitute "the best reason," or "the strongest reason," to have a child? For much of her book, Overall is content to articulate the difficulty of these questions, but toward the end she offers a series of more or less confident assertions. One should have a child, Overall writes, in order to produce, engage in, and be substantially altered by the particular kind of conditional and asymmetrical love that characterizes the parent–child bond: "[I]n this relationship lies the best reason for choosing to have a child" (212). It is more important than ever, she says, to think about why you might reproduce; but even asking the question suggests a desire for an experience that should "not be missed." Nevertheless, she adds, if you are going to have children, "please" have two, not one or three (183). (Overall suggests two rather than one because, oddly, a single child might suggest that one of the parents was not worth replacing

[183].) Overall does not want to be thought of as "pronatalist," but she counsels those who are at all inclined to have children to "just risk it" (183). This reference to "risk," coupled with the surprising "Please don't have more than two!" alerts us to our location, I would suggest, on the border of a conceptual or ethical wilderness for Overall and her readers. Prayer and danger are the watchwords of this space. It's hard not to leave Overall's book without a sense of the pervasive ethical impasse generated by an encounter with reproductive choice.

For many liberal or "humanist" thinkers committed to consent as a formative ethical category, the figure of the nonconsenting child, the child who does not, because she cannot, consent to being, seriously complicates any attempt to make a just decision to reproduce. "Questions about choosing whether to have children . . . are *also* ethical questions," explains Overall, "for they are about whether to bring a person into existence—and that person cannot, by the very nature of the situation, give consent to being brought into existence" (6). The absence of consent threatens to mark the reproductive act with a violence that a certain strand of classically humanist thought can find no way around, except by assuming that life itself is unquestionably desirable—that life is a "gift." The "gift" names an idealized form of nonconsent or nonexchange, and Overall puts it to work for reproductive ethics by reversing its conventional application. In reproduction, she writes, "the gift creates the recipient" (57).

On the one hand, the rhetoric of gift works, for Overall, to mask or displace the irrationality and the potential violence (the ethical "surprise!") of the decision to bring another into being. On the other hand, one might imagine that the absence of any consent to be brought into being would only bolster David Benatar's claims with respect to the harm done by procreation. Benatar worries that, absent any possibility of consent, procreation might be seen as a "victimless" crime: "One common basis for denying that procreation violates the rights of the person created is that prior to procreation that person does not exist and thus there can be no bearer of the right not to be created" (53). In order to defend his ethical critique of procreation, then, Benatar has to invent what he calls "a special kind of right," one that "has a bearer only in the breach" (53). The rights-bearing subject would appear simultaneously with (and would be produced by) the act of violation perpetrated by another. "I acknowledge that this is an unusual kind of right," Benatar remarks, "but coming into existence is an unusual case"

(53).[19] Benatar and Overall thus arrive at a similar conclusion from different points of departure: life is either the enigmatic gift that creates its recipient or the violence that creates the rights (and hence the rights-bearing subject) that it violates. In both instances, reproduction turns out to be a peculiarly doubling and doubled event (and it is perhaps this originary doubling that is the real source of the ethical crisis registered by these philosophers). Reproduction poses an ethical dilemma for Benatar and Overall, but for both philosophers the solution demands a fantastic temporal invention: reproduction must happen at a moment in time and must bring an absolutely new, singular being into the world; but reproduction must immediately also generate a past for that being, a past figured by Overall's enigmatic "recipient" or Benatar's "bearer in the breach." The reproductive event would, in these accounts, have to be thought of as both the first event in the life of a subject and, somehow, another event in the life of a preexisting being. Being, to put it another way, would repeat itself in the moment of its arrival. But it is precisely this deconstructive or Derridean account of originary supplementarity (the iterability of being) that Overall and Benatar attempt to disavow by temporalizing the enigma of reproduction.

Benatar's "special" right (the right that is brought into being in the moment of its violation) is introduced as part of an attempt to defend an argument in favor of humankind's self-annihilation. Benatar has to convince us that reproduction happens to something like a preexisting subject (capable of bearing rights) so that he can also convince us that reproduction (and hence all life) ought, ethically speaking, to come to an end, sooner rather than later. Violence and metaphysics join hands here on the edge of extinction. (This is another way of thinking about the gift of being as the gift of death.) Benatar's classically humanist attempt to rewrite the iterability of being as the narrative of a "full" subjectivity that precedes and commands its own reproduction (as the bearer of the right to consent) coincides with what it is hard not to call a philosophical death wish for being. (This is the philosophy of the humanist suicide bomber.) Overall's comparatively reassuring investment in life as an a priori object of desire (reproduction is the gift that creates its own recipient) may describe humanism's last attempt to avoid Benatar's nihilistic conclusions. As long as the iterability of being remains the disavowed ethical problem that must be solved (by insisting on the singular goodness or evil of life "itself" or on the possibility of separating out life's beginning—as an event of presence—from its repetition or re-presentation), then Benatar's "nuclear" option will continue to exercise its compelling attraction. But a posthumanist ethics suggests that life is neither good nor bad "in advance" of its arrival; to reproduce is to reproduce the undecidability of being and hence to reinvent the ethical every time. And how does one ever decide on the undecidable?

"Monstrous Decision"

"*What possessed us?*" asks Eva in her second letter to Franklin, dated November 15, 2000. "We were so happy!" she exclaims. "Why, then, did we take the stake of all we had and place it all on this outrageous gamble of having a child?" (12). Eva racks her brain "trying to reconstruct those few months in 1982 when we were officially 'deciding'" (12), and does her best to recapture and record the "arbitrary rhythm [of their discussions] tending toward and tending against." Why have a child? she recalls asking: "You know that euphemism, *she's expecting*? It's apt. The birth of a baby, so long as it's healthy, is something to look forward to. It's a good thing, a big, good huge event" (20). Exploring the world and writing travel books (Eva runs a highly successful business researching and writing budget-travel guides) has lost its appeal for Eva, who longs for something new: "'Motherhood,' I condensed in the park. 'Now, that is a foreign country'" (19). Eva also wants someone to give to; she wants someone else to love precisely because she loves her husband so much. And, then again, she wonders if it is somehow nihilistic *not* to want children. On another occasion, Eva suggests to Franklin that they should have a child so that they can get over talking about their own parents and siblings:

> "Now *that*," you clanged the spinach pan in the sink, "is frivolous."
> I stayed your hand. "It's not. What we talk about is what we think about, is what our lives are about. I'm not sure I want to spend mine looking over my shoulder at a generation whose lineage I'm personally helping to truncate." (23–24)

When Eva tries "rooting around" in her "mental attic" for her original reservations about motherhood, she finds what now appear to be "pygmy misgivings" that are "dumbfounding" in their naïveté, especially given "what actually happened" (26). "Yet," she continues, "as I contemplate that list now it strikes me that, however damning, the conventional reservations

about parenthood are practical," whereas contemporary decisions to reproduce seem predetermined by the incommensurably grand and unmoored
abstractions that are invoked on behalf of procreation: "After all, now that
children don't till your fields or take you in when you're incontinent, there
is no sensible reason to have them, and it's amazing that with the advent
of effective contraception anyone chooses to reproduce at all. By contrast,
love, story, content, faith in the human 'thing'—the modern incentives are
like dirigibles, immense, floating, and few; optimistic, large-hearted, even
profound, but ominously ungrounded" (26–27). Even as Eva asserts that the
only rational choice is not to have children, she also problematizes the whole
question of choice with respect to reproduction. Before any real child or
tangible experience of parenting has materialized, *We Need to Talk about
Kevin* takes on and takes apart the category of free decision: How can you
choose that which you know nothing about? How can you choose when the
only "rational" choice is simultaneously culturally coded as the choice you
shouldn't make, a kind of giving up? I choose to give up, to be precisely the
kind of individual who has no choices to make, *or* I choose to open myself
up to a kind of incalculable but potentially immensely valuable risk. Eva,
in fact, longs *not* to have a choice: "For years I'd been awaiting that over-
riding urge I'd always heard about, the narcotic pining that draws childless
women ineluctably to strangers' strollers in parks. I wanted to be drowned
by the hormonal imperative" (27). And in revealing this urge (this urge to
be driven by no choice), she recalls her idiosyncratic psychological history
of choosing precisely what she most fears or doesn't want. The choice of that
which is *not* desired functions, for Eva, as a supplement for her own perceived lack: "However intrigued by a 'turn of the page,' I was mortified by
the prospect of becoming hopelessly trapped in someone else's story. And
I believe that this terror is precisely what must have snagged me, the way
a ledge will tempt one to jump off. The very insurmountability of the task,
its very unattractiveness, was in the end what attracted me to it" (32). That
which I do not want, Eva's self-analysis implies, imposes itself on me as a
kind of limit point of my desire, so that choosing it promises the recovery
of some elusive sense of autonomy. I choose and choose that which I would
not choose, and my subjecthood is constituted by the sum of these repeated
performances of resisted-determination-as-agency. Throughout *We Need
to Talk about Kevin*, we hear Eva deciding, undeciding, and redeciding—
"*What had I done?*" (50); "I felt expendable, throw-away, swallowed by a

big biological project that I didn't initiate or choose, that produced me but would also chew me up and spit me out. I felt used" (51)—and each time, the decision is fraught with a crisis of self-assertion and desire.

It would be very easy to give in to the temptation to dismiss Eva's crises of decision as insignificant on the grand scale of things. We are not talking here about the founding of a nation-state or of God's demand that one sacrifice one's son. Shriver's Eva is troubled merely by trying to sort out her desires. But Eva's decision might also be thought of as the paradigmatic (and therefore most "mad") example of ethical choice, because it involves the production of another "real" other. If the most basic form of pro-choice language foregrounds autonomy, a certain version of ethical and deconstructive philosophy reminds us that every decision of consequence is "of the other." Derrida writes, "Levinas would probably not say it in this way, but could it not be argued that, without exonerating myself in the least, decision and responsibility are always *of* the other. They always come back or come down to the other, from the other, even if it is the other in me."[20] Eva's difficulty deciding how to decide with respect to parenthood records a more pervasive cultural anxiety surrounding the relationship between responsibility and reproduction, between nihilism and futurity. And Kevin's violence resonates with the apocalyptic tone in which much of this discussion (or nondiscussion) continues to take place.[21]

Kevin also clearly complicates the matter of responsible decision by exploring what it might mean for two people to decide together or for someone to decide *for* someone else (in more than one sense: my decision is *for* you, a kind of gift; *and* I decide *instead* of you, in your place). It is after deciding to have a child (and becoming pregnant) that Eva comes to realize that she regrets her choice and that what she has chosen is clearly and unambivalently what her husband, Franklin, desires: "It is not true that I was 'ambivalent' about motherhood. You wanted to have a child. On balance, I did not. Added together, that seemed like ambivalence, but though we were a superlative couple, we were not the same person" (55). Eva's crisis of autonomy with respect to the reproductive decision is then reanimated by her doctor's and her husband's responses to her pregnancy: "This was my introduction to the way in which, crossing the threshold of motherhood, suddenly you become social property, the animate equivalent of a public park" (52). Her profound sense that she is or should be first and foremost herself is accompanied by the simultaneous realization that this is no longer how she is perceived. Eva's decision undermines her autonomy, both because it activates a socially specific reading of the maternal body (a reading that, as a choosing subject, she might be expected to resist) and because, like any completed decision, it puts an end to the freedom that preceded and defined the possibility of choice.

Eva's response to her own "monstrous decision" (22) is, perversely enough, to make the decision again—twice. Shortly after Kevin's third birthday, Eva and Franklin come to an agreement. Eva agrees to move out of the city (Franklin's desire) if, in exchange, she gets to take a three-month research trip to Africa for A Wing and a Prayer (her travel-book company). It is while on these unhappy and unproductive travels that Eva decides that she needs to become Kevin's mother *again*:

> In a funny way, I resolved, I had to remake that arduous decision of 1982 and jump into parenthood with both feet. I had to get pregnant with Kevin all over again. Like his birth, raising our son could be a transporting experience, but only if I stopped fighting it. . . . Flying into Kennedy, I was bursting with determination, optimism and goodwill. But in retrospect, I do feel obliged to observe that I was at my most passionate about our son when he was not there. (120)[22]

Eva later chooses to have another child, in an attempt to prove to herself and her husband that the problem with Kevin is Kevin, not his mother. In this later instance, Eva's decision is both unilateral and deceptive: Eva tells Franklin of her planned and premeditated pregnancy, and he responds:

> "So you just go ahead and—a fait accompli—just—like some kind of mugging.
>   As if it had nothing to do with me."
> "It has everything to do with you. But I was right and you were wrong." (215)

If Eva rather disastrously attempts to master her own decision-making process and Franklin never gets to decide (even if he gets what he wants), where does this leave Kevin? Certainly, he was not consulted on the question of his existence. And Eva concludes that the "disturbing[ly] self-possessed" (113) child that she and her husband have produced is outraged at a primal level with his own being: "I think Kevin hated it. I think Kevin was off the scale, he hated being here so much. . . . Kevin seemed incensed that no one had ever consulted him about turning up in a crib with time going on and on" (90). Kevin is born out of a crisis of decision, and he seems to understand, very early on, that his mother does not want him to have existed. He is deprived, that is to say, of the constitutive message that would make survival or going-on-being possible. And it is just such a message, a promise or performed affirmation, that is characteristic of all of the texts I examine in this study. The message, as we have seen, structures Morrison's *A Mercy*, where it functions as both an affirmation and a registration of the profound vulnerability of black lives. As a quasi-psychoanalytic account of development, *We Need to Talk about Kevin* emphasizes not the child who must read adult ambivalence, complexity, and enigma (à la Freud, Ferenczi, Lacan, Kristeva, or Laplanche) so much as the child who must take on a kind of sheer negativity. In other words, and oddly enough, all this might simply be another way of talking about a psychoanalytically familiar child: Shriver's novel could be read as the realization of a classically Oedipal fantasy (the boy left alone with his mother, having destroyed all other rivals and distractions!).

But Kevin's complexity emerges from the fact that he is not merely a consequence of maternal nondesire (even as he surely is *also* this: I'll destroy everything until you and I are left to love one another); Kevin also figures the (wild) child as the arrival of relation without end, the arrival of an other for whom you have already taken (or been given) responsibility, even as he or she may look like an absolute nonrelation or an uncanny mirror image. Part of Eva's original fear in relationship to motherhood is that she will *fail* to produce an other—"I wanted a door to open and a whole new vista to expand before me that I had never known was out there" (80)—and that she will instead replicate her own "closed" and "stony nature" (32). This fear, too, inscribes a specifically feminist or maternal engagement with reproduction. If there is a long patriarchal history of reproducing the same while, or *by*, misrecognizing it as the other, then Shriver's account of the ordeal of reproductive choice might be said to offer us a radical revision of this very question: what does it mean to want one's own child?[23]

Drawing on an avowedly Levinasian theoretical framework, Lisa Guenther attempts to reconfigure the liberal impasse over the relationship between reproduction and consent by describing coming into being as the subject's opening onto "a future of giving-forth or responsibility for the Other."[24] "If I do not posit my own existence," she writes, "and if even my fantasies of repeating or reclaiming birth already require this birth as their most basic condition—then my selfhood remains radically exposed to Others even when I try most to deny this exposure."[25] Guenther's "exposure" recalls the exposure of unwanted infants and suggests that the "wild child" who may or may not survive such exposure also figures the posthumanist ethical subject. The "gift" of being that proceeds from a time that is not my own, she suggests, marks every subject that comes into being with a (maternal) imperative to "bear or support an Other who may or may not be my child."[26] The gift of birth, she asserts, "disengages responsibility from causation" and "self-interest."[27]

If the dominant modern (which is to say, the post-Enlightenment) approach to ethical relation insists on the protection of subjects who have rights and who give consent, an intensified relationship to reproductive choice threatens to expose a trace of nonconsent in the structure of every subject. The child's ambiguous political and legal (which is also to say ontological) status has always registered and concealed this more persistent undecidability at work in every being's violently noncontractual origin. The "wild child" has always haunted and fascinated liberal human rights theory precisely because that child emerges out of (and thus can always be reencountered in) the dystopian and frightening space of an ethical and philosophical impasse. Guenther's achievement is to take precisely what Benatar and Overall (and many other philosophers) encounter as a logico-ethical problem (the impossibility of consent to our own being) and translate it into the basis for a theory of every being's originally ethical dependence on and responsibility for (hospitality toward) the other. Lack of consent becomes, in Guenther's Levinasian reading, the pejorative liberal registration of our boundedness to one another, a boundedness that exceeds calculation. From this perspective, all that marks the reproductive act as an unreasonable, incalculable, and, indeed, unjustifiable gesture toward an other simultaneously marks parent and child with the trace of ethical relation. The possibility of ethical relation proceeds not from an act guaranteed by consent or by the gift exchange of an idealized economic transaction, but precisely from the rupture in calculation and consent that makes otherness and relation (and the future as site of a radical otherness) possible. "This dispossession for the sake of the Other," Guenther writes, "is the condition for a meaningful existence, a world that is not deprived of meaning by the privacy of the individual."[28]

But what Guenther celebrates, Shriver's Eva fears, and her son, argu-ably, acts out as a tragically destructive sociopathology. Kevin performs the incompletion of self that his birth, in Guenther's words, "disrupts in advance," not as the opening onto an ethical relation but as a disaster ("The alternative to loving was disaster," as Alice Munro puts it in the epigraph to this chapter). And in this respect, as in so many others, Kevin might be said to repeat his mother's impasse. It is Eva, to begin with, who is loath to give up the completeness that she imagines her adult life to have realized: "For the first half of my life," she writes, "I was my own creation." But her child is also imagined as a wholly separate being from the start: Kevin's arrival is experienced by Eva, in one of her memorable formulations, as a "filial mug-ging of who I once was to myself" (167). "[F]rom the instant he was laid on my breast," Eva writes, "I perceived Kevin Khatchadourian as pre-extant, with a vast, fluctuating interior life" (116). Kevin and Eva, in other words, have to learn how to survive the destructive violence of being in relation, and it is never entirely clear whether they succeed.

"The Very Center of the Moment Was Bliss"

The profound animosity that comes to characterize the once-loving rela-tionship between Kevin's parents, Eva and Franklin, proceeds, in part, from their two very different concepts of relation—differences that begin to become clear to Eva only after Kevin's birth. Eva comes to believe that her husband's desire for a child (which is to say, any child) precludes the desire for this particular child (Kevin), whereas her resistance takes precisely the opposite form. Eva cannot come to terms with what it would have meant to desire anything other than a particular child, a particular other with whom to experience relation: "I could not love *a* child; I would have to love this one" (88). Eva is "interested in Kevin as Kevin really [is]," whereas Frank-lin is entirely besotted with a fantasy object, and these differences extend to include their own particularity as named subjects: "We were no longer Eva and Franklin [and this is well before Kevin is born; in fact, it is the evening of the day when Eva tells Franklin that she is pregnant], but Mommy and Daddy; this was our first meal as a *family*, a word and a concept about which I had always been uneasy" (54). Franklin, from the very beginning, dwells in the realm of representational abstractions that Eva wants to defy with par-ticularity and proper names (the very signs of autonomy or self-possession).

But this also means that whereas her husband is "captivated by self-sacrifice," Eva is capable of feeling threatened by the very particularity and otherness of the being she will mother. "I was already victimized," she writes in the early stages of her pregnancy, "like some princess, by an organism the size of a pea" (55). Eva continues to describe this alienating discrepancy. Franklin wants a house with a yard and a tire swing for his son ("The awful revelation dawned that we were dealing with your childhood—an idealization of our childhood—that could prove, like your fantasy United States, an awesome cudgel. There's no more doomed a struggle than a battle with the imaginary" [107]), whereas Eva finds herself monstrously subjected to Kevin in his particularity:

> I do mean *Kevin* and not *the baby*. From the very beginning that child was particular to me, whereas you often asked *How's the kid?* Or *How's my boy?* Or *Where's the baby?* To me he was never "the baby." He was a singular, unusually cunning individual who had arrived to stay with us and just happened to be very small. For you he was "our son"—or, once you started to give up on me, "my son." There was a persistently generic character to your adoration that I'm certain he sensed. . . . On my part it was this broad covenant with children-in-theory that I may have failed to make and to which I was unable to resort when Kevin finally tested my maternal ties to a perfect mathematical limit on *Thursday*. (88)

For a brief moment, Eva contemplates the connection between these different ways of relating to a child and broader aspects of cultural and communal identification: "I was connected to the world by a multitude of threads," she tells her dead husband, "you by a few sturdy guide ropes. It was the same with patriotism. . . . In the particular dwells the tawdry. In the conceptual dwells the grand, the transcendent, the everlasting. Earthly countries and single malignant little boys can go to hell; the idea of countries and the idea of sons triumph for eternity. Although neither of us ever went to church, I came to conclude that you were a naturally religious person" (88).[29]

The tension between Eva and Franklin rehearses a broader cultural crisis around the collapse of one or another discourse in which reproduction and the child are justified and spoken of in proudly generic terms (patriarchal, national, theological terms). But this collapse, which is at once a symptom and a driver of technological and political transformations in the culture of reproduction, also intensifies the ethical questions surrounding the decision to have a child and affects the relationship between parents and the children whose being they are, in a certain way, more responsible for than ever. *Love* is perhaps the most loaded and difficult word used to describe this relationship, and there is a sense in which neither parent in Shriver's novel can be said to "love" Kevin initially. Franklin loves his ideal son, whereas Eva feels only frustration and animosity. But it is Eva, finally, who is forced to confront the question of ethical relation to an other—an other for whom she is responsible but with whom she enjoys no original relationship of mutual consent. Yet it is eventually only the purity of Eva's aggression that seems capable of generating anything like love (in the novel's terms): "Because after three days short of eighteen years, I can finally announce," Eva writes on the very last page of the novel, "that I am too exhausted and too confused and too lonely to keep fighting, and if only out of desperation or even laziness I love my son" (400).[30]

We Need to Talk about Kevin unfolds as, first, a drama of (reproductive) decision making and then as an increasingly disturbing series of encounters with the afterlife of that decision's madness. From the moment Eva decides to have the baby, it seems, the ordeal of decision involved in its coming into being structures the mother and child's interminable relational crises. Shriver's novel suggests, albeit in hyperbolic form, that every relationship consists in a series of more or less fraught decisions about bringing the other into being. Eva continues to struggle with her "monstrous decision" as she attempts to reconcile her own ambivalence with the exhausting work of caring for an extremely difficult infant.[31] "I couldn't have expected that simply *forming an attachment* to you," she tells Kevin, "would be so much work. I thought—I thought that part came for free" (57). Eva's active resistance to Kevin's birth during labor is met, in turn, by Kevin's refusal of her milk, leaving Eva feeling humiliated and defeated. "I shouldn't have taken it personally," Eva writes, "but how could I not? It wasn't mother's milk he didn't want, it was Mother. In fact, I became convinced that our little bundle of joy had found me out. Infants have great intuition, because intuition's about all they've got" (86–87). The attempt at establishing a primary nursing relationship is brought to a halt when Eva develops mastitis and becomes very ill. "Inimical to my sustenance," Eva continues, "he could still introduce me to corruption as if already at year zero the more worldly party of our pair" (88). Kevin is hostile, unfriendly, unreceptive to what Eva provides, but he also actively attacks that which would sustain her, as if to say, "I'm not going to help you to sustain me, thereby sustaining you; I'm waiting for your full recognition, and for the gift of my being." Eva is eventually abandoned to an unhelpful diagnosis of postnatal depression: "The term was less diagnostic than tautological: I was depressed after Kevin's birth because I was depressed after Kevin's birth. Thanks" (86). What happened, she wonders, to that "good . . . big, huge event"?

Left alone with his mother all day, Kevin screams, and Eva offers us a profuse anatomy of infant cries: "the wail of inarticulate need . . . the shriek of terror . . . that lassitudinous *wah-wah* . . . the muted, habitual mewl of a baby who may be perfectly miserable but who, whether through neglect or prescience, no longer anticipates reprieve" (89). Kevin's cry is off the charts: "[H] is loneliness displayed an awesome existential purity. . . . And I discerned no plaintive cry of appeal, no keen despair, no gurgle of nameless dread. Rather he hurled his voice like a weapon, howls smashing the walls of our loft like a baseball bat bashing a bus shelter. . . . Driving this remarkable combustion engine was the distilled and infinitely renewable fuel of *outrage*" (90). In this respect, *We Need to Talk about Kevin* offers us (all too effectively!) the nightmare enclosure of parenthood as opposed to the (surprisingly) utopian space of the parent–child relationship in *Room* or *The Road*. And, in retrospect, the unnerving violence detected in Kevin's infant crying eerily prefigures the mass murder that he eventually perpetrates.[32] The "speech act" that constitutes Kevin's murder of his peers and teacher and family, in other words, echoes this early cry in all its shattering indeterminacy; the murder is at once an event of massive meaningless destruction and a very special plea to his mother: "So do you still love me now?" Speaking to a journalist who tries to tempt her into talking ("[M]aybe you think Kevin was misunderstood?"), Eva is defiant: "Seems to me he got across his personal *worldview* better than most. Seems to me that you should be interviewing children who are a great deal less accomplished at self-expression" (95).[33] Crying, the primal version of the ethical call, turns power on its head and represents the tyrannical power of the powerless. Located as it is on the threshold of meaningful language, crying hesitates between an address to the other (conjuring Kevin's mother) and violent disruption—an attempt to destroy the world (and any relationship) with an infant's only weapon.[34] As such, infant crying is perhaps a privileged example of the liminal communication that recurs throughout Shriver's novel (and throughout the present study) and that appears to have an important relationship to the whole question of being's precarious relationship to desire and consent.

In this novel, as in other texts in this study, the crisis of reproductive decision and the emergence of a posthumanist ethics of reproduction coincide with a reflection on the precarious relationship between violence and meaning in every event of language. Every utterance maintains a relationship to the original and undecidable (material and prediscursive) infant's cry, and in Shriver's novel, Kevin embodies a certain refusal to screen that constitutive cry behind a reassuring facade of meaningful, relational, or affirmative communication. If language binds human beings together, Kevin wants none of it. Eva repeatedly comments on her son's profound apathy and self-possession (if only there were something "wrong" with him!). If at one point Eva contemplates what she would like her son to call her, she eventually realizes that she is abandoned to referring to herself in the third person, and Kevin (at age six) no longer addresses her by name at all (182). He quite literally refuses to call her into being (unless, of course, this refusal itself constitutes a call). Similarly, it is impossible to give Kevin gifts. If his father overgives highly commercialized possessions that Eva calls "plastic dirt," her own attempts at "personalized" and "homespun" offerings are no more successful. The only object that Eva can remember Kevin showing any attachment to is the squirt gun that she destroys after he defaces her study with paint. "I'd had a spooky presentiment when I finished grinding the barrel into the floor," she writes, "that since he *had* been attached to it, he was glad to see it go" (182).

Kevin outgrows his unbearable crying, but his character continues to be associated with language in its empty and dead materiality. He is a performer with a particular affinity for repetition and mimicry, and he succeeds well enough at school by doing precisely what is required of him in a rote and empty way: "He wasn't precisely disobedient, which is one detail that the Sunday magazine exposés often got wrong. Indeed, he could follow the letter of his assignments with chilling precision" (192). As quite a young child, Kevin takes to parroting his parents' (and particularly his mother's) speech patterns, and in its earliest manifestations, this mimicry constitutes an uncanny performance in which the supposedly innocent, if annoying, child is indistinguishable from a far more malicious and all-too-knowing being:

"Kevin, stop it! That's enough. Let Mommer and Daddy talk—"
"NYEH-nyeh, NYEEEE nyeh—! Nyeh nyeh-NYEEH—!"
"I mean it, Kevin, quit the *nyeh-nyeh* or we're leaving."
"Nyeh NYEE nyeh, nyeh nyeh, nyeh nyeh *nyeh-nyeh* nyeh nyeh NYEE-*nyeh!*"
I don't know why I threatened him with departure, lacking any evidence that
    he wanted to stay. This was my first taste of what would become a chronic
    conundrum: how to punish a boy with an almost Zen-like indifference to
    whatever you might deny him. (127)

As such passages might suggest, Shriver's novel, for all its eventual excess
and horror, can also be read as a hyperbolic account of familiar parental
experiences. "You doubtless found my usage of the word *war* preposterous,"
writes Eva, referring to her account of changing Kevin's diaper. "But in cor-
ralling Kevin to the changing table . . . I was often reminded of those scrappy
guerilla conflicts in which, underequipped, a ragtag rebel force manages to
inflict surprisingly serious losses on powerful armies of state. . . . If Kevin
enjoyed our trysts, I did not" (189). By deferring its narration (it appears in
the center of the novel), Eva privileges one particular episode in Kevin's toilet training and reveals the extent to which its conclusion profoundly impli-
cates her in his violence. A six-year-old Kevin is attending "Love-'n'-Learn"
kindergarten, and his mother must show up regularly to change his diapers.
("This one developmental stage that our son seemed to have skipped," she
explains, "was tyrannizing my life" [176]). Eva, who has already described
Kevin's ability to tempt others into primitive self-destructive behavior, tells
the story of a day in which he attacks her verbally when she tries to draw
him out of indifference. He then defecates *three* times in quick succession.
Defecation here is no meaningless physiological process, it is suggested,
but itself a kind of assault. An enraged Eva subsequently fails miserably in
her performance of the role of the Winnicottian good-enough mother. She
picks Kevin up and hurls him across the room; his arm is badly broken.
She whisks him away to an emergency room, and he seems to agree to keep
the story of her attack a secret from his father and from the doctors. But in
her retrospective account of this scene, Eva reads violence not as the final
collapse of relation but as a kind of authentic communication—violence
as actually quite an *excellent* way to get your point across—the moment
when all performance and false artifice give way.[35] "I was still intoxicated
from a moment that may put the lie to my preening incomprehension of

Thursday," she admits. "On its far side, I was aghast. But the very center of the moment was bliss" (195). Here, again, Eva confronts one of her initial fears about reproduction. She is never quite sure whether it is more terrifying to open up the door to reproduction's "anyone" or to risk reproducing a mirror image. When it comes to communicating with or entering into relation with an other, Kevin and his mother can come across, at times, as disturbingly twinned. In the wake of her attack on Kevin, Eva becomes the quasi-philosophical (quasi-terroristic!) narrator who can attest to the "uses" of a "domestic violence" that promises authentic relation: "For two seconds I'd felt whole, and like Kevin Khatchadourian's real mother. I felt close to him. I felt like myself—my true unexpurgated self—and I felt we were finally communicating" (196).

In "Hate in the Counter-Transference," D. W. Winnicott lists *eighteen* reasons why a mother "hates her infant from the word go": "I suggest that the mother hates the baby before the baby hates the mother," he writes, "and before the baby can know his mother hates him."[36] Winnicott's formulations are bracingly unsentimental, but they are not designed to draw our attention to a mother's failure or a child's lack; they participate in Winnicott's attempt to theorize the formative place of a certain destructive violence in the development of relationality. The excess of hatred in this scene counters our temptation to describe the parent–child relationship in the more familiar terms of gift, gratitude, or mutual (consensual) exchange. "Hate," for Winnicott, names a mode of relation that itself depends on a structurally prior encounter with "destruction" and survival and with the concomitant emergence of the self–other distinction. Relationality is dangerous and unpredictable work for the Winnicottian parent and child, and the analyst who finds him- or herself participating in this effort in a clinical setting may even have to check his patients at the door: "When the analyst knows that the patient carries a revolver, then, it seems to me, this work cannot be done."[37]

The hyperbole of Winnicott's analytic terminology is more than matched, in Shriver's novel, by the horror of a child's responsibility for mass murder. As an allegory of relation between a parent and a child, *We Need to Talk about Kevin* narrates the movement from ambivalence or outright rejection toward some kind of loving relationship, but it does so, shockingly, by suggesting that this trajectory requires passage through carnage. Mass murder, the novel seems to suggest, is the prerequisite for a loving relationship between mother and son. On the face of it, it's hard to imagine a wilder theory of relation. But Winnicott offers us a nuanced language for describing what's going on here. Destructiveness, argues Winnicott, produces the very possibility of externality, of that which is beyond the omnipotent self: "It is generally understood that the reality principle involves the individual in anger and reactive destruction, but my thesis is that the destruction plays its part in making the reality, placing the object outside the self."[38] Winnicott's account of destruction's place in the development of the capacity for relation, in other words, also describes the limits of a liberal model of individual consent for thinking the subject's relationship to his or her or their own desire to be. We do not owe our parents something for giving us life; we come into life (which is to say something like individuated being with the capacity for relation with others) only insofar as we enter into relationships that defy consent and resist reciprocal exchange. "Destruction" might be another name for this relational surplus that produces the possibility of others and thus of socialization and community (social reproduction). "In intersubjective terms," writes Jessica Benjamin, "violation is the attempt to push the other outside the self, to attack the other's separate reality in order finally to discover it. The adult sadist, for example, is searching for a surviving other, but his search is already prejudiced by his childhood disappointment with an other who did not survive."[39]

Eva's gesture of pure signification (her throwing Kevin against the wall—the equivalent of *Thursday*) does not constitute an act of survival of the other's aggression, because Eva's violence remains caught up in Kevin's relentless machinations. In Winnicottian terms, Kevin might be said to have succeeded in destroying his mother, reducing her to violence, thereby only confirming his omnipotence. (But this is, of course, a self-defeating triumph, as Kevin needs Eva to be his surviving other.) Eva describes the summer that follows her violent attack as "defy[ing] all my narrative instincts." She acts violently, and Kevin thereby assumes more of a condition of control: "I had ransomed my soul to a six-year-old" (199); "*I* shuffled and cowered as if auditioning for a minstrel show" (201). After his arm is broken, Kevin surprises his father by immediately "sauntering off" to use the bathroom (199). Eva reads this as Kevin's ultimate victory: "He had won the larger battle; acceding to the toilet was the kind of trifling concession that a magnanimous if condescending victor can afford to toss a vanquished adversary" (200). It is Eva who is left "unworthy," characterized by her "*incontinent* outpouring of tenderness" (203).[40]

One might think that the ultimate victory, from Kevin's perspective, would be the destruction of his parents' marriage several years later. But Eva comes to understand, instead, that witnessing his parents' breakup constitutes a turning point for Kevin, the world-destroying moment when he decides to commit mass murder. Eva and Franklin are arguing over the latest crisis with Kevin: he appears to have successfully accused a teacher of sexual harassment, and Eva is convinced that her son has once again provoked and staged the undoing of a vulnerable other. Franklin announces that their marriage is over; there is no decision to make; it has all already happened, short of the more practical arrangements. The couple then realize that Kevin has witnessed their interaction, and Eva observes that "he look[s] different" and that, although he is entirely clothed, "this [is] the first time in years I ha[ve] seen him naked." Franklin attempts to reassure Kevin, saying that he has misunderstood and heard something out of context. Kevin responds:

"Why would I not know the context?" He took a single swallow from his glass.
  "I am the context." He put the glass on the counter and left.
I'm certain of it: That moment, that hard swallow, is when he decided. (349)

Parents divorce, and for a certain child it is the end of the world, although usually a child's response, however disturbed and disturbing, doesn't take the form of murderous violence. Eva herself, in fact, is confused by her own assessment of the scene. If, as Eva assumes, Kevin has been attempting to break up his parents from day one, as a screaming infant, why should the end of their marriage be anything other than pleasing to him? Eva concludes that what really horrifies Kevin is the prospect of being abandoned not *by* his mother but *to* his father; he prefers his mother's authentic hostility (glimpsed beneath the performance of the good mother) to his father's apparently bottomless artificiality (150). But remaining within the terms of the fiction and, to a certain extent, within the parameters of Eva's own understanding, we might consider another (Winnicottian) possibility: Kevin is horrified by his own destructive and seemingly limitless power ("I am the context"). He tries to destroy his parents' marriage and he succeeds, and this experience of power leads, according to a dangerous and perverse logic, only to more violence. This is indeed connected to what Winnicott calls "the difficult part of my thesis, at least for me." For Winnicott, as we have seen, the individual doesn't come up against a frustrating reality that thwarts his potential as an agent, but rather there comes to be that which can be experienced as real and other only as a result of a more primary relationship to destruction.[41]

Witnessing his parents' deciding to separate, Kevin witnesses his own destructive power; but he also witnesses the repetition of an existential primal scene: his parents' separation rehearses a decision on the threshold of his own (non)being, and in response, he decides (Eva is convinced) to take life. His decision, in other words, can also be read as another form of imitation: Kevin mimics his parents' (and thus the world's) decision about his birth. Kevin's responsibility for ending his parents' relationship implies an experience of omnipotence, certainly, but this omnipotence also coincides, as Winnicott well knows, with a certain ontological precariousness. It is as if Kevin witnesses his own power to decide that he should not be (or have been). Neither Eva nor the reader knows for sure what Kevin wants, but a Winnicottian account of the child's destructive violence suggests that what he wants and needs is a surviving other—someone who could be responsible for the decision regarding his own being. Winnicott notes that it is the analyst/mother's role to *survive* the analysand/infant's destructiveness without either giving way or retaliating. Either of these responses would merely confirm the analysand/infant's omnipotence (there is no other and thus no relation).

Kevin's violence, read figuratively and in accordance with a Winnicottian protocol, repeatedly appears to direct itself toward his mother, Eva, in an effort, not fully cognized by either, to test her ability to survive and thus to function as his enabling other. The tyrannical, omnipotent infant, Winnicott suggests, cannot come to "use" any other (no matter how completely dependent he or she may be) until the infant is able to "use" that other as an object that has survived destruction: "In the sequence one can say that first there is object-relating, then in the end there is object-use; in between, however, is the most difficult thing, perhaps, in human development. . . . This thing that there is in between relating and use is the subject's placing of the object outside the area of the subject's omnipotent control" (89). This process of becoming a self capable of using others seems to require the distinction it simultaneously brings about, and "destruction" is Winnicott's term for the logical violence that effects and constitutively informs this coming into being via the other.[42] Surviving Kevin's violence becomes, for Shriver's Eva, a kind of repeated encounter with her responsibility for his singular being, and the difficulty Eva has deciding whether or not to have a child in the first place anticipates (or parallels, given the complex narrative structure of the novel) the repeated encounters Eva has with her son's apparent resistance to being and to being in relation. Kevin's destructive violence therefore also subjects Eva to repeated encounters with what neither she nor we can definitively ascribe to a desire-not-to-be. Kevin's violence functions, that is to say, as a desperate and almost inarticulate plea to have been brought into being by the other's desire: I want you to have wanted me, Kevin's aggression says, prior to and in excess of my desire to be; I want you to have wanted my being in excess of any calculation or justification or consent. But as such, Kevin's violence could also be said to repeat and confront Eva's own desire for the other to bring *her* into being as a parent. Eva and Kevin are locked in a deadly power struggle in which each waits for the other to call him, or her, into being: as a beloved child, as an authentic mother. "I need you to make being possible and desirable for me," says the unwanted child. "Why else would I go on being? Or, since you have so insistently demonstrated your nonlove, I won't trust any second-rate tokens of affection." And the reluctant mother pleads in turn: "If only you would recognize me, I could be your real mother rather than merely playing a role. I would even accept recognition that took the form of violent rejection, if only I could be certain that it was a cry or call, a distorted bit of language addressed to *me*." Each awaits the gift of full recognition from the other; each awaits the other's decision regarding reproduction.

The particular question that the figure of Kevin poses for both the reader and Eva (if, that is, one doesn't give in to a reading of Eva as an entirely deranged and violent parent) is whether his threat is a profound and pure rejection of life and relation or whether his aggression represents its own kind of overly meaningful plea and ultimate defense against vulnerability: "How can I believe that you love me if you don't hate me?" or "Will you still love me if I do the worst thing?" or "Is there a 'you,' and if there is not a 'you,' how can there be a 'me'?"[43] When ten-year-old Kevin is unwell, he briefly presents himself as an entirely different character, a vulnerable little boy who loves and needs his mother:

> When I tucked him in, he huddled gladly with the blanket to his chin, and when I slipped the thermometer between his flushed lips . . . he suckled the glass with gentle rhythmic contractions, as if finally, at the age of ten, having learned to nurse. . . .

> ... Kevin wasn't just cranky or tired, he was a completely different person. And
> that's how I achieved an appreciation for how much energy and commitment
> it must have taken him the rest of the time to generate this other boy. (236)

The episode suggests the possibility of a narrative breakthrough and hints at the development of a progressively affirmative relationship between Kevin and his mother. But this is clearly not the only story that Shriver tells. Instead, what we are given again and again is evidence of Kevin's uncanny capacity for destructive nonrelatedness.

Ethical Misreading

We Need to Talk about Kevin and Kevin, I would contend—both Shriver's novel and her character—share something with the philosopher David Benatar in his attempt to understand the "moral duty not to procreate" (14). Benatar tries to persuade his readers that nobody should ever make the choice to have a child, and this because, in the balance, no human life is ever worthwhile. We merely sentimentally manage to convince ourselves otherwise, and therefore it would be to everyone's benefit to end things as soon as it might be humanely possible. Benatar would convey to all of us the message Kevin gets from his mother and returns to her with his very person: I don't know that I should go on being. I don't know that I would choose being, if the choice had been mine. But "we find ourselves in a kind of a trap," Benatar writes, "[for] we have already come into existence" (220).

It is hard to get one's head around Benatar's simultaneously human-centered account (all based, as it were, on a kind of calculation of the question of human happiness) and his relative haste to dispose of us all: "I do not think that there should ever have been any people. Given that there have been people, I do not think that there should be any more" (182); "It strikes me, therefore, that the concern that humans will not exist at some future time is either a symptom of the human arrogance that our presence makes the world a better place or is some misplaced sentimentalism" (200). For "what is so special," he asks, "about a world that contains moral agents and rational deliberators?" (199). ("*Nyeh. Nyeh. Nyeh. Nyeh. Nyeh. Nyeh. Nyeh*"!) Because Benatar asserts that he is a philanthropist rather than a misanthrope, he does admit to the peculiarity of his gesture ("It may seem like an odd kind of philanthropy—one that if acted upon, would lead to the end of all *anthropos*" [223]) and to its probable futility ("[I]t is quite likely that my views either will be ignored or will be dismissed" [225]). But surely the peculiarity of this provocative speech act merits more consideration. This cheerful philosopher would disabuse us of any sense of the worthwhile nature of "the whole human thing" (to use Eva's words), yet the very philosophical nature of his communication necessarily and structurally conveys a different message. There is, in other words, a rather radical disjunction between the constative and the performative dimensions of Benatar's utterance. Simply put: I will engage in the world-making work of speaking to others and awaiting their reply, even as I will make the argument for the end of human being. Perhaps Benatar, like Shriver's Kevin, would like to see if we can survive his provocation and destruction. In all fairness to Benatar, maybe that is what it means to be a philosopher (or a novelist): prove to me that I am not omnipotent by surviving the force of my argument! But if Benatar's philosophy recalls Kevin (which is also, in some sense, to recall Eva, who dreads the mere repetition of her own monstrous being), Benatar's writing reminds us that there is a reproduction of life and futurity in every relational event, no matter how crossed that attempt may be by a desire to communicate resistance to being. In *We Need to Talk about Kevin*, Eva Khatchadourian reads her son as not wanting to go on being and as murderously resentful of others who have an attachment to being. Yet both Eva and the novel refuse to relinquish Kevin; instead, Kevin's resistance is "misread" as a registration of the groundlessness of being that is also a cry for recognition and for the love that would make going-on-being not only possible but worth everything. Eva doesn't *know* that Kevin deserves something other than abandonment on his own merits; nor is he necessarily in any way—be it knowable or unknowable—*truly* worthy of such care (this would be a humanist ethic or a humanist solution). Instead, what I am calling Eva's (and the novel's) misreading can be said to participate in an ethical ordeal precisely because it proceeds without any guarantee of referential felicity. This kind of reading has the power to produce the speech act it only apparently responds to, although not inevitably. There is a kind of ethical madness at play here, as there is in every reading worthy of the name. But to avoid such misreading would be to take the risk of making a different mistake: I missed the call of the other because I was not entirely convinced that it was meant for me, or even that it was a call.

Shriver's narrative combines its epistolary address to Kevin's dead father with a series of conversations between mother and son that take place when Eva goes to visit Kevin in the correctional facility after his conviction:

> I do. I go at every opportunity. . . .
> You're astonished. You shouldn't be. He's my son, too, and a mother should visit her child in prison. I have no end of failings as a mother, but I have always followed the rules. If anything, following the letter of the unwritten parental law was one of my failings. (39)[44]

Chronologically, the prison visits follow the main events of the novel, but their formal narrative relationship suggests a different temporality, one in which the visits function as an alternative or a supplementary text. If one story ends in disaster, the other opens up a certain possibility for relation—a parenting relation, between a mother and her now adult, but really childlike, son: "He has five grim years left to serve in an adult penitentiary, and I cannot vouch for what will walk out the other side. But in the meantime, there is a second bedroom in my serviceable apartment. The bedspread is plain. A copy of *Robin Hood* lies on the bookshelf. And the sheets are clean" (400). This narrative structure preserves, if somewhat obscurely, two different ways of thinking about relation (one that stresses the destructive impasse and one that offers a hopeful process) while simultaneously resonating with a particular theoretical understanding of the psychoanalytic clinical scene. As Winnicott has suggested, the scene of analysis *repeats* the scene of the mother–child relation, unless this relation could be said never to have happened, in which case it effects a certain literalization: "[F]or the neurotic the couch and warmth and comfort can be symbolical of the mother's love; for the psychotic it would be more true to say that these things are the analyst's physical expression of love. The couch is the analyst's lap or womb, and the warmth is the live warmth of the analyst's body. And so on."[45]

The first account we are given of Eva's visit to Kevin alludes to a series of visits that have already taken place: "Kevin himself has been surprised by my dogged appearances, which is not to say, in the beginning at least, pleased" (40). Kevin appears to be "surprised" that Eva still exists after his act of mass destruction (it is a sign that he is not omnipotent). He is surprised, as we might say colloquially, that she is still "there" for him.[46] But he will continue to test this presence by attempting to destroy his mother psychologically;

having survived his "real" violence, how much violent talk can she bear? Will she respond to the shocking things he says with the hate they seem to deserve?[47] And what is Eva's pose? She would seem to be engaged in a kind of therapy with her son, refusing to abandon him to his sociopathic self-presentation and to a diagnosis of "empathic deficiency" (56). Thus, her very carefully orchestrated therapy is constructed as an attempt at authenticity: what if I stop playing my role (the good mother) and you stop playing yours (the monstrously indifferent and radically unmotherable sociopath)?

> Once I was no longer fussing with my coat, he said, "You may be fooling the neighbours and the guards and Jesus and your gaga mother with these goody-goody visits of yours, but you're not fooling me. Keep it up if you want a gold star. But don't be dragging your ass back here on my account." Then he added, "Because I hate you."
>
> I know that children say that all the time, in fits: *I hate you, I hate you!* eyes squeezed with tears. But Kevin is approaching eighteen, and his delivery was flat.
>
> I had some idea of what I was supposed to say back: *Now, I know you don't mean that,* when I knew that he did. Or, *I love you anyway, young man, like it or not.* But I had an inkling that it was following just these pat scripts that had helped to land me in a garish overheated room that smelled like a bus toilet on an otherwise lovely, unusually clement December afternoon. So I said instead, in the same informational tone, "I often hate you, too, Kevin," and turned heel. (44)

When Eva next visits Kevin, he confronts her directly: "You never wanted to have me, did you?" (56). But this response counts, for Eva, as progress—a sign of Kevin's recognition of, and interest in, her interiority, even as it raises the specter of incurability for their relationship, since, for Kevin, being is so profoundly vexed from the start. His question also appears to confirm one explanation for his horrific act. Deprived of the constitutive message that would make survival, or going-on-being, possible, Kevin chose to stage spectacular violence: "When you're putting on a show," he tells his mother when she asks him why he did not kill her, too, "you don't shoot the audience" (394). Kevin's violence functions as a kind of speech act or returned message, even as this message flirts frighteningly with the possibility of non-response: sheer destruction threatens to mean nothing or to mean this: "I am only your mirror. You decided to conceive me. I decided to kill everyone—look at me!" But Kevin's apparently definitive sense that he might not have been wholly and simply desired into being is not the only story here. After all, who, in their specificity, could ever have been desired? Our particularity is inseparable from a radically undesired and unanticipated coming-into-being. Kevin, in other words, might be read as a highly figurative inscription not of a simple (though tragic) failure of maternal desire but of a more intractable (and formative) crisis of consent and of being-in-relation. Our being cannot rid itself of the trace of performative violence and incoherence that makes us only belatedly desired—only retroactively, and hence imperfectly, called into our particular being.

For Eva, as I have suggested, ethical crisis coalesces around the question of her ambivalence with respect to reproduction. She does not know what to do with the power to choose whether or not to reproduce, and her decisions (including her decision to have another child) are, paradoxically, as much about fantasized forms of circumventing the decision (I choose what I do not want so as not to be tyrannized by the decision; I choose again and again in order to try to prove to myself that my previous choices were good ones) as they are about acting decisively. Eva never comes to terms with her inability to choose reproduction. Her character, we might say, is the anthropomorphized embodiment of an impasse concerning the reproductive "decision" (or the relationship between reproduction and decision). It is this crisis that, as I have suggested elsewhere in this book, has been exacerbated by political and technological transformations affecting the culture of reproduction in the last fifty years. As the relationship between choice and reproduction has become intensified (by progressive feminist and queer politics, by technological advances in the field of assisted reproduction and, in different ways, by a pervasive liberal-capitalist discourse of privatization), the limits of a humanist model of consent and rationalization have become harder to ignore. What are the grounds upon which to bring another into being? Does one invent ethics anew with every reproductive decision, which is also to say with every decision to performatively "misread" the other's personhood as a referential given? How might one be said to choose a wild child? Eva's local struggle cites this grander philosophical challenge, whereas Kevin's violence—his sociopathological wildness—allegorizes the harm done by a liberal-humanist disavowal of its own limitations. Being demands the other. In Winnicott's terms, Kevin needs Eva to survive and to want survival: if Eva is able to survive the son who destroys just about everything and everyone else—her whole meaningful world—then perhaps she can, indeed, function as an other beyond his omnipotent power, capable of providing her son with love and recognition and of rescuing him from his monstrous self. But this would also be to recognize the Winnicottian mother as the social other that every child has to come into relation with, like it or not: the social survives the violence of my individual (monstrous) exceptionality and thereby comes to recognize and love me. In testing the limits of her willingness to survive his acts of destruction, the child also tests the limits of the mother's commitment to being as being in relation. This everyday crisis of being and relation is what *We Need to Talk about Kevin* allegorizes so extravagantly and what Shriver's novel reminds us we still need to talk about.

5

"Dis-ap-peared"

Endangered Children in Denis Villeneuve's *Prisoners* and Alice Munro's "Miles City, Montana"

In a widely influential 1954 essay titled "The Crisis in Education," Hannah Arendt distanced herself from the critique of pedagogical and parental authority then under way, on the grounds that this "revolutionary pose" actually masked a widespread "estrangement from the world."[1] "It is as though parents daily said," writes Arendt, "'In this world even we are not very securely at home; how to move about in it, what to know, what skills to master, are mysteries to us too. You must try to make out as best you can; in any case you are not entitled to call us to account. We are innocent, we wash our hands of you.'"[2] Arendt's essay responds to what historian Michael Grossberg has described as the expansion of "liberationist" definitions of children's rights in the postwar period.[3] Invoking the work of British political philosopher David Archard, who distinguishes between "liberationist" and "caretaking" approaches to children's rights, Grossberg suggests that these terms actually name the poles of a persistent twentieth-century conflict. Hence, whereas liberationist definitions of children's rights expanded from the 1940s to the 1970s, children in the last decades of the twentieth century and into the twenty-first have been increasingly imagined as endangered and in need of special protection. This protection does not pursue the kind of conservative "preservation" that Arendt was trying to articulate in 1954. "Exactly for the sake of the new and revolutionary in every child," Arendt wrote, "education must be conservative; it must preserve this newness and introduce it as a new thing into an old world, which, however revolutionary its actions may be, is always, from the standpoint of the next generation, superannuated and close to destruction."[4] "The Crisis in Education" makes a deceptively simple case, then, for a parental (or, more specifically, generational) responsibility to protect the child's revolutionary "wildness." In this chapter, I want to consider how certain paradoxes of rights and responsibility play themselves out in representations of children and their adult caretakers in the passage from a "liberationist" moment committed to individual choice and freedom for children and women to a protection-ist, neoliberal, and late-patriarchal cultural moment that we still inhabit. Is there a theory of rights, I want to ask, that cannot be reduced to either a simple demand for individual freedom (freedom to choose, freedom from adult control, freedom as a mode of being) or a discourse of protection (the right to be protected or to protect one's own)? How might representations of vulnerable children or protective parents inform a posthumanist (which is also to say a post possessive–individualist) concept of rights? Specifically, I'd like to examine how a certain model of child protection can be seen to undo itself in a grueling contemporary film, Denis Villeneuve's *Prisoners* (2013), before turning back to an earlier moment to read what I would contend is a more profound consideration of both children's rights and the failure to pro-tect children from rightlessness and precarious being, Alice Munro's short story "Miles City, Montana" (1986). In each of these texts, as I hope to show, a certain figuration of the wild child, a child who cannot be domesticated or protected, troubles and informs an attempt to exercise parental responsibil-ity and inscribes an enigmatic resistance to liberal-humanist models of indi-vidual right and responsibility.

From Liberation to Protection

Since the late nineteenth century, Grossberg explains, "rights" have "assumed greater and greater importance as a primary way for Americans to determine the meaning of childhood."[5] After 1945, liberationist rights claims became increasingly bound up with the demands of other civil rights movements as children's rights advocates "fought to include the young in the era's roster of self-determining persons who could make claims recognized by law."[6] This trend peaked in the 1960s and 1970s, with the most radical of advocates call-ing for the end of children's subordinated legal status.[7] Although these more radical claims were never generally accepted, Grossberg argues, they were indicative of a consistent movement toward "greater autonomy and self-determination for the young."[8] At the same time, others have disparaged what Mormon legal scholars Bruce C. Hafen and Jonathan O. Hafen, for example, refer to as "abandoning Children to Their Rights." Children, they seem to imply, have a right *not* to have rights:

> [A] growing clamor over legal rights for children may create the illusion that parents, teachers, and other adults owe children only what the law demands of them. The increased appearance of autonomy for children becomes then essentially the default position that results from reducing our sense of adult responsibility for children. The assertion that untutored, unguided children already enjoy all the autonomy they need may relieve adults of demanding obligations, but that assertion is ultimately a profound form of child neglect. Children cannot raise themselves.[9]

In many ways, as Grossberg suggests, the 1989 United Nations Convention on the Rights of the Child marked the culmination of, and limit point in, an attempt to combine caretaking and liberationist approaches to children's rights. The convention "carefully balanced" the two schools of thought, but it also "stirred up latent American opposition to international agreements that might infringe on national sovereignty," with the result that the United States, infamously, refused (along with Somalia) to ratify the convention. "In the United States," Grossberg asserts, "the limits of liberationist rights had been reached."[10]

For philosopher and psychoanalyst Elizabeth Young-Bruehl, however, the unambiguous progress signaled by both the UN Declaration on the Rights of the Child (1959) and Convention on the Rights of the Child (1989) has not been enough to counter a progressive exacerbation of "childism" in the United States. In her 2012 book, *Childism: Confronting Prejudice against Children*, Young-Bruehl suggests that childism must be combated by deploying a combination of clinical psychoanalysis (which allows for a specialized form of listening to children or to adults' narratives of their own childhood) and sociopolitical analysis: "This is something that children themselves cannot tell us about. Their insight is at the micro-level of their families. . . . Our task is to apply theoretical concepts, analysis, and history to their insights in order to broaden our inquiry to the macro-level of social attitudes, legislation and policy. For this, we need to examine their parents."[11] Young-Bruehl's historically specific claim, which is also, she notes, a story about her own generation, is that post–World War II baby boomers became "deeply

conflicted in relation to their children, as well as to the future more generally, with progressive and regressive tendencies waging a constant battle."[12] A
generational ambivalence toward children became manifest at a policy level
in the acquiescence to an antichild trend "that began during Richard Nixon's presidency, was normalized during the Reagan years, continued during
the Clinton years, and escalated dramatically during the George W. Bush
administration."[13]

But Young-Bruehl's most provocative claim (and most germane for the
present study) is that the child as victimized, vulnerable, and in need of protection gradually came to substitute for all other understandings of subjects
with precarious rights. "Most child advocates have focused narrowly and
wrongly on protecting individual children from child abuse," she writes.
"This focus narrows the idea of children's basic rights to simply Protection and so does little or nothing to help the nation's children as a group."[14]
In other words, politically generated scenarios of criminal child abuse and
individual vulnerability calling out for adult protection have gradually displaced efforts to think in terms of a more child-friendly climate of socially
engineered policy and planning. The historical narrative she tells begins
with the "discovery" of child abuse—by Dr. C. Henry Kempe, who explored
"battered child syndrome"—which led not to a larger set of state-supported
developmental programs but instead to the far more narrowly conceived
Child Protective Services. Richard Nixon's veto of the Comprehensive Child
Development Act and Walter Mondale's alternative legislation marked a
turning point: "After the 1971 veto, the Comprehensive Child Development
Act's main Senate sponsor, Walter Mondale (D., Minn.), decided to push
the problem of child abuse forward on its own. "Not even Richard Nixon
is in favor of child abuse," he quipped. After hearings and much deliberation, Senator Mondale's proposal eventually emerged in 1974 as the Child
Abuse Prevention and Treatment Act."[15] Young-Bruehl notes the irony: "[L]
egislators who objected to American children being 'federalized' into developmental programs, because the authority of their parents would be under-
mined and their minds would be tinkered with, agreed to institute as the
sole service universally available to children an *investigative* service, invasive
of family life and privacy by definition."[16] At the same time, as Paula Fass has
documented, the "privatization of responsibility" in the post-1980 United
States generated a new discourse of hyperprotection around the figure of the
child. "One would be hard-pressed," writes Fass, "to find a stretch of time in

American history in which anxieties about children were more intense than in the two decades from 1980 to 2000, and this includes periods of severe depression and long wars with serious ramifications for the civilian population."[17] "A grossly inflated and misplaced sense of crisis," adds Steven Mintz, "became widespread in the last quarter of the twentieth century, reflecting genuine worries—for example, over children's well-being in a hypersexualized society—and more generalized anxieties—over street crime, family instability, and shifts in women's roles."[18]

Young-Bruehl's psychohistory, which includes a diagnosis of the type of childism most characteristic of the Nixon administration ("obsessional"), as opposed to that which was most representative of the Reagan administration ("narcissistic"), concludes with what she argues was the sudden disappearance of the 1980s and 1990s panic over forms of childhood sexual abuse. "[M]uch of the anxiety that had developed around childhood sexual abuse and SRA [satanic ritual abuse]," she writes, "was rechanneled into a panic over terrorism following the attacks of September 11. The attackers struck many commentators as a new kind of Satanist—cold-blooded religious fanatics like Osama bin Laden, infidels, or as I suggested before, politicized pedophiles."[19] In many ways, the protection and security discourse directed at the figure of the child came to incorporate the figure of the absolutely vulnerable American citizen after September 2001, but it continued to do so, Young-Bruehl ultimately argues, at the expense of the very child (and, by implication, the citizenry) whom such measures claimed to protect. Narratives of absolute vulnerability that call on a paternal or patriarchal model of individual protection and on a figuration of absolutely criminalized or demonized threat are also ways of theorizing relation within a polity and of disavowing the limits of patriarchal omnipotence and control. But this is also to say that certain models of protection are characterized by an "autoimmune disorder" whereby the protection itself becomes increasingly indistinguishable from the threat it ostensibly seeks to dispel.[20]

In response to these and other crises of protectionism, early twenty-first century theorists of human rights have begun to question the relationship between vulnerability and agency in dominant liberal (or humanist) theories of "human" rights and "humanitarian" intervention. Scholars and activists have raised concerns about the political and philosophical presuppositions at work behind various models of protectionism; not surprisingly, the child, as one of our privileged figures for the uncertain border between the autonomous subject and the vulnerable object of protection, has often been at the center of these reconsiderations. "The child as symbol of innocence and potentiality—of that which precedes the corruption of society—," writes Rony Brauman in a critical reflection on dominant human rights discourse, "calls out for protection." [21] The sense of crisis around the theory and practice of protection expressed by scholars like Young-Bruehl and provoked and addressed by aspects of critical human rights theory is nowhere better conveyed than in Denis Villeneuve's 2013 film, *Prisoners* (made from a 2009 screenplay by Aaron Guzikowski).[22] The film builds toward, and attempts to extricate itself from, a harrowing scene of torture executed by a protective patriarch but inflicted on a vulnerable man-child. "The easy catharsis of righteous payback," notes A. O. Scott in his *New York Times* review of the movie, "is complicated at every turn, and pain and uncertainty spread like spilled oil on an asphalt road."[23] It is extremely difficult *not* to think of the central plot of *Prisoners* as a displaced figuration of the ethical crisis presented to Americans by revelations concerning the post-9/11 torture of terrorist suspects authorized by the U.S. government (think here of the ubiquitous "ticking time bomb" motif).[24] But for the viewer, the horror beyond the horror of the torture comes with the revelation that the torture victim, Alex, was himself an abducted and abused child. If, as Elizabeth Young-Bruehl argues, post-9/11 anxieties eventually came to displace panic regarding the abuse of children, *Prisoners* seems to unfold in a sociopsychological landscape located on the uncertain border of this epistemic shift. "Crimes are specified, and criminals are discovered," writes Scott, "but empirical solutions are not enough to dispel the feeling that an uncontained atmospheric menace broods over this wintry landscape."[25]

A Child Is Being Tortured

Denis Villeneuve's *Prisoners* is set in small-town Pennsylvania in what appears to be the recent, though unspecified, past. It depicts an everyman figure, Keller Dover, who, in the course of trying to save his daughter's life, engages in the abduction and torture of a child-man whom he comes close to killing.[26] "If *Prisoners* . . . upholds some of the conventions of the angry-dad revenge drama," writes A. O. Scott, "it also subverts them in surprising, at times devastating ways."[27] It is a thriller, writes David Denby, "that digs into the dark cellars of American paranoia and aggression."[28] But how are we to assess the film's profoundly disturbing central scenario? Does Villeneuve's movie (and Guzikowski's script) ultimately offer up a critical reading of its torture scenes? Or does the movie simply register an "autoimmune" ethical crisis (the responsibility to protect a child cannot be exercised without doing violence to an "other child") that it is unable or unwilling to think beyond? (This is a return of the scenario in *The Road* when the man is faced with the distinction between his child and *the* child, or "other little boys.") And, finally, how might *Prisoners*, with its proliferation of vulnerable children and desperate or dangerous adults, function as a commentary on contemporary parent–child relations and reproductive ethics? I want to try to answer these questions by interpreting the representation of torture in *Prisoners* both as a darkly allegorical engagement with the ordeal of reproductive ethics ("The 'why have children?' decision is, therefore, a big issue. . . . It more broadly raises questions about the value of humanity and the future of the planet," Christine Overall writes)[29] and as an instantiation of the central paradox of conventional international human rights language as explained by Werner Hamacher in his 2004 essay "The Right to Have Rights."[30] To what extent are the moral crises of *Prisoners* the same crises that trouble dominant liberal models of human rights, and how might attention to the figure of the vulnerable child at once distract from and intensify our engagement with these ethical demands?

Two neighboring families in small-town Pennsylvania are celebrating Thanksgiving together when their two young daughters, Anna and Joy, are abducted. The protagonist of *Prisoners*, Keller Dover—doubled with yet differentiated from the film's violent and heroic police detective, Loki—will do anything to bring his daughter, Anna, home. Dover's neighbors (Joy's parents), Nancy and Franklin, will become complicit in Dover's crime, but Dover's own wife and son will not know anything of his actions for most of the film. Dover is a Christian survivalist, always prepared for any disaster. Although in better times his wife pokes fun at his overly stocked bunker-like basement (complete with gas masks), in her desperation she sobs and laments, "You made me feel so safe. You told us that you could protect us from anything." Dover's entire world, it would seem, is bound up with a fantasy of absolute protection that makes it impossible to tell where his own being ends and his child's begins.[31]

But Dover's desperate protective efforts eventually lead him to take his own prisoner: Alex Jones, a mentally disabled young man who clearly has some connection to the girls' disappearance but who refuses to give any information to the police and cannot be definitively tied to the abduction. Released from police custody, Jones whispers minimal messages that only Dover can hear ("They only cried when I left them"), contributing both to Dover's desperation and isolation and to his sense of absolute justification. (Dover is both seduced and persecuted by such messages in what one might call—looking ahead to my reading of Munro—a Laplanchean mode.) Dover believes that he must act unilaterally; the state and the law will not play the role of the good protective father for him. But the film both participates in and seems to open up some critical distance from the symptomatic aspect of Dover's situation. That is to say, both Dover and the film seem incapable of teasing apart the desire and the fear at work in this narrative of paternal protection. Dover is on his own, and his family—with an emphasis on the possessive pronoun—is in danger. An anguished Dover recites the Lord's Prayer (as he does when he and his teenage son go hunting in the movie's opening scenes) and, almost simultaneously, tortures Jones, whom he has taken captive and chained up in the bathroom of an abandoned building. The building, we later learn, was also Dover's childhood home. Dover ultimately walls Jones up in a shower stall so that he can continue to torture him with scalding and freezing water without killing him and also without having to see his face. "I've made my choice," Dover tells his friend and neighbor Franklin Birch. "He [Jones] is not a person anymore. He stopped being a person when he took our daughters." Yet his words to his captive repeatedly belie this very assertion: "I know you are scared and I know you want to go home. If you aren't going to talk, Alex, I'm going to have to hurt you." Struggling to keep up the work of interrogation, Dover ultimately tapes a picture of the kidnapped girls to the wall in the torture chamber to remind him of the justification for his own brutal actions.

The extremely disturbing quality of the torture depicted in *Prisoners* both calls for and renders precarious a figurative or allegorical interpretation. In this abandoned building, a father is confronted by the faces of children: his own face in the bathroom mirror of his childhood home; the face he wants desperately to see, that of his absolutely vulnerable daughter; and the face he cannot bear to see, that of the child-man victim of his own violence. Children are saving children from children in this fantasmatic scenario, and children are surrounded by parents who fail to protect. If the daughters of Dover and his neighbor stand in here for the hegemonically conceived recipients of humanitarian aid (Brauman's "child as symbol of innocence and poten-tiality—of that which precedes the corruption of society"),[32] Jones—the film's wild child—is caught somewhere between childhood and adulthood, between rightless monstrosity and victimized vulnerability, and would seem to demand another (posthumanist?) approach to the concept and subject of fundamental rights. The elaborate narrative construction of the torture scene in *Prisoners*, I suggest, generates a confrontation between a protec-tionist, paternal "good guy" and a child-man whom that father has to other as "not a person" in order to fulfill his responsibility to his family. In other words, what takes place in this abandoned home is a confrontation between a late-patriarchal father and a posthumanist wild child.

Alex Jones may be the most affecting "wild child" in Villeneuve's movie, but he is not an isolated exception. *Prisoners* is populated by a series of dam-aged adult-children: the orphaned detective was abused by priests in a boys' home; an alternative suspect turns up who is suspicious precisely because he is engaged in an elaborate and grotesque reenactment of his own scene of childhood torture; and Dover himself turns out to have had a traumatic ado-lescent past. The temporal feel of *Prisoners* (all the events take place within a single week) is thus of the urgency of time passing—when a child dis-appears, time is of the essence, and this provokes both Loki and Dover to violence—but there is also an alternative temporality, in which time doesn't pass so much as repeat itself, or persist, suspending any future while events wait to be read, detected, and apprehended.[33] "Villeneuve throws us into a complicated skein of abductions going back years," writes David Denby, "without losing the urgency of the present."[34] Dover strives to produce a utopian and timeless family but becomes caught up, instead, in a seemingly endless (and thus suspended) scene of torture that invokes a perverse scene of parent–child intimacy. The timing of the recovery of his own abandoned child, Anna, also presents itself as an odd analogue for the timing of parental failure, only here the timing runs in reverse. Keller Dover does not confront the time to abandon the child but seeks, instead, the time to undo abandon-ment, the time before there is no time and before it is too late.

Because the kidnapped girls are ultimately rescued, we might be led to believe that the torture depicted in *Prisoners* (unlike the "enhanced inter-rogation techniques" deployed by American security forces at Guantanamo Bay and at so-called "black sites" throughout the world) is justified. But

Dover's status is left uncertain. In the movie's denouement, Dover himself is abducted and secreted away in what may become his own grave (a terrifying pit that surely also allegorizes the ethical impasse Dover finds himself in long before he is physically captured), and we are led to believe that the horrors we have been witnessing might all be traced back to a monstrous maternal figure, Alex Jones's "aunt" and guardian, Holly Jones, and the terrible loss that she and her husband have refused to come to terms with. Thus, Dover's burial also suggests the mother's womb-as-tomb, from which Dover can only wait to be reborn (he is not quite as "lucky" as Max in *Where the Wild Things Are*). Holly Jones tells Dover the story of how she and her husband were once devout Christians with a young son. They lost their son to cancer and subsequently began to wage a war with God that began with the abduction of Alex, twenty-six years earlier. "Making children disappear," Holly Jones tells Dover as she drugs him and disposes of his car keys and cell phone, "is the war we wage with God . . . makes people lose their faith . . . turns them into demons like you. . . . [I] had to slow down since my husband disappeared. . . . I do what I can . . ." One might say that the film places at its origin the kind of extraordinarily painful loss that nobody can be held responsible for while simultaneously suggesting that, within a certain fantasy economy, sociopathic killers are preferable to cancer. But, of course, there is also a recognizably gendered story at work here in which female figures are either all good or all bad (pure victims or murderous mothers), whereas masculinity struggles with a simultaneous experience of impurity and the inability to tolerate this compromise. The vulnerable or evil female characters function, in other words, to purify and justify the masculine subject. Nevertheless, for all its monstrous hyperbole, the film figures the loss of a child as the loss that undoes subjectivity and the very possibility of the world. In this sense, it remains closely intertwined with the fantasies that sustain the parental characters we have encountered in Donoghue's *Room*, McCarthy's *The Road*, and Morrison's *A Mercy*.

Is Keller Dover an exemplary parent, willing to do anything for the sake of his child, or an archetypally self-possessive American patriarch, determined to preserve and defend all that he considers "his"?[35] "*Prisoners* is a challenge," writes David Denby. "[Y]ou have to decide who's right and who's wrong at every turn, and, when it's over, ambiguity, rather than the satisfactions of harmony, reigns. Life stays out of joint. This movie suggests that it's never really been any other way."[36] But the challenge of *Prisoners*, I would suggest, is not unrelated to the challenge presented by orthodox human rights discourse, particularly insofar as that discourse attempts to preserve a distinctly humanist model of individual rights in the face of multiple challenges to its ethical and political efficacy. This is where Werner Hamacher's deconstructive and post-Marxist account of the subject of a "right to have rights" dovetails with the fears and uncertainties that animate Villeneuve's film.

Hamacher picks up on Arendt's famous critique, in *The Origins of Totalitarianism*, of an international human rights policy that, by 1951, had reduced millions of stateless persons to a more profound state of rightlessness than ever before. This situation did not simply amount to a failure to extend human rights to all, Hamacher asserts (teasing his account out of Arendt's analysis); rather, this state of affairs was and is bound up with the very "paradoxical" structure and concept of such rights: "Human rights said to be inalienable and thoroughly independent are thus de facto made dependent on a particular, that is, alien power to guarantee them, and are thus exposed to the arbitrary will and the special interests of this power. Herein lies the fundamental and unresolvable paradox of human rights, a paradox that allows Arendt to speak of 'the perplexities of the rights of man.'"[37] Looking at laws of denaturalization and denationalization during the first part of the twentieth century, Arendt is able to show that to be deprived of one's (nationally determined) legal status was also to be deprived of one's most basic human rights. Hamacher elaborates:

> Arendt explains this catastrophic turn of national governments against the universalism of human rights by pointing out that a global power to guarantee those rights was lacking. Her argument implies the further explanation, however, especially in light of Marx's critique of the first human rights declarations, that this perversion is made possible by the internal structure of human rights themselves. Not only were the so-called denaturalization laws enacted by the same powers that had included human rights in their constitutions . . . [b]ut, moreover, it was the human rights themselves that sanctioned this flagrant contradiction in that they allowed, as rights of property and security, for the defense against every attack (and even every presumed attack) on the integrity of the private person or the nation-state. (351)

It is this "structural perversion" or "horrendous paradox" within conventional human rights discourse (whereby the very rights that are being

enshrined seem to threaten the rights of others) that Hamacher emphasizes in his discussion of Arendt's critique. This is, in fact, the very paradox that the authors of the 1948 human rights charter themselves tried to
ward off in the final article of their declaration: "No determination contained within the present declaration may be interpreted in such a way that
any state, group or person is given the right to exercise a capacity or take an
action, the aim of which would be the annihilation of rights and freedoms
introduced in this declaration" (quoted 351). Hamacher refers to this article
as a "hermeneutic protection clause" that announces the limits of the rights
discourse it seeks to defend: "Human rights *themselves*," he writes, "cannot
prevent . . . their own use toward the destruction of precisely these human
rights" (351).

It is precisely at this point in Hamacher's argument, the point at which
he exposes the limits of orthodox liberal human rights theory and begins
to speculate on a posthumanist alternative (grounded in the "right to have
rights"), that the figure of the child might be said to come back into view.
Arendt introduces the concept of a "right to have rights" that, Hamacher
argues, does not belong either to the "catalog" of human rights or to the
political rights thereby generated. And whereas Arendt herself refers to the
right to have rights as "the right of every individual to belong to humanity," (quoted 353), Hamacher pushes further: "[T]he right to have rights,"
he suggests, is a "protoright in which it is left open *what* a human may be,
who a human may be, and which rights may be granted to him aside from
this unique one of belonging to humanity and of formulating his rights
correspondingly." He continues: "The only reality that is laid down in this
right is that of this very possibility—of having rights, of using, transform-
ing, and expanding them. It is the possibility offered to the existence of each
and every one whoever or whatever he, she or it may be" (353). The subject of a "right to have rights," Hamacher explains, the subject of what he
calls a "bare existence," departs from classically humanist modes of political thought insofar as it need not be thought of as referring to bare *human*
existence but, instead, as "a naked existence without further qualification"
(354). For Hamacher, the very category of the human gives way here: "[A]
lone out of its freedom from predicates is mere existence capable of becoming a social existence that is not determined in advance by the appurtenance
to a species, a group, a nation, a state, or even just a language. 'Unqualified
mere existence,' which also comprehends the being of animals and of natural

and artificial things, is the only universal that is at once utterly singular. . . . By it alone a universal order, a world . . . would have to orient itself" (354–55). If classical human rights are finally only egoistic, bourgeois property-owning rights (Marx) or alienable political rights entirely dependent on a given nation-state, "the right to have rights" claims a belonging irreducible (precisely as a *claim* or as *performative*) to either natural or political sources of legitimation. "This right is thus valid for all of those," Hamacher explains, "who were in the past excluded from civil rights and human rights or who were able to be excluded *de jure* because they were not viewed as humans, but rather—whether metaphorically or not—as animals, machines, as either beneficial to life or life-threatening" (354).[38]

As I have been arguing throughout this study, the child of a Kantian liminality on the border of the fully human and the animal has always functioned as a crucial intermediary figure for humanist philosophies of being and right; the child has functioned as both an ontological and a (merely) temporal figure in and of the conceptual space between the fully consenting, rights-bearing, self-possessed individual human and the beings (Hamacher's "he, she or it") of the animal or natural world. Between consent and nonconsent, in other words, one encounters the figure of the child as quasi-rational, quasi-consensual, quasi-animal. The concept of a right to have rights thus prompts a rethinking of Aristotle's *zoon logon echon* (the human as the being with reason) as what Hamacher calls *"zoon euchèn echon,"* where *euché* means "prayer, plea, wish, claim, vow, also curse or malediction" (356). In other words, (human) being, in this account, remains dependent on an irreducibly performative and relational (hence always precarious) structure of address. "And to this extent," Hamacher writes, "the language of the *euché* is the language of the *may*, of the *volo ut sis* of the Augustinian definition of love that is quoted by Arendt in her *Vita Activa*" (356). The *volo ut sis* (the *I want you to be*) describes the precarious address that responds to or "makes" a child (that infant being on the cusp of language), as well as the performative dimension of all being-in-relation. The posthumanist theorization of a right to have rights identifies an exit from the "horrendous paradox" of liberal human rights discourse and practice, but it does so by exposing the concept of the human to its own indeterminacy and to its own dependence on a radically social supplement.

One of the ways in which contemporary fictional narratives have registered this conceptual struggle, as I have been suggesting throughout this book, is via allegories (often hyperbolic or intensive allegories) of the parent–child relationship. How does a parent protect his or her child from the world without becoming him- or herself part of what every child needs to be protected from? How does the parent protect his or her *own* child without doing a violence to what can always be figured as "the other child"? In *Prisoners*, the torture practiced by Keller Dover on the child-man, Alex Jones, functions to undo being and to produce a nonsubject who could not possibly have the rights attributed to the liberal self-possessed individual. Torture forces the "primal apostrophe," the infant's cry, back over the threshold from relation to isolation, from potentially meaningful communication to sheer pain and mere materiality ("The alternative to loving was disaster").[39] Dover thus performs violently the very opposite of the parenting function: he unmakes (human) being. Yet he does this ostensibly to reveal truth, to access knowledge and to protect his daughter. In *Prisoners*, the paternal intervention functions as a more violent form of the postapocalyptic father's performative declaration in *The Road* ("He doesn't remember any other little boys"),[40] but it is in its very violence, its very hyperbole, perhaps, that it becomes exposed to its own undoing.

This is also to say that *Prisoners*, like the other narratives looked at in this book, alerts us to the possibility that the ethical uncertainty at work in its disturbing scenarios also belongs to the very category of the child: the child's ideological function as border figure between the human and the animal always threatens to come into view at the site of a constitutive uncertainty with respect to the kind of being that may or may not have rights of any kind. In *Prisoners*, Keller Dover makes, protects, and nurtures fragile being. That is "my job," he might say, echoing the father in McCarthy's *The Road* ("My job is to take care of you. I was appointed to do that by God. I will kill anyone who touches you. Do you understand?").[41] But Dover's child is simultaneously his possession and, to switch registers, the site of his own imaginary totalization. (This is to recall Lee Edelman's work on the ideological child: "The Child, that is, marks the fetishistic fixation of heteronormativity; an erotically charged investment in the rigid sameness of identity that is central to the compulsory narrative of reproductive futurism.")[42] And this identificatory structure becomes all the more obvious when we recall that every individual committed to protecting children in this film is also a damaged child. The adults, who are also figurations of the social per se, are out to save themselves, retroactively. Child protection, in *Prisoners*, comes to figure what Hamacher (following Marx) refers to as the "structural psychosis" of liberal human rights theory—its participation in two ethical registers at once: "human-against-human" and "human-for-human" (349). In this respect, Keller Dover's torture of the man-child, Alex Jones, couched as it is in a story full of nuanced religious references, might also be read as another provocative take on the story of Abraham and Isaac.

Prisoners opens with a scene of sanctified violence, as Dover guides his son in his first deer kill. Dover's recitation of the Lord's Prayer blesses the act, rendering it a meaningful sacrifice. But whereas, in Abraham's story, the sacrifice of the child is avoided at the last moment and an animal becomes the substitute, in *Prisoners* we proceed from the hunting of an animal to be consumed to the torture of a vulnerable human being. This torture is located conceptually in a space between vigilante justice, coded as higher and better than any contingent human system of law, and a space of no justice (Hamacher's "presocial and antisocial *bellum omnium contra omnes* of Hobbes' state of nature" [348]). Torture, as I have suggested, appears here as the absolute other to parenting, to relation, and to the very possibility of sociality; torture is an exercise in unmaking the other, inflicting severe harm that not only undoes being but also is designed to elicit the very cries to which one will fail to respond.[43]

The fantasy at play in Dover's horrific "work" is that torture will restore everything to its place: the father will get his world back and will preserve his family, frozen in time, in a world in which only "animals" (and not animal-persons) are sacrificed. This would be a world in which God is in "his" place—a world of suspended time, full presence, and no loss in which a property-owning and/or God-fearing father figure would be capable of providing absolute protection.[44] But this dystopian/utopian scenario also allegorizes a conventional parental crisis. In Keller Dover, *Prisoners* depicts a paternal refusal to play the *fort-da* game typically associated with the child's entry into language and culture. He also refuses to be the Winnicottian good-enough (m)other who will deploy the art of timing and fail her child. This story of child abuse, kidnapping, and murder, in other words, also tells the story of a *parent* who won't separate, who will not accept an economy of substitution and loss (so meticulously depicted, for example, in *Room*), and who is mired, as a result, in the fantastic opposition between an idealized self-fulfillment (associated with the child's absolute protection) and a separation that looks like complete devastation. This *fort-da* game of parenthood is inseparable, as I have argued throughout this book, from ethical relation, and one way of differentiating the narratives under consideration is to distinguish those in which a paternal figure *resists* from those in which a maternal figure painfully *concedes* to the various forms of loss that such a relation demands.

Accounting for *Prisoners* also requires us to try to distinguish between the behavior of its central characters and the lingering affectual experience of the movie. Does the figure of the tortured child stay with us at the end of Villeneuve's film? Does the suffering child, in other words, allegorize a kind of unforgivable excess, representative, as well, of another scene, the American torture of "political prisoners" after 9/11 as part of the "global war on terror," or do we come to see things in the same way as Keller Dover, whose mortal and moral status at the end of the film is profoundly uncertain? Is Keller Dover a paranoid man who stumbles into the world of his own worst imagining and who becomes, as a result, monstrously violent? Or is he a particular figuration of the vigilant post-9/11 subject who believes in torture as necessary for a kind of superlegal justice? Although *Prisoners* might be said to include a critical perspective on Dover's paranoia and potential for extrajudicial violence, it would be hard to ignore the possibility that the film finally offers him symbolic redemption. Dover both gives his life and gets to keep it (this is one way of reading the film's ambiguous ending). He abducts and tortures a disabled and traumatized man, yet his wife, Grace (a figure of pure suffering and love), despite knowing this, tells the police detective (and the film tells its audience?) that her husband is "a good man." At the end of the film and what may be the end of Dover's life, Grace reinscribes her husband in the symbolic order, as if she is writing his epitaph.[45] And, of course, what makes this fantasy of paternal redemption and absolute protection at all possible is the jolting narrative displacement of Dover's violence onto the (anti)maternal source of all the film's horror: Holly Jones. Holly Jones is behind the kidnapping of Dover's daughter and of other children, and she goes to her grave cursing everyone. This grotesquely gendered solution nevertheless replays a predictable and symptomatic gesture: mothers, not fathers, are ultimately or sovereignly responsible for our lives and our deaths (which is to say, for our very being).[46]

But there is also an oppressively *abyssal* logic to responsibility in *Prisoners*: behind Holly Jones lurks the preeminent example of a father who fails to protect and who thereby opens the floodgates to all this horror. The traumatic seduction/persecution which for Laplanche is part of the very structure of subjectivity is hyperbolized here and set in relationship to a historically specific set of politicophilosophical crises. Laplanche writes, "That God is enigmatic, that He compels one to translate, seems obvious in the entire Judeo-Christian tradition of exegesis. Whether this enigma presupposes that the message is opaque to Himself is plainly a different question. Does God have an unconscious?"[47] Behind the monstrous mother, in other words, is the divine father as abandoning God. And this figure, I would argue, combines a sensitivity to waning patriarchal power with a nuanced engagement with the ethics of reproduction. For Holly Jones, the suffering and death of her child can be read only according to a narrative of divine betrayal and antagonism: the father failed to honor any promise of protection. But this intensive (though not fantastic) experience of loss also allegorizes a critical encounter with the precariousness of every promise and, hence, with the groundlessness of being. The meaningfulness and value of our being is not promised in advance or protected by any teleological certainty of redemption any more than an everyday promise is bound to be kept.[48] *Prisoners* exposes, by allegorizing, the violence that accompanies a paternal determination to protect children and promises from going astray. But its somewhat predictable response to this paradox of care takes the form of a misogynist displacement onto the person of Holly Jones. With this same move, any explicit recognition of the maternal ethics that would disrupt—by diagnosing—patriarchal Christianity can appear only in the form of a maternal monstrosity. It is as if the dead mother from *The Road* (who, as I have suggested, figures and quarantines the death drive for the patriarchal father in McCarthy's novel) has come back to life in the form of a serial child killer.

Read in this way, *Prisoners* can be understood as a rich and complexly symptomatic dramatization of a clash between lingering versions of a patriarchal humanist discourse of protection and responsibility and all that appears destabilizing and, indeed, monstrous in the discourse and practice of a posthumanist maternal ethics. From the perspective of a critical engagement with the film's father figure, the daughter's abduction allegorizes, counterintuitively, a deep conceptual challenge to the world of patriarchal, possessive individualism. But at the almost voiceless and unreadable center of this tormented narrative is Alex Jones, the movie's compelling invocation of the posthumanist wild child. With his undecidable status (Is he legally

an adult? Does he require care like a child? Is he capable of moral judgment?) and his almost complete lack of socialization (his abuse at the hands
of Holly Jones and her husband seems to have locked him into a childhood
from which he cannot escape), Alex distressingly revises aspects of Victor
of Aveyron. Dover's furious yet conflicted antagonism toward Alex gives us
an unforgettable portrait of the liberal-humanist patriarch coming undone
at the site of this particular wild child. As such, the powerfully disturbing
scenario that *Prisoners* inflicts on us also poses a question that, as I hope to
show, shapes the subtle narrative twists and turns of one of Alice Munro's
most effective stories: How do we reconcile the desire and demand to protect children with the ethical uncertainty of what it means to have brought
them into being in the first place?

"Where Are the Children?"

Alice Munro's "Miles City, Montana" is also about a failure to protect children (as are many Munro stories), even if its violence takes a far less desperate and assaultive form. The story's title invokes and preserves that not-
quite-foreign place (from the perspective of the Canadian writer) just south
of the border where a child almost disappears. This child is not, however,
abducted by a religious fanatic or monstrous mother; rather, she is nearly
the victim of a mundane accident: her parents delegate their authority, and a
teenage lifeguard isn't watching when Meg, the narrator's three-and-a-half-
year-old daughter, almost drowns. Everyday horror and the banality of the
limits of parental protection coincide in this story with a subtle reflection on
reproduction as "consent" to the suffering and death of children. But, unlike
Prisoners, with its temporally disorienting landscape of adult children,
Munro's story offers us three distinct temporal and conceptual moments: a
childhood trauma that involves the death of another child, a later scene from
the adult life of the narrator (and the childhood of her children), and finally
the event of narration that could be thought of as a scene of psychoanalysis in which the significance of the earlier moments is shifted. In *Prisoners*,
childhood is at once inescapable and invisible; the childhood of adults won't
stay in the past, even as the child at the center of the events, Dover's daughter, is constituted only by the desire to protect her. Munro's story, with its
clearer sense of temporal distinction, nevertheless prompts us to ask (with
Laplanche) how there can ever be a child at all, given that the child is always

constituted by the address and desire of the other. Once again, Laplanche's emphasis on the priority of a third term (understood as a seductive, traumatizing, and constitutive address), and on the primal bond (understood as the adult–child relation in its mutating historical forms), will be particularly useful when read in conjunction with what this extraordinary literary text has to offer. I want to elaborate on this correlation between Munro and Laplanche, then, while paying particular attention to the historical and maternal specificity of Munro's "Miles City, Montana": if Villeneuve's father is the post-9/11, postfeminist patriarch, Munro's mother is crucially situated at an earlier moment, on the cusp of a new feminist possibility and concomitant ethical crisis.[49] Published in 1985 and set partially in the early 1960s, the story is preoccupied not only with accidental death but also with accidental birth and with the newly exposed status of responsibility for the lives of others that accompanies the emergence of new reproductive choices and technologies. This setting prompts a consideration of Munro's distinctive and psychoanalytically inflected understanding of both the discourse of protection and maternal ethics.

"As we know," Jean Laplanche writes in *New Foundations for Psychoanalysis*, "psychoanalysis does tend to work backwards from the Oedipal relationship to the mother–child relationship. . . . And yet the mother–child relationship is changing very quickly. Without wishing to look too far into the future . . . it should be recalled that more and more children are being brought into the world by artificial means."[50] Such reflections, Laplanche adds, require that psychoanalysis reconsider the historical contingency of the Oedipal structure: "After all, what will remain of the classic Oedipal triangle—not triangulation—in a few decades, or a few hundred years? Is anyone prepared to bet on the survival of the Oedipus on which Freud bases his arguments? Is anyone prepared to claim that human beings will cease to be human beings if it does not survive?"[51] Laplanche's words, as I have already had occasion to note, continue to speak to an early twenty-first-century moment in which we find ourselves located between a mythic past (Oedipus) and an only partially imaginable and technologically saturated future: "It used to be a woman without fallopian tubes: no baby. Now we have almost four million babies from in vitro fertilization," says the doctor at his Santa Monica fertility clinic in *Future Baby*.[52] But for all his attention to what is changing about parenthood, Laplanche remains attentive to what he presents as inevitable or noncontingent: the seductive relationship (which is also, and for the same reasons, a relationship of care and dependency) between adult and child.

Alice Munro's fiction, I would argue, understands the parent–child relationship in terms that are remarkably similar to those given by Laplanche, even as her writing supplements his account by incorporating a markedly feminist ethical perspective. If feminism necessarily involves a move beyond the patriarchal-Oedipal model, Munro would have us understand that any such move also exposes the subject to her vulnerability to, and responsibility for, the other—and this while simultaneously holding open the promise of a kind of (depressive) reparation.[53]

"Miles City, Montana" is set in 1961—or rather, this year dates the conventional past-tense-as-present that appears to fill the space being narrated. The narrator and her husband, Andrew, and their two children (ages six and three and a half) are driving from Vancouver to Ontario through the United States to visit their families and "present" themselves: "That summer, we were presenting ourselves, not pictures."[54] The first section of the story consists of an account of an episode from the narrator's childhood (she was six years old, the same age as her older daughter in the more recent past that constitutes the present of the story). The episode centers around the appearance of a dead child named Steve Gauley: "My father came across the field carrying the body of the boy who had been drowned. There were several men together, returning from the search, but he was the one carrying the body" (84). The distinctive phrasing here, the way in which the verb "to drown" is given in a potentially transitive form ("the boy who *had been* drowned," as opposed to "the boy who *had drowned*"), opens up the space of responsibility. Is there someone to answer for this loss? It will turn out in the context of this story that there is more than one way to answer the question. But what strikes us all the more forcefully is the way in which this scene stages a "gift of death": "Here you go," says the father, effectively, to his six-year-old daughter ("*he* was the one carrying the body"); "Here is death. Here is a dead child. This is for you." Death is given as an enigmatic, traumatizing yet seductive signifier; Laplanche writes, "I would say that the question of the enigma of death is brought to the subject by the other."[55] Yet, almost immediately, the narrator undercuts the reliability of this scene as she remembers it:

His [Steve Gauley's] face was turned in to my father's chest, but I could see a
nostril, an ear, plugged up with greenish mud.

I don't think so. I don't think I really saw all this. Perhaps I saw my father carrying him, and the other men following along, and the dogs, but I would
not have been allowed to get close enough to see something like mud in his
nostril. (84)

The "unreliability" of this memory, I would suggest, has less to do with
an either/or distinction between reality and fantasy and more with what
Laplanche would refer to as the third term, or the reality of the message.
This gift/message/address was enigmatic in its original occurrence and, as
it is returned to, after a second scene, it retains its enigmatic status, coded
now as a recognizably fantastic excess ("I don't think I really saw all this").
The drowned boy is, in fact, one of many significant and enigmatic parental
messages in "Miles City, Montana." Indeed, the narrator discusses at length
her and her husband's relationship to such instances of signification as the
children of their own parents: "It was as if at some point we had received an
unforgettable indigestible message—that we were far from satisfactory, and
that the most commonplace success in life was probably beyond us. . . . [B]
ut Andrew's mother, my own mother and father couldn't have meant [this].
All they meant to tell us was 'Watch out. Get along'" (97).

In this same opening section of the narrative, we learn that Steve Gauley's
death took on an added weight or "shame," because he did not have a mother
or any close female relative to mourn him: "It seemed a worse shame (to
hear people talk) that there was no mother, no woman at all—no grandmother or aunt, or even a sister—to receive Steve Gauley and give him his
due of grief" (85). The motherless child and his death are tinged with shame
insofar as he and it exceed symbolic recuperation.[56] Instead, this family unit,
which is almost not a family unit (minimal reference is made to a mother's desertion), consists of Steve Gauley and his "accidental" father: "His
fatherhood seemed accidental, and the fact that the child had been left with
him when the mother went away, and that they continued living together,
seemed accidental" (85). This is a father who provides and protects minimally, "just enough and just in time—and their life was held together in a
similar manner; that is, just well enough to keep the Children's Aid at bay"
(85). As there is no mother or father to adequately play a protective role,

the narrator's own parents preside over the funeral, thereby providing their daughter with another instance of enigmatic signification. For the narrator's childhood self, death is divided into two moments: the event of the drowning itself, insofar as it is represented by the recovered corpse presented by the father, and the symbolic and partial recuperation of the boy's life in the ritual of the funeral presided over by both parents.[57]

The narrator tells us what she can remember of this event: a row of children, including herself, each holding a single narcissus ("which must have come from a pot that somebody forced indoors") and singing a children's hymn, "When He Cometh, When He Cometh, to Make Up His Jewels." The narcissus signifies in excess of any realism (the death of the child effects the "death" of a certain self-satisfied narcissistic completion; Steve Gauley drowns, and there is another near death by drowning later in the story), whereas the nineteenth-century hymn is an intensified instance of sentimentalized theological redemption: pure children sing of pure children transfigured and preserved. There is no death: "'They will shine in their beauty, bright gems for his crown'" (86).[58] Both the narcissus and the hymn signify a certain painfully heightened and "forced" artificiality. As a child, the narrator is subjected to a Christian message (here we might recall the father's recitation of the Lord's Prayer in *Prisoners*) that is insistently conveyed and simultaneously not quite believed, and, in response, what she chooses to dwell on is a disturbing excess of unprocessable affect that "could not be understood or expressed" (86). Her white stockings, also presumably experienced as excessive and artificial, are "disgustingly itchy," and the narrator's registration of this excess is "mixed up with another feeling" concerning "[a] dults in general but my parents in particular."[59] The narrator suggests that children are often "disgusted" with the very bodies of adults, "[t]he size, the lumpy shapes, the bloated power. The breath, the coarseness, the hairiness, the horrid secretions" (86). "Bloated" (an important Munro word in this story, as it conveys both an insistence on and a departure from sheer materiality) refers back to Steve Gauley's corpse ("it would have been bloated and changed and perhaps muddied all over after so many hours in the water" [84–85]), which is otherwise absent from the funeral scene. Then again, the very embodiment of adults conveys death and decay to the observing child: "They stood side by side opening and closing their mouths for the hymn, and I stood removed from them, in the row of children, watching" (86). The narrator returns to this scene and its surplus of affect at the very end of the story in order to give it, by repeating it, some kind of meaning.

In the story's later, second scene, the narrator and her family are in the midst of a car trip, and everyone is hot and tired. After some sharp words, the narrator and her older daughter, Cynthia, jointly conjure up a swimming pool, only to bump up against a reasonably obliging reality: "But there was a pool. There was a park, too, though not quite the oasis of Cynthia's fantasy" (97). The pool is closed for lunchtime, but a lifeguard, accompanied by her boyfriend, agrees to watch the children while they swim. Temporarily relieved from her more vigilant maternal role, the narrator is suddenly disrupted, awakened, by her reception of a message: "*Where are the children?*" (99). This message is italicized, isolated as its own paragraph, not introduced with any kind of tag phrase, and thus it is akin to what one might call a superego message: You must answer this question now! In fact, you must answer this question before there is any reason to have asked it; once it has been asked, you have already failed; you are already too late. (It is notable, in this regard, that the children are "*the children*" and not Cynthia and Meg; the narrator's failure is, in other words, something more than particular.)[60]

The events that follow are temporally distorted, and, as a distorted memory, this scene repeats the opening scene of the narrative (as it is recalled), where the narrator's father and the other men return from their search with the child's dead body:

> "Cynthia!" I had to call twice before she knew where my voice was coming from. "Cynthia! Where's Meg?"
>
> It always seems to me, when I recall this scene, that Cynthia turns very gracefully toward me, then turns all around in the water—making me think of a ballerina on point—and spreads her arms in a gesture of the stage. "Dis-ap-peared!"
>
> Cynthia was naturally graceful, and she did take dancing lessons, so these movements may have been as I have described. She did say "Disappeared" after looking all around the pool, but the strangely artificial style of speech and gesture, the lack of urgency, is more likely my invention. (100)

"Disappeared," or "Dis-ap-peared!," is at once an evasive performance of a nonanswer and, in another sense, the only real "answer" that there could be, the dreaded answer: she is dead. "Disappearance," in other words, is death in its least disguised form, for even a corpse, like Steve Gauley's, is in some sense a substitute, a compensation, a thing in the place of a lack. This is perhaps how we should understand the formal excess of the signifier's materiality in Munro's text, both in the offset message addressed to the mother *("Where are the children?")* and in the disjointed "Dis-ap-peared!," separated out into its constituent syllables. These words themselves might be said to occupy the same place as the corpse, the child's body, in the story's first scene.[61]

But what does happen at the pool? The parents are elsewhere, not watching; the lifeguard is kissing her boyfriend; Cynthia is "seduced" by this scene and is paying no attention to her younger sister. Meg sees a comb at the bottom of the deep end of the pool and tries to reach it, not knowing that the water is deep. The narrator, simultaneously (she later decides) with Meg's narcissus-like plunge, receives the message *("Where are the children?")*, and her husband, almost immediately and just as magically, bounds over the fence (100–101). And while this near disaster is unfolding, Meg, it turns out, doesn't really need rescuing. Instead, she falls into the water and swims:

> "You swam, Meg," said Cynthia, in a congratulatory way. (She told us about
> the kissing later.)
> "I didn't know it was deep," Meg said. "I didn't drown." (102)

So, while on one level this scene repeats the story's earlier account of the drowning of Steve Gauley, there is also a sense in which, this time, *nothing* happens. What the two moments rehearse, I would argue, is a Freudian-Laplanchean structure of signification whereby a first moment, a sexual trauma implanted without any capacity to process the message, is followed, much later, by what is, in a certain sense, a nonsexual nonevent that has the capacity not only to be experienced but also to trigger a return of the first moment. Embedded in the second scene, too, is Cynthia's repetition of the narrator's own reception of the parental message. Cynthia's watching of the lifeguard and her boyfriend inscribes a miniature version of a primal scene but one that, more profoundly than many a psychoanalytic account, conjoins sexuality and death: seduced by sex, one misses—or causes—death; or to reproduce (and here one risks sounding like contemporary philosopher and antinatalist David Benatar) is merely to reproduce more mortal tragic beings. Life, as Benatar might say, is a tragic "accident." In the first scene of a drowning, the narrator-as-child receives the gift of death as enigmatic signifier, and its subsequent insertion into a religious context (death as sacrifice) fails to dissolve its enigmatic status. In the second scene, in her very failure to protect, the mother (belatedly) gives her own children this gift—and this is a mother who prefers the role of "watcher" to "keeper," who is pleased to have her husband attribute to her a maternal "extra sense" while simultaneously wanting "to warn him—to warn everybody—never to count on it" (105).

I want to pause for a moment to consider the motif of reflection that "Miles City, Montana" picks up on here. Meg's near-fatal gaze into the water reminds us, perhaps, of the omnipotence—the sense of fearlessness and immortality—that belongs to early childhood. But if Narcissus is a figure for self-love, he is also invoked as a poor reader, incapable of distinguishing a false, shadowy imitation from reality. Meg is drawn into the dangerous water not by her image, directly, but by the banal (yet mythologically loaded) comb that lies on the floor of the pool and that looks, to her, far closer than it actually is. As a rewritten Narcissus scene, however, Meg's fall also recalls the "forced" narcissus flower that the narrator remembers being required to hold at Steve Gauley's funeral—and it is precisely at this point in the narrative, after the fact of her daughter's "rescue" and while chiding herself for indulging in a "trashy" and "shameful" imagining of her daughter's death, that the narrator recalls the drowning and Steve Gauley's funeral. She is able to bring new knowledge and new conceptual language to her comprehension of the events, but in her telling, the narrator seems to attribute this knowing to her past self. It is, in other words, a markedly dislocated return to the first scene, partaking, I would argue, of a space and time that are neither those of the first nor those of the second experience, but rather more akin to the space of analysis:

> When I stood apart from my parents at Steve Gauley's funeral and watched them, and had this new, unpleasant feeling about them, I thought that I was understanding something about them for the first time. It was a deadly serious thing. I was understanding that they were implicated. Their big, stiff, dressed-up bodies did not stand between me and sudden death, or any kind of death. They gave consent. So it seemed. They gave consent to the death of children and to my death not by anything they said or thought but by the

very fact that they had made children—they had made me. They had made
me, and for that reason my death—however grieved they were, however they
carried on—would seem to them anything but impossible or unnatural. This
was a fact, and even then I knew they were not to blame.

But I did blame them. (103)[62]

Parents consent to give their children the gift of death, and the narrator-
as-child protests on behalf of "Steve Gauley" and "all children." Children
"by rights . . . should have sprung up free, to live a new, superior kind of
life, not to be caught in the snares of vanquished grownups, with their sex
and funerals" (104). Steve Gauley is a figure for romantic childhood—"free,"
"superior," innocent of sex and death, like "all children"—a wild child who
couldn't possibly survive, who couldn't possibly be protected other than as
an ideal, a fantasy, a psychic trace. On the realist level, the communal and
accepted understanding of Steve Gauley's death is that he died because he
wasn't looked after by a responsible parent: "He was neglected, he was free,
so he drowned. And his father took it as an accident, such as might happen
to a dog [or a deer]" (104).[63] In an unusual turn in her already unusual thinking, the narrator-as-child sees this all quite differently. Steve Gauley's father
makes no promises (and in this sense he isn't a father—the narrator refers
to him somewhat ambiguously as a "grownup"), and so he breaks no promises: "[H]e was the only grownup that I let off the hook. He was the only
one I didn't see giving consent. He couldn't prevent anything, but he wasn't
implicated in anything, either—not like the others, saying the Lord's Prayer
in their unnaturally weighted voices, oozing religion and dishonor" (104).
The motifs of accident and (ir)responsibility that are woven throughout this
intricately patterned story recur here not only in the form of an accidental
death but also as a hint about the accident of birth: the accident that takes
place in the absence of reliable birth control and more profoundly, perhaps,
the exposure of birth as something other than a divine plan—every human
life riven by contingency and insecurity. This sense of the limits of choice
and responsibility also marks the closing lines of "Miles City, Montana": "So
we went on, with the two in the back seat trusting us, because of no choice,
and we ourselves trusting to be forgiven, in time, for everything that had
first to be seen and condemned by those children: whatever was flippant,
arbitrary, careless, callous—all our natural, and particular, mistakes" (105).
Adults have some kind of "choice," figured here as the choice of which road

to take, "the interstate" or "Highway 2," a minimal choice, of course, but one with suggestive figural significance, as in "The Road Not Taken"; but children have "no choice"—either about their being or about their continued reliance on (parental) others.

The subtle suggestion of violence and compulsion in this claustrophobic family space recalls but markedly differs from the scene of torture that traps Keller Dover and Alex Jones in an abandoned bathroom together. The overwrought wild child of the patriarchal imaginary of *Prisoners* is replaced, in Munro's story, first by Steve Gauley, whose lack of a mother and a responsible father leaves him "free" and "unprotected," but ultimately by more apparently ordinary children, like the narrator's daughters. The limits of (patriarchal) parental ownership and protection are not demonized in "Miles City, Montana," even if they can terrify, and no god or monster waits in the wings to translate the enigmatic (or wild) message that brings a child (and a parent) into being.

"A Woman's Sacrifice or a Sacrifice of a Woman"

God, the father, promises Holly Jones and her husband protection from death and unbearable loss, yet he fails to provide this protection. And it is this failure that generates her evil. What was received as God's most meaningful gift, a child, now becomes the source of the suffering of as many families as possible. God gave us the gift of an unbearable wound, say Holly and her husband, and we will in turn inflict it mercilessly on humanity. Keller Dover, in his place, also inherits an intolerable psychical message. At the very beginning of the film (and, as such, this scene could be said to preside over the entire film), Dover looks on and recites the Lord's Prayer as his teenage son shoots his first deer. The scene represents both masculine self-sufficiency and a certain intimacy with sanctified death. One thinks here of the animal sacrificed in the place of the child (in, for example, the Abraham and Isaac story). But in this moment, Dover also passes on the message he received from his own father: "You know, the most important thing your grandpa ever taught me—be ready . . . whatever it ends up being. I'm proud of you son. It was a nice shot." It is only later that we learn that Dover's own father committed suicide, shooting himself in the head, and that the body was discovered in the family home by the teenage Dover and his mother. Here, then, would be another instance of a father failing to protect himself and his family. Keller receives an almost unbearably mixed message: You can save yourself from death, his father tells him, or I can save you from death, by being "ready" for "whatever it ends up being"; but also: You cannot save yourself, and neither can I. What, then, is the legacy or message? Is Dover locked in a doomed attempt to prevent that which has already happened? Is this one way to figure Laplanche's version of the seduction that structures every parent–child relationship, the seduction of an enigmatic message? And is this why Dover returns to his family's home to imprison and torture Alex Jones?[64]

Keller Dover, like the other child-men in Villeneuve's film, cannot be said to enjoy an *analytic* relationship to repetition. Instead, these characters' repetitions are a form of madness that turns protectors into torturers and killers. God the good father becomes a senseless and vengeful killer; Holly Jones and her husband, once loving parents, become abductors and torturers; Keller Dover's father and then Keller himself become the violence they promise to protect against; and even Detective Loki is caught in this pattern, for if Loki ultimately rescues Dover's daughter, he also becomes responsible for the suicide of yet another tormented adult-child victim—Bob Taylor.

Alice Munro's parent-narrator in "Miles City, Montana" also describes a repetitive return to scenes from her past that register a failure of protection and an exposure to the enigma and the limits of parental responsibility. But hers is a portrait of the subject not just of repetition but also of the ability to read moments in relationship to one another. It is this possibility of reading that "gives" an adult the childhood he or she could not "have" as a child. Nevertheless, Munro's story does not imply that it is easy to evade the snares of symptomatic repetition—far from it. Instead, a kind of symptomatic repetition—true to psychoanalytic form—is bound up with any possible analytic insight. In this opposition (analytic repetition versus symptomatic repetition), analysis hardly produces certainty and unquestionable knowledge. As readers of Munro will know, moments of insight in Munro's fiction are typically destabilized as their own instances of repetition: the subject will repeatedly encounter her own failures, blindness, and uncertainty (and Munro's analeptic and proleptic manipulations of temporality effect this quite brilliantly). But Munro's fiction does not seek to embody these failures and blindnesses in a diabolical God or a monstrously gendered other or even in an evil child. Nor does it imagine that failures of parental responsibility can be avoided by building a wall of protection or by staying at home (in the family, in the patriarchy, within the logic of an ideological repetition). Rather, the repeated encounters with failure and insight that punctuate Munro's narratives suggest that a kind of parental failure is indissociable from parental responsibility and from what it means to be a parent and an adult. The adult (Christian) disavowal of the gift of death that the young narrator of "Miles City, Montana" loathes in her parents becomes, in *Prisoners*, the terrifyingly autodestructive violence of a desperate father before being displaced, in turn, onto the monstrously inconsolable love of a bereaved mother. The movie, in other words, records a culture of protection addicted to one or another attempt to wall off the interminable ethical crisis of reproduction and parenting. Does the gift of death surround being like a dystopian netherworld from which a good father might be able to protect his family (and thus himself) by remaining at home, "in the shelter of its essence or *telos*"?[65] Does this home become a prison, a torture chamber, or a grave? Or, like Munro's mother-narrator, do we "go on," "trusting to be forgiven," surviving, occasionally appearing to have preternatural parental powers of protection while simultaneously wanting "to warn everybody" "never to count on it"?

"Miles City, Montana," like Morrison's *A Mercy* and Donoghue's *Room*, distinguishes the maternal from the patriarchal precisely around a certain opening onto the gift of life as a gift of death. This, too, helps to explain why it is a monstrous maternal figure that comes to "solve" the ethical dilemma of the father in Villeneuve's *Prisoners*. In this respect, Holly Jones bears a disturbing relationship, as I have noted, with the dead mother in *The Road*, whose desire to kill herself and her child (in order to avoid an apocalyptic horror) is translated by the patriarchal gaze into an antitheological, nihilistic renunciation that the father cannot bear. In *Prisoners*, this patriarchal othering of the maternal takes the form of imagining a woman so racked by pain and loss that she can effectively substitute for the good father who has engaged in torture and has thus risked losing his moral standing. The mother who has given up on God—hence, given up on patriarchal protection—is here depicted as a bringer of death and suffering.[66] In Munro's story—and this is surely what makes it literary (rather than simply symptomatic or ideological)—the maternal association with the gift of life as a gift of death (the reproductive ethical ordeal) appears not in monstrous drag or even as the stuff of patriarchal nightmare or desire. The moment of the near drowning of her daughter occurs as the mother in "Miles City, Montana" experiences herself and her world in their "forlorn" singularity and coincidental relationality. Leaving the car to go in search of a drink, the mother sees the world with the attention and curiosity of the writer she will become:

> Dazed with the heat, with the sun on the blistered houses, the pavement, the burned grass, I walked slowly. I paid attention to a squashed leaf, ground a Popsicle stick under the heel of my sandal, squinted at a trash can strapped to a tree. This is the way you look at the poorest details of the world resurfaced, after you've been driving for a long time—you feel their singleness and precise location and the forlorn coincidence of your being there to see them. *Where are the children?* (99)

In *The Gift of Death*, after describing scenarios in which one or another male figure, from Abraham to the lawyer in "Bartleby the Scrivener," is involved in a sacrificial relationship to absolute ethical duty and responsibility, Derrida comments, "It is difficult not to be struck by the absence of woman in these two monstrous yet banal stories."[67] This absence prompts a crucial question:

> Would the logic of sacrificial responsibility within the implacable universality of the law, of its law, be altered, inflected, attenuated, or displaced, if a woman were to intervene in some consequential manner? Does the system of this sacrificial responsibility and of the double "gift of death" imply at its very basis an exclusion or sacrifice of woman? A woman's sacrifice or a sacrifice of a woman, according to one sense of the genitive or the other? Let us leave the question in suspense.[68]

"Miles City, Montana" (like Morrison's *A Mercy*, Shriver's *We Need to Talk about Kevin*, and Donoghue's *Room*) contemplates the sacrifice of children and the limits of parental responsibility. But where McCarthy's *The Road* and Villeneuve's *Prisoners* might be populated with characters who are paralyzed by an opposition between sacrifice as nihilism and sacrifice as a fantasized promise of absolute protection (for the self and the child-self), Munro's story participates in an attempt to think an alternative, posthumanist, and postmetaphysical maternal ethics of the gift of death. At the moment when her child is alone, unprotected, and exposed to the possibility of death by drowning, Munro's mother figure is preoccupied by a peculiarly writerly exposure to the world (of Popsicle sticks and trash cans) in all its vulnerability and specificity: "you feel their singleness and precise location and the forlorn coincidence of your being there to see them." Posthumanist ethics is an ethics of "forlorn coincidence" and it places in suspense, in the suspense of a decision about reproduction that can never, finally, be made, the "precise location" of a parental responsibility that, promising and failing, encounters every child in its "singleness," every child as the "world resurfaced," and every child as incurably wild.

Nim Chimpsky at the LaFarge home. Photograph by Harry Benson. http://www
.mongrelmedia.com/film/project-nim.aspx. Courtesy of Harry Benson.

Afterword

The Pretense of the Human from Victor of Aveyron
to Nim Chimpsky

"What is it about an infant's crying," writes Alice Munro in "My Mother's Dream," "that makes it so powerful, able to break down the order you depend on, inside and outside yourself? It is like a storm—insistent, theatrical, yet in a way pure and uncontrived. It is reproachful rather than supplicating—it comes out of a rage that can't be dealt with, a birthright rage free of love and pity, ready to crush your brains inside your skull."[1] Whereas Munro's infant arrives with a capacity for (Winnicottian) destruction and devastation, for Immanuel Kant, the crying infant announces precisely its *human* specificity: "Even the child who has just wrenched itself from the mother's womb seems to enter the world with loud cries, unlike all other animals, simply because it regards the inability to make use of its limbs as *constraint*, and thus it immediately announces its claim to freedom (a representation that no other animal has)."[2]

Kant imagines a three-step progression in the natural history of infant crying that Derrida refers to in *The Animal That Therefore I Am* as "at the same time extra-lucid and totally wild."[3] Initially, Kant argues, the human baby must not have cried at birth (should one hesitate to write "human baby," as this infant was the infant of "a time before time" and a "pure state of nature"?). Curiously, in the next epoch, just as the "parents accede to culture, nature makes the disturbing cry of the newborn possible."[4] There is then a third moment, which Derrida recognizes as "extraordinary" ("Kant is no longer speaking of the animal in general and he takes into account a structural difference between nonhuman types of animal") and as "merely" having "the status of a reverie with no tomorrow," no future.[5] Kant writes, "This remark leads us far—for example, to the thought that upon major upheavals in nature this second epoch might be followed by a third, when an orangutan or a chimpanzee developed the organs used for walking . . . handling objects, and speaking."[6] If Kant were to seriously entertain such an upheaval, Derrida writes, "[it] would require a redistribution of the whole logic of this anthropocentrism, and by extension Kant's whole work." "[O]ne understands a philosopher only by heeding closely to what he means to demonstrate, and in reality fails to demonstrate, concerning the limit between human and animal."[7] But has Kant's "major upheaval in nature" already taken place? Or, rather, was this major upheaval ever going to take place "in nature" as opposed to in our thinking about nature, about the human and, as this study has suggested, about the child?

The classically humanist (wild) child functions, as I have suggested, as a way to cordon off the wild animal from the civilized, rational adult, who is also a subject of language. The humanist child is also, as the telos of creation, a justification in and of herself for reproduction; her being coincides absolutely with her raison d'être, and Kant's infant's cry seems to announce this fact with a kind of violent unequivocality: her "malicious" "shrieking" speaks the human child's early and unlearned possession of a "concept of justice."[8] The posthumanist wild child no longer functions to conceal or disavow the ethical and ontological uncertainty that haunts this Kantian infant, and the present study has sought to identify the features of this (posthumanist) wildness in a number of related senses. But what has not been considered, at least not overtly, is the child as animal in a more immediate sense. This is precisely the subject taken up by three recent novels—Karen Joy Fowler's *We Are All Completely beside Ourselves* (2013), Colin McAdam's *A Beautiful Truth* (2013), and Kenneth Oppel's *Half Brother* (2010)—all of which feature characters who adopt a chimpanzee as if he or she were a human infant (and much will turn, needless to say, on the status of this "as if").[9] McAdam, in one of his novel's many lyrically compelling passages, deploys the imperative voice to write of Walter (a human father) and Looee (the adopted chimpanzee son):

Look at the chimp years later handing the last of his milk teeth to the man who
says I am not going to give you a treat for that, there is nothing more useless
than a tooth outside a mouth.
Call him father.
Call him son.
Walt's heart was warm, his house was his, he was happy with the questions of
his days.[10]

All three works, moreover, to a greater or lesser degree, return to the 1960s
and/or 1970s and to the work of various research scientists who set out to
challenge Noam Chomsky's "primary thesis that language is inherent only in
humans."[11] In what follows, I want to take up briefly the striking relationship
of this kind of experimentation to Jean Itard's pathbreaking work with "wild
child" Victor of Aveyron at the turn of the nineteenth century. But I ultimately want to argue that the more recent novels, with a particular focus on
Half Brother, adopt a critical position with respect to the liberal-humanist
understanding (and ultimate abandonment) of these experimental, nonhuman subjects. In commenting or signifying on these experiments, Oppel's
novel participates in the work of articulating a posthumanist ethics even as it
also joins *The Road* and *Prisoners* in addressing (with much less hyperbole)
some of the motifs and implications of patriarchy in crisis. If the fathers in
The Road and *Prisoners* are desperate, insecure, and insistent—it is truly the
end of the world—it would seem to take the experience of the child protagonist of Oppel's novel to think the future and social reproduction differently.

Oppel's book, which was written explicitly for children (or, rather, "young
adults"), is narrated by thirteen-year-old Ben Tomlin, who moves with his
parents from Toronto to Vancouver where his father, a behavioral psychologist, will undertake research on a chimpanzee that he plans to care for like a
member of the family. The year is 1973, and Dr. Richard Tomlin's academic
focus is on language acquisition and on challenging Chomskyan linguis-
tics; he would like to prove that "language" is not the exclusive property
of human beings: "This isn't a typical animal behaviour study. This is the
first proper human attempt to talk, actually *talk,* with another species. . . .
No cages. No labs. He's one of us now. He has a crib and clothes and toys.
And most important, he has a family" (22). Ben's mother, Sarah, is a graduate student who plans to write a doctoral dissertation on cross-fostering.

Ben explains, "Dad knew how smart chimps were, and wanted to see if they could learn American Sign Language, just like deaf people. . . . It turned out finding one wasn't all that easy. You couldn't just buy one at a pet store. . . . Dad wanted a brand new chimpanzee. A fresh slate; that's what he'd called it" (13). For all its apparent commitment to undermining human supe-riority (Tomlin wants to prove that language is not exclusive to humans), the father's research project nevertheless emphasizes a kind of pioneering hubris (he will be the "first" to talk to another species) that may not survive the chimp's failure to perform as expected. Eventually the experiment loses its funding, and Ben's father loses his interest. Simultaneously, the chim-panzee, Zan, becomes far more difficult and dangerous for Ben, his mother, and the team of graduate students to care for. (Ben's father, tellingly, isn't involved in the day-to-day care of the chimp—in Sara Ruddick's sense, he is no mother!) But all this is going on as the novel's central human character, Ben, is negotiating his own struggle with adolescence. In Oppel's young-adult novel, this negotiation is depicted as an ethical trial bound up with a historically specific crisis of masculinity and, more specifically, a crisis of fatherhood. Richard Tomlin tries to justify his lack of relationship to Zan both by claiming that "[i]n the wild, the fathers don't have anything to do with the babies" and by adding, ironically, "I'm not an animal person." But he is confronted by his wife: "'This experiment,' said Mom, 'relies on cross-fostering. Raising Zan human. You are supposed to be his *father*. Now, how would you describe being a father, I'm just interested to know. What kind of obligations and responsibilities and activities does that entail? In your esteemed opinion?'" (132).

To Ben's horror, Zan is sold to a supposedly humane researcher, Helson, whose stance is decidedly against treating chimps like human beings: "We don't pretend they're humans here," says Helson. "They're chimps and they live like chimps, and there's a lot more dignity in that than dressing them up in children's clothes" (271). In one of the novel's most disturbing scenes, Zan is indeed stripped of his clothes and toys and is forcefully reduced to mere animal being: "It was like we'd just given him his name—and now we were taking it away from him" (258). Unhappy with this arrangement that they have at first consented to (they suspect, among other things, that Hel-son plans to sell Zan to a biomedical research facility), Ben, his mother, and Peter, a graduate student with a particularly close bond to Zan, stage a res-cue mission and steal Zan back from Helson. It is only after a failed attempt at flight into the woods with Zan ("returning" to the wilderness is an impossible fantasy) that Ben reconciles himself to giving his "half brother" ("he was half brother, half stranger to me") to an animal sanctuary (363). Ben hopes that one day Zan will "forget that he was ever human" (375).

Half Brother marks its departure from the classical humanist (Kantian) tradition by carefully depicting the exchange of "human" and "animal" attributes across the classical divide. Humans, for example, are shown to be mercilessly violent. The novel begins with the juxtaposition of two mothers: the chimp mother, who is nurturing her infant ("He was eight days old and his mother was holding him, nursing him. He was cuddled against her and she made comforting sounds" [1]) and who is shot with a tranquilizing gun and watches, dazed and paralyzed, as her infant is whisked away; and the human mother, Ben's mother, to whom the infant chimp is subsequently given. Elsewhere, the novel depicts numerous traits that humans and animals share and express, such as destructive rage, loyalty, and sexual desire, and in a later passage, we are given an extended account of how a troupe of chimpanzees mourn their dead (290). Both chimps and humans, we are reminded, bite and show remorse for wounds inflicted, and humans, the narrator reminds us, can possess a certain "animal" intelligence (Peter says of Helson, "He can practically *smell* your thoughts" [327]). Struggling with masculinity and with his own transition to adolescence, Ben wonders if he should be imitating humans or animals. Meanwhile, we, the readers, cannot be sure that we know the difference. Peter provides Ben with an alternative to Richard Tomlin in this decidedly Oedipal narrative, but Oppel also cleverly equates the pinnacle of patriarchal civilization with the most "animal" manifestation of maleness. Is being a "dominant" male or "alpha" male a human or an animal trait—a natural or cultural trait? Toward the end of the novel, Ben's father and Helson face off: "It was like being back in the chimp house. . . . In a colony there was only one alpha male, but here there were two. I could almost smell their pheromones, transmitting themselves over the phone lines" (352).[12]

Most profoundly, I would argue, Oppel's novel displays a subtle interest in the relationship between personhood, language, and imitation. It shares, in other words, *Room*'s sense of constitutive relationality and of the complex function of storytelling (the "as if") with its refusal of an easy opposition between play and the "real." Central to the debate over Nim's language skills is the question of authenticity and its relationship to deceptive imitation.

Ben is told that Zan has only "tricked" the researchers into believing that he was learning language, but Ben, who increasingly thinks of Zan as a person, undertakes his own research: "[T]he dictionary said you had to be human to be a person. Maybe the dictionary was wrong" (159). Aspects of imitation are at play in all of the novel's other concerns, including education, masculinity, identity, responsibility, and love; a denigration of imitation is used by those wielding authority to justify abandoning the animal—precisely by designating *imitation* as the name for how animals fail to access full human being. As such, the novel picks up on aspects of the actual research work conducted by Columbia University behavioral psychologist Herbert Terrace with Nim Chimpsky. Elizabeth Hess's *Nim Chimpsky: The Chimp Who Would Be Human* (2008) tells Nim's life story and offers an account of Terrace's research, and Hess's work is, in turn, a crucial source for James Marsh's powerful documentary *Project Nim* (2011).[13] And, of course, Terrace's study, as it is represented in these sources, also calls to mind the far earlier efforts of Jean Itard to coax Victor, the "wild boy of Aveyron," out of his silence and isolation.[14]

Itard, a French physician and educator of the deaf, whose work influenced Maria Montessori, among others, believed that the human was constituted largely by education. His hypothesis was that his work with the "savage" Victor would refute the claims of his own mentor that Victor suffered not only from an original deficiency in culture but also in his very nature. Itard writes, "I never shared this unfavourable opinion and in spite of the truth of the picture and the justice of the parallels I dared to conceive certain hopes. I founded them for my part upon the double consideration of the cause and the curability of this apparent idiocy" (7). Itard assigns a privileged place to "speech" and bemoans his limited success: "If I had wished to relate only happy results I should have suppressed from this account this fourth aim [the attempt to teach Victor to speak], the means I have employed in order to reach it and the slight success I have obtained in it" (25–26). But he also describes his efforts to teach Victor nonvocal modes of signification (Victor learned very basic reading and writing) while looking carefully for other signifiers of the human, including affection, a sense of justice, and disinterested expressions of love. Although convinced by Victor's display of "an inner sense of justice . . . that eternal basis of the social order," Itard's efforts prove to be less successful by other measures:

I will disclose the animal side of his nature with the same fidelity as I have described the civilized side. I will suppress nothing. Although he has become sensible to gratitude and friendship, although he appears to feel keenly the pleasure of usefulness, Victor remains essentially selfish. . . . But what appears still more astonishing in the emotional system of this young man, and beyond all explanation, is his indifference to women in the midst of the violent physical changes attendant upon a very pronounced puberty. (96)

Imitation is a category of some complexity for Itard, since it is a "faculty" that needs to be taught so that Victor can learn at all ("[I]t was necessary once more to retrace our steps and to try and rouse from their inertia the imitative faculties by submitting them, as we had the others, to a kind of gradual education. . . . Writing is an exercise in imitation, and imitation was yet to be born in our savage" [83]), even as imitation is that which a "normal" and adult human subject with an interiority and an entirely rational cognitive function must be able to transcend. Hence, Itard is led to categorize what he calls a "special kind of imitation": "Here was no longer a routine repetition of what the pupil saw being done, such as can be obtained up to a certain point from certain imitative animals, but an intelligent and reasoned imitation, as variable in its method as in its applications, and in a word, such as one has a right to expect from a man endowed with the free use of all his intellectual faculties" (84–85). Itard worked with Victor for five years and wrote two reports outlining his experiences, but he struggled with the adolescent Victor, and in 1805 Victor was given over entirely to the care of Mme Guérin, who had been looking after him all along. Victor and Mme Guérin moved into a house around the corner from the Institute for Deaf-Mutes and lived there for the next seventeen years. "From this moment on," writes Roger Shattuck in *The Forbidden Experiment*, "Victor slips into obscurity."[15] Itard, Shattuck concludes, abandoned the work (and Victor) in the face of two obstacles: Victor's "egotism" or inability to purely transcend his own interests, and Victor's frightening sexuality: "[W]ould I not have been afraid to make known to our savage," Itard writes, "a need which he would have sought to satisfy as publicly as his other wants and which would have led him to acts of revolting indecency. Intimidated by the possibility of such a result, I was obliged to restrain myself and once more to see with resignation these hopes, like so many others, vanish before an unforeseen obstacle" (99).

In *Half Brother*, Richard Tomlin's experiment involves raising Zan like a human in a human family to see whether he can develop something like language; but this procedure inevitably renders the family, the human, and what we call language parallel subjects of inquiry. Only days into the experiment, Ben listens in on a conversation among some of his father's new colleagues: "A silver-haired fellow with a pipe was saying, 'It's a fascinating journey you're embarking on. I've done a little reading on chimpanzee cognition, and it seems they're very good at imitating'" (37). Tomlin immediately rises to the challenge: "'Absolutely,' said Dad. 'So the key is to make sure they're not just imitating the signs, but making them independently'" (37). Tomlin and the others depicted here all subscribe to a distinction between "language" and "mere communication." "Language," in their account, involves a grasp and understanding of grammar and syntax, as well as the ability to initiate conversation. When asked, "And what of Noam Chomsky?" Tomlin replies that although he is a "huge admirer" of Chomsky's work, Chomsky is "dead wrong" in believing that only humans can learn or "have" language. Such a departure from the current orthodoxy on Tomlin's part is registered as "very controversial—even obscene" (38).

But when do human beings decide to designate a practice or utterance as *nonimitative*, to grant it originary or transcendent status? One morning Ben comes across Zan awake and playing with his dolls arranged in a semicircle around him, "the baby, the chimp, the chick, G.I. Joe." Ben is stunned to see that Zan is "*signing* to them. With one hand he offered the chick his empty bottle of milk, and with his free hand he signed *drink*. He held the bottle to the chick's mouth for a moment, then dropped it impatiently and signed *hug*. He picked up the chick and clutched it to his chest" (134). Ben tells his parents about what he has seen, and they are suitably impressed: "It means he's not just imitating us" (134). Obsessed with this distinction, the researchers call in more experts until, inevitably, Zan is relegated to the secondary, shadowy realm of imitations and his language learning is dismissed. The project is going to be shut down, Dad tells Ben, because "Zan's not learning language." Ben recalls, "It was like being told something so obviously untrue, you didn't know what to say. *The sun won't be coming up today, Ben. Your mother and I are aliens from another planet. Sorry . . .*" "'Who says?' I said. 'Who says he's not learning?'" (235).[16]

It is at precisely the point when the animal (in the case of *Half Brother*, it is the chimpanzee) threatens to undermine the distinction between real speech and imitation that he, she, or it is sent back to that conceptually "natural" space before or outside of what is said to be true language. This is also the space from whence the child emerges on the way to becoming the adult human being who takes it upon himself or herself to decide who does or does not count as a being with language. The animal is returned to nature, then, to protect a certain version of humanist thought from coming face to face with its own wildness. The wilderness that is the animal's home is thus, too, the home of all the violence and stupidity that a logocentric tradition associates with imitation and mere repetition—all that threatens to reveal an originally contaminating relationship between force and signification. But the "natural" or instinctual aggression of the animal that is so often figured as the other to language needs to be recognized, as it is throughout *Half Brother*, not as a displaced name for the false, repetitive element of every act of signification but as the disavowed form of the very meaningful address that humanist logocentrism wants to guard for the human alone. The animal, in other words, helps the human to manage the trick of a relationship to language that both relies on and rejects the wildly contaminating relationship between repetition (or imitation) and invention (expression) in the structure of language and thus of "personhood." Whether as perpetrator of a wild aggression or a deceptive mimicry, the animal is associated with all in language that works against its assimilation to a logocentric model of meaning. "How should one conceive of the relation between what language does and what it says?" asks Jonathan Culler in a recent return engagement with Austin's speech-act theory. "This is the basic problem of the performative—the question, yet to be resolved, of whether there can be a harmonious fusion of doing and saying or whether there is an ineluctable tension here that governs and undermines all textual activity. Whereas once it was assumed that aesthetic achievement depended on harmonious fusion, the ineluctability of tension now seems better established."[17] Culler's "ineluctable tension that governs and undermines" names, economically, the wildness that a humanist tradition attempts to displace onto the animal and to contain (temporarily) in the liminal personhood of the child. And this tension can also be disavowed by idealizing animal violence as its own form of pure and uncontaminated, singular expression.

In Marsh's *Project Nim*, both Laura-Ann Pettito and Stephanie LaFarge read Nim's violence as full of meaning and as an intense and aggressive response to (maternal) abandonment. When Pettito, a research assistant, opts to leave Terrace's project after being treated badly ("It's the humans I wanted to leave, not the chimp"), Nim jumps down from the second floor of the house and slams her head into the pavement ("He wasn't my child. He wasn't my baby. You can't give human nurturing to an animal that can kill you"). When, years later, LaFarge, Nim's adoptive "mother," visits Nim in the animal sanctuary and insists on entering the cage despite numerous warnings, he grabs her and violently drags her before she eventually escapes. LaFarge's daughter comments, "The fact that he didn't kill her meant a lot, because he could have, and he would have been dead because they would have shot him." LaFarge assesses the situation: "I had abandoned him and he had managed to grow up, and I had walked back in as if I had not abandoned him and he said 'No. This is my space and I'm going to put you in your place, but I'm not going to hurt you.'" *Project Nim* allows us to listen to these women as they read, some thirty-plus years later, Nim's "speech." As contemporary viewers, we in turn must read the critical space produced by the film's representation. If the women read Nim's violence as a direct act of address, the film encourages us to hold on to a state of suspense between idealization and a more nuanced account of the meaning or nonmeaning of violence.

An idealizing fantasy of seamless communication and ontologically grounded being also informs the deep unease produced by those speech acts which structure the relationship between a parent and a child—the promises, calls, acts of naming, and expressions of desire and recognition that bring the child, repeatedly, into being. Judith Butler writes

> My infantile body has not only been touched, moved, and arranged, but those impingements operated as "tactile signs" that registered in my formation. These signs communicate to me in ways that are not reducible to vocalization. They are signs of an other, but they are also the traces from which an "I" will eventually emerge, an "I" who will never be able, fully, to recover or read these signs, for whom these signs will remain in part overwhelming and unreadable, enigmatic and formative.[18]

Narratives of parental protection and care, as I have argued throughout this book, dramatize the conflicts and uncertainties that are at play in every speech act and that are exposed by the philosophical engagement with language and performativity from Austin to Derrida and Butler and beyond.

In both *Half Brother* and *The Road*, the motif of parental promise and protection is also inverted at crucial moments, such that the adult/parent figure is shown to be dependent on something like the promise of meaning that a child (or child-animal) is expected to provide (this is also apparent, in a somewhat different way, in all the other texts featured in this study). When the male researcher declares that the experiment with chimpanzee communication is over and that Zan (or Nim) "tricked me," he expresses a kind of disavowed lament for the failure of language to ever function "honestly." The father in McCarthy's novel needs his son to perform the possibility of goodness and thereby guarantee the existence of God and of a future, as if the boy were himself a walking promise—a speech act to ground and sanctify all language in a postapocalyptic world of near meaninglessness. (Shriver's Kevin absolutely refuses to play this role and he, too, is associated with a disturbing capacity for aggressive imitation and a violent embrace of meaningless communication.) The reproductive transformations that provide some of the contextual backdrop for this book also materialize or phenomenalize the philosophical challenges presented by a new exposure to the "ineluctable tension" at work in each and every speech act. The radicalization of choice, that is to say, needs to be seen as an ongoing encounter with aporias of intentional subjectivity and meaningful expression. Wrested, increasingly, from the discourse of religion, patriarchy, or ethnonationalism, human reproduction has been revealed to us as an act of meaning making exposed to the complexity and tension of other attempts to represent ourselves and build relation. It is precisely this correlation of language theory with psychoanalytic theories of profound relationality and new encounters with the social and technological possibilities of reproduction that helps describe the contours of what I have called, following others, a maternal ethics.

Half Brother demonstrates some of the ways in which the animal/human distinction is bound up with language not because it shows that humans have it and animals don't but insofar as it dramatizes the way in which forceful performative utterances, often passing as descriptive constative utterances, *produce* the animal/human distinction. The difference between humans and animals, in other words, is that humans are those beings who insist on a difference between human beings and animals.[19] "[A] saying of the event that makes the event is passed off as a saying of the event."[20] After

playing or experimenting with what would appear to suggest another possibility, Ben's father lays down the law with performative force: "Ben, he's
not your little brother and never will be. He's an animal. He's a different species" (239). Ben's appropriately wild response is to bite his father.[21] Tomlin
ends his experiment in much the same way that Herbert Terrace ended the
experiment with Nim. In a move that journalist Elizabeth Hess describes
as surprising, Terrace declared Project Nim a failure: "In the end, Terrace
became convinced that his highly intelligent chimp was a mimic, nothing
more," reports Hess. "His vocabulary was 'pure drill,' Terrace told the *New
York Times*. 'Language still stands as an important definition of the human
species.' . . . 'Nim fooled me.'"[22] The animal imitates, but it also "fools," which
is to say that it imitates "real" language. Derrida writes of Lacan, "A balance sheet separates the accounting of what has to be accorded the animal
(pretense and the trace, inscription of the trace) and what has to be denied
it (deception, lying, pretense of pretense, and erasing of traces)."[23] There is
a wildness to the *mis en abyme* of this relationship between language and
imitation that comes into play whenever the nonhuman animal or the child
comes before the humanist subject for evaluation and classification. The
wildness of the posthumanist "animal" or the posthumanist "wild child"
is inseparable from an irreducible mimetic interference at work within the
structure of every language event.

In *Half Brother*, Tomlin's son, Ben, doesn't want to give up the experiment with Zan. "[W]hat could be wrong with teaching language to an intelligent animal?" Ben asks when he is first introduced to the possibility of a
negative response to his father's project. "We were making Zan's life *better*,
and maybe we could make the lives of all the chimps better" (93). When
his father (echoing Herbert Terrace) says later that "Zan tricked us," Ben
is indignant: "'*He* tricked *us*?' I said. 'We treat him like a human baby and
pretend we're his real family, and *he's* tricking us?'" (216). Fooling, or tricking, functions, for both Ben and his father here, as a moral and a taxonomic
category dividing the good from the bad, the true from the false. But Ben's
mother approaches this somewhat differently. While much of the Oedipal
story of *Half Brother* is played out among male characters, Sarah Tomlin is
granted a privileged insight that would be hard not to identify with the novel's implied author. This junior scholar and parent gestures toward a non-
Chomskyan theory of language when she suggests that the consulting "preeminent" linguist from Berkeley, who has lost faith in the Zan experiment,

"has a very, very rigid view of language. He doesn't even have his own children. . . . [H]e has no first-hand knowledge of how children learn language" (245). This disconnection from children, Ben's mother suggests, is what allows the "expert" to disavow the ways in which the human itself is constituted through imitation.[24]

All language speaks the desire that there be language, all language articulates a hope for or promise of language, and thus all language, as irreducibly phatic, includes an irreducible meaninglessness. This is the wildness of language that the animal and the child are mobilized to contain either by confirming an unbridgeable divide or by performing the recapitulation of an evolutionary advance from primitive to rational communication. The phatic registers a wild interference with the Kantian dream of human rationality: "Phatic statements make us aware of the actual air between us or the electromagnetic field that makes it possible to listen to recorded music, or see a movie."[25] But this wildness is indissociable from the relational per se. The animal and the child therefore also reveal the originally relational aspect of language and being. Language is only ever shared, but there is no sharing without repetition and without the material supplement of the signifier. The child's wildness thus also names the child's precarious dependence on the relational contingency of being. (Colin McAdam captures this concisely in his description of the first encounter between infant chimp and human mother in A Beautiful Truth: "Looee reached for Judy before conversation began.")[26] The "animal" cry, the sound or stuff of signification without meaning, speaks relation (the desire for relation, rather than the Kantian confirmation of "freedom") before (or as soon as) it means anything else. The child occupies the border between a language of violence and imitation ascribed to the "animal" and a language of meaning claimed by the human. But this is also the border between a notion of being's dependence on relation and a fantasy of reason's singular self-sufficiency or full presence to self. This is why the wild child I have both identified and imagined through a range of textual readings can also be located at the temporal and conceptual limit of a phallogocentric humanism that is crucially invested in both the animal's distance from language and the adult human being's transcendence of constitutive relationality.

The pathos of the child's invocation of a constitutive relationality can be glimpsed in a fleeting moment of J. L. Austin's foundational writing on performative speech acts. One of Austin's surprising and recurring gestures is to compare "unsophisticated primitive language" with what happens in "more developed" societies. "If I say something like 'I shall be there,'" writes Austin, "it may not be certain whether it is a promise, or an expression of intention, or perhaps even a forecast of my future behavior, of what is going to happen to me; and it may matter a good deal, at least in developed societies, precisely which of these things it is. And that is why the explicit performative verb is *evolved*—to make clear exactly which it is, how far it commits me and in what way, and so forth."[27] Why does it matter more in "developed societies" that our utterances make things certain? What does it mean to refer to the performative as a product of human evolution? Does Austin really believe that, on some level, the members of a "primitive society" don't need to understand each other as well as "we" do? Because nothing they have to do is important enough to require efficient social organization? Primitive society, Austin seems to suggest (like the "animal"), does not worry as much about the future and whether or not we can master it in advance by knowing, for example, who will be where and when. Primitive people might appear to promise, but it is not as important to know when a promise has been made in such a state. The utterances of primitives, like those of children (and, notoriously, those of actors in a theater), do not matter as much, Austin consistently implies; they do not need to be managed as carefully as the words of sophisticated, evolved adults speaking "normally" and "seriously." "Serious theorists of speech acts maintain that a promise must always promise something good," adds Derrida, quasi-seriously.[28] With enough thought and sufficient development, says Austin, evolved speakers will be able to tell each other where they will be or what they are doing in such a way that the addressee will understand, exactly, what the other is trying to say. Hence, evolution, for Austin, moves in the direction of less and less semantic ambiguity and a more accurate correlation between signifiers and signifieds. Evolution tames language. The primitive speaker, like the child (and the "animal"), is more at home in a world in which words do not need to be so "clear"—"exactly." But this alien "world," as I think much contemporary narrative fiction registers in one way or another, is increasingly *the* world, even if some can register it only in the mode of apocalypse.

From a linguistic perspective, then, wildness would name a persistent incoherence at the level of the sign, a kind of ecological white noise equivalent to the intimation that signification can never be purged of the possibility of error or meaninglessness without simultaneously losing its power to mean anything at all. Every child is wild precisely insofar as he or she always threatens to expose this constitutive semiotic meaninglessness. Speech-act theory proffers a relatively sophisticated form (perhaps it would be better to say a pointedly reverse form) of magical thinking: it is desperately determined to distinguish the constative from the performative—language as conveyer of meaning from language as maker of relation, the logocentric from the phatic. Hence, the scenes of violence that often punctuate narratives in which primates are experimentally introduced to human language are misread by the researchers involved as "signs" of an irredeemable wildness (a natural wildness to which the animal must—and even wants to—be returned). But these scenes can also be read in reverse. Humans refuse to read the animal's violence as text—as direct, meaningful address—and instead they retreat into the "primitive" space of a logocentrism that wants to believe (magically) in the opposition between matter and sign, force and signification. Exiled to this counterecological animal-free zone, the human puts its hands over its ears and makes noise so as not to hear the language of the animal other outside. Every child is wild insofar as he or she remains, even if only partially or temporarily, a child of this outside.

At the end of *Half Brother*, Sarah Tomlin (in a significant departure from "nature") assumes, specifically in Ben's eyes, the role of the dominant chimp and voices an alternative approach. Ben reflects, "I'd never seen Mom look so seriously and so coldly at Dad. It was riveting, and terrifying too, because it was the kind of look one chimp gave another. It meant: *Only one of us is going to win this, and it's going to be me*" (342). "Zan's not human," Sarah says, "But we *taught* him he was. We raised him like a child. Our child. And we have responsibilities to him now" (342). Sarah Tomlin's position is crucially neither that of her husband, for whom Zan is unequivocally animal, nor that of her son, for whom Zan is a person and perhaps even more of a "person" than the scientists who "tricked" him: "He lived with us and trusted us, and we lied to him every day. We fooled him into thinking we were his real family, and that we would always love him and take care of him. We did this so he'd perform all his tricks for us. But later, when his tricks weren't useful any more, we locked him in a cage and got rid of him" (259). We adult human beings, Sarah says, are responsible for this being whom we treated *as* human. And her words resonate on another level, too. Responsibility begins with the *as if* of parental recognition—for everyone. We are called into being when our acts of phatic noncommunication, our "animal" cries, are (mis)read as

meaningful utterances. Every child, in other words, is a wild child responding to the ruse of personhood. Every adult (everyone) is responsible for all
those others whom they first and continuously call into being *as if* they were
persons. This is what it means to recognize a posthumanist ethics of lan-
guaged becoming and of the wildness of every child.

In fact, it turns out that Oppel's adolescent protagonist, Ben, shares a very
particular relationship to the call into personhood with his "half brother,"
Zan. He, too (recalling Kevin in Lionel Shriver's novel), could be said not
to have been unambivalently desired and therefore fully summoned into
being. Ben overhears a conversation between his parents: "'Richard, you
didn't even want your own *child*,' Mom said. . . . 'I didn't want a child right
then,' said Dad. 'We were in the busiest stages of our educations. A lot of men
would've walked away. I stuck it out.' '*Stuck it out,*' said Mom. 'That's really
heroic'" (246). Ben, Kevin, and Zan, in different ways, highlight aspects of
coming into personhood that remain resistant to the logic of contractual
reciprocity or rational determination. We are all, more or less, tricked into
our being, as subjects of a reproductive decision that can never be fully justified (Benatar's "coming into existence is never worth its costs"),[29] or as subjects of Laplanche's enigmatic parental message, or as beings who imitate
our way into particularity and relation.

Responsibility emerges out of the contamination of the performative and
the constative—it is a responsibility *for* this enigmatic contamination. And
it describes every parenting experience: every child is produced as "human"
by being raised "like a child," and every child inherits the enigma of this
message. The lesson that Ben learns from Zan and from his mother (and
that differentiates him from his father) is that we are all subjects of this imitation. What might be called Ben's risky identification with the feminine in
Half Brother, his exposure to a maternal ethics, is also what allows us to read
him as another kind of posthumanist wild child. Oppel's adolescent is an
allegorical amalgam of boy and chimp, emerging at the frayed end of patriarchal humanism. (As if to enforce this point, Zan saves Ben from a potentially fatal fall but in so doing breaks his hand, and Ben is left with a weak-
ened thumb and thus a hand more like a chimp's [372].)

What I have argued in the previous chapters is that the wildness of language and of the child, the wildness that a dominant humanist tradition
repeatedly seeks to send back to nature or to childhood, appears in contemporary fiction in displaced and externalized form whenever children and

adults are placed in intensified conditions of relational crisis. Contemporary fiction allegorizes the phatic wildness of language and being via narratives of adults and children at the social limit—on the edge of disaster. From the perspective of the adult, the child can always appear like the arrival of an infelicitous speech act (the child of an intention that always exceeds or falls short of the event it purportedly refers to). The child occupies a point of interference, incoherence, or irresponsibility—a point of phatic disturbance that I have chosen to abbreviate as wildness. Children are wild, then, not just because they evoke patriarchy's end or the limits of humanist sovereignty but also because they powerfully expose the limits of every speech act, every address to the other, and every attempt to say, "I will be there," and to know, exactly, what such a promise will have meant.

Acknowledgments

I would like to thank Jean Wyatt and Rebekah Sheldon for their generous and insightful responses to my manuscript. Their comments were enormously helpful, and while I revised I engaged in internal conversation with them both. Thanks also to Danielle M. Kasprzak at the University of Minnesota Press for her support and warmth and for shepherding me so painlessly through the publishing process.

Notes

Introduction

1. *Where the Wild Things Are,* directed by Spike Jonze (Warner Bros., 2009).

2. D. W. Winnicott, *Playing and Reality* (New York: Routledge, 1991), 90.

3. Jacques Derrida and Élisabeth Roudinesco, "Disordered Families," in *For What Tomorrow . . . : A Dialogue,* trans. Jeff Fort (Stanford, Calif.: Stanford University Press, 2004), 36.

4. Adam Phillips, *The Beast in the Nursery: On Curiosity and Other Appetites* (New York: Doubleday, 2010), 50.

5. See Timothy Morton's account of "Nature" in, among other places, *Ecology without Nature: Rethinking Environmental Aesthetics* (Cambridge, Mass.: Harvard University Press, 2007) and *The Ecological Thought* (Cambridge, Mass.: Harvard University Press, 2010).

6. Immanuel Kant, *Kant on Education* (Ueber Paedagogik), trans. Annette Churton (Boston: Heath, 1906), 30.

7. Tamar Schapiro, "Childhood and Personhood," *Arizona Law Review* 45, no. 3 (2003): 586–87.

8. Philippe Ariès, *Centuries of Childhood: A Social History of Family Life* (New York: Vintage, 1962), 411.

9. Adriana S. Benzaquén, *Encounters with Wild Children: Temptation and Disappointment in the Study of Human Nature* (Montreal: McGill-Queen's University Press, 2006), 143. See, too, Jean-Jacques Rousseau's foundational *Emile; or, On Education,* trans. Allan Bloom (1762; repr., New York: Basic Books, 1979). Rousseau is often credited with inventing the idea of childhood as a discrete object of study and concern. Rousseau's child seems to require something like a wilderness-protection area: "If we want to pervert this order, we shall produce precocious fruits which will be immature and insipid and will not be long in rotting" (90).

10. Ariès, *Centuries of Childhood,* 412, 413.

11. Jean Itard, *The Wild Boy of Aveyron*, trans. George Humphrey and Muriel Humphrey (New York: Meredith, 1962), xxi.

12. Ibid., 36–37.

13. Cary Wolfe, *What Is Posthumanism?* (Minneapolis: University of Minnesota Press, 2009), xv.

14. Ibid., xxv. See also Karen Barad: "[M]y use of 'posthumanism' marks a refusal to take the distinction between 'human' and 'nonhuman' for granted, and to found analyses on this presumably fixed and inherent set of categories." *Meeting the Universe Halfway: Quantum Physics and the Entanglement of Matter and Meaning* (Durham, N.C.: Duke University Press, 2007), 32.

15. In other words, although Haraway uses the dog to challenge the conventional sentimental logic of the child, whom one loves "unconditionally," her thinking, in an additional turn, might be reapplied to a theorizing of the child figure, or more precisely to the child–parent relation. "The Companion Species Manifesto," *Manifestly Haraway* (Minneapolis: University of Minnesota Press, 2016), 93–198.

16. Ibid., 103–4.

17. Karen Barad, "Posthumanist Performativity: Toward an Understanding of How Matter Comes to Matter," *Signs* 28, no. 3 (2003): 802.

18. Barad, *Meeting the Universe Halfway*, 32.

19. It is striking how many of the assertions made and accounts offered in Barad's "Posthumanist Performativity" might have been written by Judith Butler herself even as they are explicitly or implicitly presented as critiques (and extensions) of her thought. It might be worth reiterating here that Butler's *Gender Trouble* intervenes precisely as a critique of a constructivism that would either reposit an opposition between materialism and idealism or favor one or the other side of that opposition. I think Butler would agree with Barad that "[m]atter is always already an ongoing historicity" ("Posthumanist Performativity," 139). See also the introduction to Butler's *Bodies That Matter* for her response to charges of "somatophobia" ([New York: Routledge, 1993], 10). Barad's (far from uncommon) characterization of (feminist) poststructuralism fails to appreciate the extent to which poststructuralism was always a form of the posthumanism she prizes. Similar gestures in the work of Rosi Braidotti proceed from a somewhat reductive definition of language; see, for example, *The Posthuman* (Cambridge, U.K.: Polity Press, 2013), 37, and *Nomadic Theory* (New York: Columbia University Press, 2011), 5, 20. For Derrida, "the traits that can be recognized in the classical, narrowly defined concept of writing . . . are valid not only for all orders of 'signs' and for all languages in general but moreover, beyond semio-linguistic communication, for the entire field of what philosophy would call experience, even the experience of being: the above mentioned 'presence.'" "Signature Event Context," in *Limited Inc*, trans. Samuel Weber and Jeffrey Mehlman (Evanston, Ill.: Northwestern University Press, 1988), 9. See also Cary Wolfe's assertion that "the [Derridean] trace structure of signification crosses species boundaries and exceeds the question of the subject, human or animal." *Animal Rites: American Culture, the Discourse of Species, and Posthumanist Theory* (Chicago: University of Chicago Press,

2003), 80. For another version of the tendency I've identified in Barad and Braidotti, see Stacy Alaimo and Susan Hekman, eds., *Material Feminisms* (Bloomington: Indiana University Press, 2009). "Our thesis," Alaimo and Hekman write, "is that feminist theory is at an impasse caused by the contemporary linguistic turn in feminist thought" (1).

20. Francis Fukuyama, *Our Posthuman Future: Consequences of the Biotechnology Revolution* (New York: Picador, 2002), 7.

21. Bruno Latour, *An Inquiry into Modes of Existence: An Anthropology of the Moderns*, trans. Catherine Porter (Cambridge, Mass.: Harvard University Press, 2013), 10.

22. Schapiro, "Childhood and Personhood," 576.

23. Maggie Nelson, *The Argonauts* (Minneapolis: Graywolf Press, 2015), 143 (emphasis in original).

24. John Stuart Mill, *On Liberty*, in *The Basic Writings of John Stuart Mill* (New York: Modern Library, 2002), 112.

25. Viviana A. Zelizer, *Pricing the Priceless Child: The Changing Social Value of Children* (Princeton, N.J.: Princeton University Press, 1985). See also Steven Mintz, *Huck's Raft: A History of American Childhood* (Cambridge, Mass.: Belknap Press of Harvard University Press, 2004), for a slightly less pronounced version of this argument.

26. Zelizer, *Pricing the Priceless Child*, 3.

27. Ibid., 6.

28. Cormac McCarthy, *The Road* (New York: Vintage, 2006), 273.

29. The intensified ethical and political engagement with reproduction and parenting that I want to explore in contemporary North American fiction can be linked, in part, to certain profound changes in the politics and technology of the family and of reproduction that can be traced back to the introduction and legalization of new birth control techniques in the 1960s and early 1970s. The birth control pill was approved by the Food and Drug Administration in 1960, but it was not until 1972, in *Eisenstadt v. Baird*, that birth control became legal for all Americans. See Rickie Solinger, *Pregnancy and Power: A Short History of Reproductive Politics in America* (New York: New York University Press, 2005). For the Canadian context, see Heather Latimer, *Reproductive Acts: Sexual Politics in North American Fiction and Film* (Montreal: McGill-Queens University Press, 2013).

30. In *Everything Conceivable*, a study of the impact of new reproductive technologies, Liza Mundy argues, for example, that assisted reproduction is "having a social impact as profound as the widespread availability of the birth control pill in the 1960s, and the passage of *Roe vs. Wade*, legalizing abortion in the United States, in 1973." *Everything Conceivable: How Assisted Reproduction Is Changing Men, Women, and the World* (New York: Knopf, 2007), 22. In the twenty-first century, she asserts, "the radical thing may not be to end a pregnancy, but to begin one" (23).

31. Israeli bioethicist Carmel Shalev specifically addresses the question of a right to reproduction in *Future Baby*, directed by Maria Arlamovsky (NGF, 2016): "[F]rom

desire, to need, to entitlement is a very quick movement. But the fact that we desire things doesn't mean we have the right to something. . . . What do we mean when we say that we have a right to parenthood—does it mean by whatever means?"

32. Solinger, *Pregnancy and Power*, 9.

33. Ibid.

34. Michelle Goldberg, *The Means of Reproduction: Sex, Power, and the Future of the World* (New York: Penguin, 2009), 201.

35. Allan Carlson, quoted in ibid., 203.

36. Goldberg, *The Means of Reproduction*, 203, 204.

37. Ibid., 207. See, too, Donna Haraway's discussion of the multiple and varying effects of technological "development" and reproductive commodification in *Modest_Witness@Second_Millennium.FemaleMan©_Meets_OncoMouse™* (New York: Routledge, 1997). "The age of designer fetuses," writes Haraway, "is also the age of sharp disparities in reproductive health, and therefore of sharp disparities in technoscientific liberty" (201).

38. Quoted in Susan Markens, *Surrogate Motherhood and the Politics of Reproduction* (Berkeley: University of California Press, 2007), 173.

39. Haraway, *Modest_Witness*, 211.

40. One form that this intensive parenting has taken is the "attachment parenting" of William Sears and Martha Sears. This form of intensity, with its celebrity advocates, is also associated with markedly antifeminist views. See their *The Attachment Parenting Book* (New York: Hachette, 2001). Consider, too, the proliferation of webcams in day-care centers and homes that allow parents to monitor their children (and their children's caregivers) remotely and around the clock.

41. Paula S. Fass, "Is There a Story in the History of Childhood?," introduction to *The Routledge History of Childhood in the Western World*, ed. Paula S. Fass (New York: Routledge, 2013), 13.

42. Jennifer Senior, *All Joy and No Fun: The Paradox of Modern Parenthood* (New York: Ecco, 2014), 7–8. In *Pregnancy and Power*, Solinger, too, addresses the complexity of reproductive "choice," in revising the simplistic liberal narrative of the transition from oppression to freedom. "The birth control pill," writes Solinger, "was not a simple gift" (173). Also see Latimer's *Reproductive Acts*: "[R]eproductive technologies, such as abortion, cloning, and in vitro fertilization, are also social technologies, and they therefore constantly shift the parameters of who or what is considered worthy of social protection and human rights" (162). See also Karin Lesnik-Oberstein's *On Having an Own Child: Reproductive Technologies and the Cultural Construction of Childhood*. (London: Karnac, 2007). Lesnik-Oberstein argues "that a whole array of ideas around the having and wanting of children are bound up with the very existence of reproductive technologies, whether or not they are actually used" (xxii).

43. This quotation and the following one, from Barbara Katz Rothman, are taken from Arlamovsky's *Future Baby*. Numerous cinematic texts (documentary and fictional) have taken up these issues in recent years. Ken Scott's sperm-donation comedy *Starbuck* (Entertainment One, 2011) suggests that one must father a multitude

before taking up responsibility for a single child. See, too, Sebastian Silva's intriguing *Nasty Baby* (The Orchard, 2015); Max Zähle's *Raju* (Film Movement, 2012), on transnational adoption; and John Sayles's *Casa de los Babys* (IFC Films, 2003). Sayles depicts a conversation that does not quite take place between two mothers, one who has given up her baby and another who has come to adopt, one speaking in Spanish and the other in English. The "treasure" that gets passed from one mother to the other is the materiality of the signifier in the form of her daughter's name, Esmeralda. For a powerful critique of egg "donation" and transnational surrogacy, see Zippi Brand Frank's documentary *Google Baby* (HBO, 2011), about a business arrangement involving the creation of embryos in the United States that are then shipped to India, where impoverished women serve as "gestational carriers." For a comic depiction of reproductive (ir)responsibility, see Alexander Payne's film *Nebraska* (Paramount Vantage, 2013), in which an adult son, David (Will Forte), turns to his elderly father, Woody (Bruce Dern), for words of wisdom concerning the decision both to get married and to have a child. This wisdom is, to say the least, not forthcoming.

44. The United Nations "Declaration of the Rights of the Child" was adopted in 1959 (although it was largely based on the "World Child Welfare Charter" endorsed by the League of Nations in 1924 and originally drafted by the International Save the Children Union in Geneva in 1923). In 1989, the UN "Convention on the Rights of the Child" established a set of civil, political, social, health, and cultural rights that would be protected under international law. See the website of the Office of the UN High Commissioner for Human Rights, http://www.ohchr.org/EN/Professional Interest/Pages/CRC.aspx.

Currently, 196 countries have signed on to the treaty. The United States government played a role in drafting the convention and signed it in 1995. However, conservative resistance has so far succeeded in blocking any effort to have the convention ratified by the United States. All other UN countries are party to the treaty. Among other reasons, American opponents of ratification claim that the treaty undermines parental authority. See "Convention on the Rights of the Child" on the website of Amnesty International (USA), http://www.amnestyusa.org/our-work/issues/children-s-rights/convention-on-the-rights-of-the-child-0.

45. Joel Feinberg, "The Child's Right to an Open Future," in *Whose Child? Children's Rights, Parental Authority, and State Power*, ed. William Aiken and Hugh LaFollette (Totowa, N.J.: Rowman & Littlefield, 1980), 124–53. See, too, David Archard, *Children: Rights and Childhood* (New York: Routledge, 1993). Archard addresses the tension that some identify within the United Nations "Convention on the Rights of the Child" between "participation and protection rights" for children: "[O]ne kind of right represents children as subjects or agents, capable of exercising for themselves certain fundamental powers. . . . The other kind of right represents children as patients or objects, potential victims of forms of harmful treatment" (60).

46. For a striking discussion of the intersection between environmental crisis and questions of sexual reproduction, see Naomi Klein, *This Changes Everything: Capitalism vs. the Climate* (London: Allen Lane, 2014). "What I was learning about

ecological crisis," writes Klein, "informed the responses to my own fertility crisis; and what I learned about fertility began to leave its mark on how I saw ecological crisis" (423).

47. Barad, *Meeting the Universe Halfway,* 220–21, 447n50.

48. Rachel Bowlby, *A Child of One's Own: Parental Stories* (Oxford: Oxford University Press, 2015), 4. See, too, Charis Thompson's *Making Parents: The Ontological Choreography of Reproductive Technologies* (Cambridge, Mass.: MIT Press, 2007).

49. Bowlby, *Child of One's Own,* 5, 26.

50. Ibid., 4.

51. See chapter 5 of Barad's *Meeting the Universe Halfway* for a discussion of gynogenesis, which "differs from parthenogenesis in that stimulation (but not fertilization) by sperm is required to stimulate the eggs to develop into an embryo" (446n46).

52. Bowlby, *Child of One's Own,* 43. See chapter 7 of Carole Pateman's *The Sexual Contract* (Stanford, Calif.: Stanford University Press, 1988); and, more recently, Andrew Solomon's story of the formation of his family in *Far from the Tree: Parents, Children, and the Search for Identity* (New York: Scribner, 2012), for examples of these historically distinct approaches. Pateman writes, "Contract transformed classic into modern patriarchy, but with the invention of the surrogacy contract, one aspect of classic patriarchy has returned" (214). And Solomon declares, "I espouse reproductive libertarianism, because when everyone has the broadest choice, love itself expands" (700). Of course, this historical transition is more complicated than either of these writers depicts. For a contemporary feminist critical account, see Barbara Katz Rothman: "In our modern systems, we have extended the patriarchal privilege to women. Children are, we are told, half his and half hers, comprised equally of father's and mother's nuclear genetic contribution. If that is true, babies might as well grow in the backyard. Or in any convenient hired belly. Or outsourced to India. With this understanding of kin, of who is and who is not 'really' related, wombs and pregnancies are meaningless." "The Legacy of Patriarchy as Context for Surrogacy; or, Why Are We Quibbling over This?," *American Journal of Bioethics* 14, no. 5 (2014): 37.

53. Bowlby, *Child of One's Own,* 28. For a crucial feminist account of transnational reproductive politics, see Goldberg's *Means of Reproduction.* Goldberg's work reminds us that, in an earlier moment, the United States exported birth control and abortion technology to the third world. In the twenty-first century, the transnational outsourcing of surrogacy is perhaps the most disturbing development among the various recent "innovations" in the realm of reproductive "technology." For a particularly egregious example of one kind of transnational reproductive arrangement, see Frank's *Google Baby.* For other recent accounts, see Arlamovsky's *Future Baby*; Alex Kuczynski, "Her Body, My Baby," *New York Times Magazine,* November 28, 2008, on one wealthy woman's surrogacy arrangement (complete with the unremarked-upon inclusion and exclusion of the nanny); Rothman's "Legacy of Patriarchy"; and her review of *Wombs in Labor: Transnational Commercial Surrogacy in India,* by Amrita Pande, *American Journal of Sociology* 121, no. 2 (2015): 653–55.

54. See Joan Raphael-Leff, "The Gift of Gametes—Unconscious Motivation, Commodification, and Problematics of Genealogy," *Feminist Review* 94 (2010): 117–37, for an additional psychoanalytically oriented take on these issues.

55. Bowlby, *Child of One's Own*, 17.

56. Barad, *Meeting the Universe Halfway*, 136.

57. Ibid., 137.

58. See, for one example among many, Joyce Byers's fierce attempt to communicate with and rescue her son Will from the "upside down" in Matt Duffer and Ross Duffer's web television series *Stranger Things* (21 Laps Entertainment, 2016). Byers finds herself in a partnership with police officer Hopper, who was not successful in rescuing his own child. See also Jill Lepore's account of the shared rhetoric of the Democratic and Republican National Conventions in the summer of 2016: "In an age of atrocity, the unruliness of the people and a fear of the future have combined with terror, naked terror, to make the love of children an all-purpose proxy for each fraying bond, each abandoned civic obligation, the last, lingering devotion" ("A Tale of Two Conventions," *New Yorker*, August 8 and 15, 2016, http://www.newyorker.com/magazine/2016/08/08/a-tale-of-two-conventions).

59. Wolfe writes, "My sense of posthumanism is thus analogous to Jean-François Lyotard's paradoxical rendering of the postmodern: it comes both before and after humanism" (*What Is Posthumanism?*, xvi). See also Timothy Morton's formulation that the "world is a fragile aesthetic effect around whose corners we are beginning to see." *Hyperobjects: Philosophy and Ecology after the End of the World* (Minneapolis: University of Minnesota Press, 2013), 99.

60. Lee Edelman, "Against Survival: Queerness in a Time That's Out of Joint," *Shakespeare Quarterly* 62, no. 2 (Summer 2011): 148. See also Lee Edelman, *No Future: Queer Theory and the Death Drive* (Durham, N.C.: Duke University Press, 2004).

61. There have, of course, been numerous direct critical responses to and engagements with Edelman's provocations. See, for example, Judith Halberstam, "The Antisocial Turn in Queer Studies," *Graduate Journal of Social Science* 5, no. 2 (2008): 140–56; Elizabeth Freeman, "The Immediate Country; or, Heterosexuality in the Age of Mechanical Reproduction," in *The Wedding Complex: Forms of Belonging in Modern American Culture* (Durham, N.C.: Duke University Press, 2002), 178–209; Kenneth Kidd, "Queer Theory's Child and Children's Literature Studies," *PMLA* 126, no. 1 (2011): 182–88; and José Esteban Muñoz, *Cruising Utopia: The Then and There of Queer Futurity* (New York: New York University Press, 2009). Muñoz writes, "[The] future is only the stuff of some kids. Racialized kids, queer kids, are not the sovereign princes of futurity" (95). It's also worth noting the relationship between Edelman's approach and that taken by Lauren Berlant in "America, 'Fat,' the Fetus," in *The Queen of America Goes to Washington City: Essays on Sex and Citizenship* (Durham, N.C.: Duke University Press, 1997), 83–144. Rebekah Sheldon, in *The Child to Come: Life after the Human Catastrophe* (Minneapolis: University of Minnesota Press, 2016), "builds on Lee Edelman's invective against the figure of the child and the future he signifies" (4) but also departs from Edelman by offering a more specific historical account of American culture from the 1960s to the present. Even more

crucially, Sheldon offers her readers a feminist posthumanist account as an alternative to Edelman's Lacanian articulation.

62. Solomon, *Far from the Tree*, 1. This "stranger" recalls Morton's "strange stranger": "The strange stranger . . . is something or someone whose existence we cannot anticipate" (*Ecological Thought*, 42); and, in turn, Derrida's *Of Hospitality: Anne Dufourmantelle Invites Jacques Derrida to Respond*, trans. Rachel Bowlby (Stanford, Calif.: Stanford University Press, 2000), 25. See also Irina Aristarkhova, *Hospitality of the Matrix: Philosophy, Biomedicine, and Culture* (New York: Columbia University Press, 2012), for an account of the ways in which discourses of hospitality work by disavowing connection to the maternal.

63. Edelman, *No Future*, 19.

64. Kathryn Bond Stockton, *The Queer Child; or, Growing Sideways in the Twentieth Century* (Durham: Duke University Press, 2009), 13.

65. Ibid., 2, 9.

66. Ibid, 8. In reading Stockton's inventory, I'm tempted to prioritize the Freudian child, or rather to propose that the broadly conceived psychoanalytic child isn't just one among others. This version of the child draws on Freud's relatively early insights into perversion and into the nondevelopmental aspects of our "stories." I also have in mind the "child" as an amalgam of various strains of psychoanalytic thought. In this respect, one might say that Stockton is more faithful to Freud than I am, and indeed she registers, as one must, the ways in which Freud's text is both protoqueer and heteronormative.

67. Kidd, "Queer Theory's Child," 187. Kidd also refers to Edelman's archive as "flamboyantly adultist" (184). "How is children's literature queer?" Kidd asks; "Let us count some ways" (185).

68. Jacqueline Bhabha, "The Child: What Sort of Human?," *PMLA* 121, no. 5 (2006): 1533. See, too, Rony Brauman's somewhat provocative reference to "the previously unnoticed propensity, shared by dictators and humanitarians, for having themselves publicly displayed in the company of children." Brauman continues: "The child as symbol of innocence and potentiality—of that which precedes the corruption of society—calls out for protection. In this regard, he or she embodies not so much a particular kind of humanity, but rather the ideal social body, that congealed whole of which tyrants and humanitarians alike have been known to dream." "Contradictions of Humanitarianism," trans. Bridget Conley and Emily Apter, *Alphabet City* 7 (2000): 48.

69. McCarthy, *The Road*, 5. For a powerful related claim, see Sheldon, *Child to Come*: "[O]n the one hand, the child, in her innocence and plentitude, promises another generation of species-survival posed as physiological self-similarity even as she begs for protection against the many and varied harms of contemporary industrial practices. On the other hand, while the child appears to vouchsafe the future of the species, her connection to reproduction opens onto the interlocking biological and physical systems whose liveliness compose us as much as we compose them" (177).

70. Philip Roth, *American Pastoral* (London: Vintage, 1998), 85. The language here picks up on the daughter's stutter, itself a marker of the linguistic wild space inhabited by the liminal child from Victor to Billy Budd to Roth's Merry Levov.

71. See, among other places, Derrida's references to survival in *Learning to Live Finally: The Last Interview,* trans. Pascale-Anne Brault and Michael Naas (Hoboken, N.J.: Melville House, 2007), and in *The Beast and the Sovereign,* trans. Geoffrey Bennington, vol. 2 (Chicago: University of Chicago Press, 2011).

72. For Sendak's comments, see Alison Flood, "Maurice Sendak Tells Parents Worried by Wild Things to 'Go to Hell,'" *Guardian,* October 20, 2009, https://www.theguardian.com/books/2009/oct/20/maurice-sendak-wild-things-hell. See, too, Spike Jonze and Dave Eggers, "Desperately Seeking Sendak," *Guardian,* November 22, 2009, https://www.theguardian.com/film/2009/nov/22/maurice-sendak-wild-things-jonze.

73. Maurice Sendak, *Where the Wild Things Are* (New York: Harper, 1963), 7.

74. D. W. Winnicott, "The Theory of the Parent–Infant Relationship," *International Journal of Psychoanalysis* 41 (1960): 587. Some of the remapping of Freud by object-relations theorists is, of course, undertaken, with a distinctly linguistic emphasis, by the Lacanian tradition. In drawing both on the Klein/Winnicott/Benjamin nexus and on the work of Jean Laplanche, I want to make (nondoctrinaire!) use of both modes of thought.

75. Max's globe (a gift from his father) and the plaque's words ("To Max / Owner of This World") together hint at the etymological and politico-epistemological distinction between the globe and the world. See Victor Li's discussion of Derrida's use of "mondialization" rather than "globalization" in "Elliptical Interruptions; or, Why Derrida Prefers Mondialization to Globalization," *CR: The New Centennial Review* 7, no. 2 (2007): 141–54.

76. Sendak, *Where the Wild Things Are.* Sendak said that publishers wanted him to change the word *hot* to *warm* when referring to Max's dinner, because they were worried that Max would burn himself—or because they were worried that children would worry that Max would burn himself. Sendak resisted this "dopey" alteration: *hot* sounded better. And everything about the book, he said, is "hot" as opposed to "warm" (quoted in Flood, "Maurice Sendak Tells Parents").

77. Winnicott, *Playing and Reality,* 91.

78. Ibid., 98.

79. Jean Laplanche, *New Foundations for Psychoanalysis,* trans. David Macey (Oxford: Basil Blackwell, 1989), 90.

80. Jean Laplanche, interview by Cathy Caruth, *Postmodern Culture* 11, no. 2 (January 2001): 2. It is worth noting that there are ways in which Winnicott and Laplanche might also be thought of as oppositional figures. Winnicott, on the one hand, asks how the self ever has access to an other; how can I ever "use" the other and experience myself the joys of being "used" (as opposed to being confined to a realm of merely subjective projections)? For Laplanche, there is always, on the other

hand, too much other. See Laplanche's critical comments on this aspect of Winnicott's thought in his interview by Caruth.

81. This gloss of Laplanche resonates with Karen Barad's account of the sensual and (self-)relation in a recent essay on her "virtual engagements and entanglements" with Derridean thought. See "On Touching—The Inhuman That Therefore I Am," *differences: A Journal of Feminist Cultural Studies* 23, no. 3 (2012): 206–23.

82. Jean Laplanche, *Essays on Otherness* (London: Routledge, 1999), 126.

83. Laplanche, interview by Caruth, 7.

84. Laplanche, *Essays on Otherness*, 60.

85. See also Jane Bennett's emphasis on human–nonhuman assemblages and her formulations concerning ethics in *Vibrant Matter: A Political Ecology of Things* (Durham, N.C.: Duke University Press, 2009). Bennett's emphasis on "magical thinking" and "anthropomorphizing" might also be brought into a productive relationship with the theorization of the child and the child–parent relation: "[M]aybe a bit of anthropomorphizing will prove valuable. Maybe it is worth running the risks associated with anthropomorphizing . . . because it, oddly enough, works against anthropocentrism" (120).

86. See John Fletcher and Nicholas Ray's introduction to their edited collection *Seductions and Enigmas: Laplanche, Theory, Culture* (London: Lawrence & Wishart, 2014), 32.

87. Ibid., 36.

88. D. W. Winnicott, *Deprivation and Delinquency*, ed. Claire Winnicott, Ray Shepherd, and Madeleine Davis (New York: Routledge, 1984), 192.

89. Winnicott, *Playing and Reality*, 40.

90. For a phenomenal tutorial on Winnicott's account of destruction and survival, see the romantic comedy *Lars and the Real Girl*, directed by Craig Gillespie (MGM, 2007).

91. Winnicott, *Playing and Reality*, 10.

92. Ibid., 90.

93. Ibid., 2.

94. Ibid., 93.

95. Ibid.

96. Ibid. (emphases in original).

97. Lionel Shriver, *We Need to Talk about Kevin* (New York: Harper Perennial, 2006), 128.

98. See Barbara Johnson, "Apostrophe, Animation, Abortion," in *A World of Difference* (Baltimore: Johns Hopkins University Press, 1987), 184–99; and Jacques Lacan, *Écrits: A Selection*, trans. Bruce Fink (New York: Norton, 2002), from which Johnson quotes.

99. Quoted in Flood, "Maurice Sendak Tells Parents."

100. Alice Munro, "Miles City, Montana," in *The Progress of Love* (London: Vintage, 1996), 86, 103.

101. A common response to Jonze's movie was a complaint that, unlike Sendak's book, the movie was not for children but was, rather, a film about childhood. Sendak himself resisted such distinctions. "I won't lie to children," said the author (who also once wrote a book called *Pierre* for children—with its famous refrain, "I don't care!"—and illustrated a work of the same title by Herman Melville). Sendak, quoted in Emma Brockes, "Maurice Sendak: 'I refuse to lie to children,'" *Guardian*, October 2, 2011, https://www.theguardian.com/books/2011/oct/02/maurice-sendak -interview.

102. Otto Rank, *The Trauma of Birth* (New York: Harcourt, Brace, 1929), 5.

103. Maggie Nelson's *The Argonauts* (Minneapolis: Graywolf Press, 2015) culminates with an apostrophic address to an unborn child that is indicative of the intensive and critical mode of posthumanist parent–child relation described in this study: "I want you to know, you were thought of as possible—never as certain, but always as possible—not in any single moment, but over many months, even years, of trying, of waiting, of calling—when, in a love sometimes sure of itself, sometimes shaken by bewilderment and change, but always committed to the charge of ever-deepening understanding—two human animals, one of whom is blessedly neither male nor female, the other of whom is female (more or less), deeply, doggedly, wildly wanted you to be" (142). See also *Lion,* directed by Garth Davis (Weinstein Company, 2016), in which another woman's child becomes the "wild" child of a woman in the first world. Saroo lives his life in Australia as an unwitting mistranslation who comes to desire a return to his source. This is a life story shaped by global inequality and new technology (Google Earth). The "child" here also represents a commentary on psychoanalytic stories, in that he understands himself to be "all" to two mothers.

104. Alice Munro, "My Mother's Dream," in *The Love of a Good Woman* (Toronto: McClelland & Stewart, 1998), 293–340, 337.

105. Jacques Derrida, *The Animal That Therefore I Am*, trans. David Wills (New York: Fordham University Press, 2008), 106.

106. Barad, *Meeting the Universe Halfway,* 265. The clinical space of psychoanalysis (and specifically theorizations of the performative force of that space) might be another place to look for an account of the material/discursive production of the other. See Jean Laplanche, "Transference: Its Provocation by the Analyst," in *Essays on Otherness*, ed. John Fletcher (London: Routledge, 1999): 214–33.

107. Sara Ruddick, *Maternal Thinking* (Toronto: Demeter Press, 2009), 40. My discussion of "maternal ethics" throughout this study is informed by Ruddick's *Maternal Thinking* and Lisa Guenther's *The Gift of the Other: Levinas and the Politics of Reproduction* (Albany: State University of New York Press, 2006). See, too, the last chapter of Aristarkhova, *Hospitality of the Matrix,* on male pregnancy represented by contemporary artists Virgil Wong and Lee Mingwei as an "enactment (as opposed to a simulation) of a hospitable relation between self and other" (168).

108. David Vann, *Sukkwan Island,* in *Legend of a Suicide: Stories* (New York: HarperCollins, 2008), 36–208. For another depiction of a father who attempts to

save his wild child from the social, see Smith Henderson, *Fourth of July Creek* (New York: Ecco, 2014).

109. Toni Morrison, *A Mercy* (New York: Knopf, 2008), 161.

110. Emma Donoghue, *Room* (Toronto: HarperCollins, 2011), 236.

111. Hannah Arendt, "The Crisis in Education," *Between Past and Future: Six Exercises in Political Thought* (New York: Viking, 1961), 191.

112. George Saunders, "The Semplica Girl Diaries," in *Tenth of December* (New York: Random House, 2013), 126. In this semi-allegorical tale, in which women from developing countries come to the United States to be tethered and strung up as lawn ornaments, Saunders contemplates, or has his narrator fail to adequately contemplate, the global inequalities that make "family" possible. For a scholarly take on some of these same issues, see Pheng Cheah, "Biopower and the New International Division of Reproductive Labor," *Boundary 2* 34, no. 1 (2007): 90–113. On the failed parental promise, see also the fiction of Lorrie Moore, particularly "Terrific Mother" and "People Like That Are the Only People Here: Canonical Babbling in Peed Onk," in *Birds of America* (New York: Vintage, 2010); "Referential," in *Bark* (Toronto: Bond Street Books, 2014); and *A Gate at the Stairs* (Toronto: Bond Street Books, 2009).

113. For a different account of the "postmodern wild child," see James Berger's comments on works by Oliver Sacks and Don DeLillo: "The cognitively and linguistically impaired figures in these narratives—whom I call 'postmodern wild children'—illustrate contemporary tendencies toward desires for terror and transcendence in response to traumatic damage to the symbolic order." James Berger, *The Disarticulate: Language, Disability, and the Narratives of Modernity* (New York: New York University Press, 2014), 342.

114. Laurie Anderson, "Born, Never Asked," *Big Science* (Warner Brothers Records, 1982).

115. Judith Butler, *The Psychic Life of Power: Theories in Subjection* (Stanford, Calif.: Stanford University Press, 1997), 8.

116. Nathaniel Hawthorne, *The Scarlet Letter* (1850; repr., New York: Norton, 1962), 62.

117. Ibid., 63.

118. Hester and Pearl intricately prefigure Morrison's Sethe and Beloved. And, without question, *Beloved* haunts this present study and is its origin or "dream navel." For an account of Hester's connection to enslaved women and antislavery feminists, see Leland S. Person, "The Dark Labyrinth of Mind: Hawthorne, Hester, and the Ironies of Racial Mothering," *Studies in American Fiction* 29, no. 1 (2001): 33–48.

119. Hawthorne, *Scarlet Letter*, 63.

120. Ibid.

121. Laplanche, interview by Caruth, 22.

122. Hawthorne, *Scarlet Letter*, 123.

123. Ibid., 70.

124. Emma Donoghue, *Room* (Toronto: HarperCollins, 2011), 283.

125. Sigmund Freud, *The Case of Schreber, Papers on Technique, and Other Works*, vol. 12 of *The Standard Edition of the Complete Psychological Works of Sigmund Freud*, ed. and trans. James Strachey (London: Hogarth Press, 1958), 208.

126. See Dorothy E. Roberts on the reproduction of "race" and contemporary race-based biomedicine. Although new technologies and new social policies ask us to think about "race" differently and historically, they also, as Roberts makes clear, engineer its persistence. "Race, Gender, and Genetic Technologies: A New Reproductive Dystopia?," *Signs* 34, no. 4 (2009): 783–804. See also Alys Eve Weinbaum, *Wayward Reproductions: Genealogies of Race and Nation in Transatlantic Modern Thought* (Durham, N.C.: Duke University Press: 2004).

127. Morrison, *A Mercy*, 59.

128. The contemporary significance of Morrison's historical fiction is exposed when read alongside Ta-Nehisi Coates's memoir *Between the World and Me* (New York: Spiegel & Grau, 2015). Coates, like the mother in *A Mercy*, sends a message to his child—the memoir is written in the form of a letter—and Coates doesn't know whether his son will "receive" it. Coates powerfully depicts the intensity of parental love: "Black people love their children with a kind of obsession. You are all we have, and you come to us endangered. I think we would like to kill you ourselves before seeing you killed by the streets that America made" (82). He also depicts "the state of nature" or wildness produced by social policy at once flawed and purposive.

129. Shriver, *We Need to Talk about Kevin*, 400, 397.

130. *Prisoners*, directed by Denis Villeneuve (Warner Home Video, 2013), DVD.

131. Another crucial maternal narrative to consider in this context is Cynthia Ozick's *The Shawl* (New York: Knopf, 1983). In this instance, a powerless mother fails to save her child from death in a concentration camp, and this failure (as in Morrison's *Beloved*) is connected to her child's separation from her mother and her emergence as a linguistic subject.

132. Donoghue, *Room*, 125.

133. Ibid., 237.

134. Toni Morrison, *Beloved* (New York: Vintage, 1987).

135. See also Alice Munro, "Trespasses," in *Runaway* (Toronto: McClelland & Stewart, 2004), 197–235; "Deep-Holes," in *Too Much Happiness* (Toronto: McClelland & Stewart, 2009), 93–115; and "My Mother's Dream" for narratives of children who are figured as surviving their own deaths. Their survival is, in turn, bound up with a meditation on social change and on accompanying shifts in parent–child relations. See my "Seduction and Subjectivity: Psychoanalysis in the Fiction of Alice Munro," in *Critical Insights: Alice Munro*, ed. Charles May (Ipswich, Mass.: Salem Press, 2012), 68–86; and "'Life after Life': Survival in the (Late) Fiction of Alice Munro" (forthcoming in *Ethics and Affects in Alice Munro*, ed. Amelia DeFalco and Lorraine York [New York: Palgrave Macmillan, 2018]). For a condensed representation of the history of modern childhood, see Alice Munro, "The View from Castle Rock" in *The View from Castle Rock* (New York: Knopf, 2006), 27–87. This story might also be

productively read alongside Zelizer's *Pricing the Priceless Child*. In Munro's narrative, the working-class mother is bemused when the middle-class doctor refers to her new baby as her "treasure" (71).

1. Is There a Space of Maternal Ethics?

1. Emma Donoghue, *Room* (Toronto: HarperCollins, 2011), 226. All further references to this text will be parenthetical.

2. For an unfathomable real version of the horrendous events depicted in *Room,* see the case of a young woman and two girls held captive by Ariel Castro in Cleveland from 2002 to 2013. See particularly the account of the child born in captivity and the child's bewilderment when faced with "freedom." Tom Watkins, "Neighbor Angel Cordero Played a Key Role in Cleveland Women's Escape," CNN, May 9, 2013. In a recent interview by Sybil Steinberg, Donoghue cites another instance of a captivity story that influenced her: "Held Captive: *PW* Talks with Emma Donoghue," interview by Sybil Steinberg, *Publishers Weekly,* July 12, 2010, 40. See, too, Elaine Showalter's article in the *New York Times Book Review* on the genre of the captivity narrative, "Dark Places," June 6, 2013.

3. Emmanuel Levinas, *Otherwise Than Being; or, Beyond Essence*, trans. Alphonso Lingis (Pittsburgh: Duquesne University Press, 1998), 124.

4. Thomas Keenan, *Fables of Responsibility: Aberrations and Predicaments in Ethics and Politics* (Stanford, Calif.: Stanford University Press, 1997), 20.

5. Maurice Blanchot, quoted in ibid., 21–22.

6. Keenan, *Fables of Responsibility,* 22.

7. Emmanuel Levinas, "Substitution," in *The Levinas Reader*, ed. Sean Hand (Oxford: Blackwell, 2009), 107.

8. See, for example, the essays collected in *Feminist Interpretations of Emmanuel Levinas*, ed. Tina Chanter (University Park: Pennsylvania State University Press, 2001).

9. Lisa Guenther, "'Like a Maternal Body': Levinas and the Motherhood of Moses," *Hypatia* 21, no. 1 (2006): 122.

10. Levinas, *Otherwise Than Being,* 91.

11. Guenther, "'Like a Maternal Body,'" 125.

12. Ibid., 128.

13. Here, I can't resist anticipating my discussion of abortion by quoting Margaret Little, who uses the word *room* in a way that can't but signify with readers of Donoghue's novel: "One of the most common reasons women seek abortions is that they do not have room in their life just then to be a mother, but they know if they continue the pregnancy they will not be able to give up the child. . . . One may decline to enter a relationship that, once extant, changes the contours of your psyche such that you couldn't leave it." "Abortion, Intimacy, and the Duty to Gestate," *Ethical Theory and Moral Practice* 2, no. 3 (1999): 312. Little suggests, contra Levinas and maternal ethics, that one has the "right" to say "no" to that which would alter the self.

14. If Old Nick marks a relationship to certain, for the most part older, literary genres, he also marks the novel's participation in the genre of psychoanalytic narrative: he is the Oedipal father who violently intervenes in the mother–child scene of bliss.

15. Adrienne Rich, *Of Woman Born: Motherhood as Experience and Institution* (New York: Norton, 1986), 256–80; Sara Ruddick, *Maternal Thinking: Toward a Politics of Peace* (Toronto: Demeter Press, 2009), 65–67.

16. Carole Pateman, *The Sexual Contract* (Stanford, Calif.: Stanford University Press, 1988), 182.

17. There would be no *Room* if it were not for Jack's narration. Yet the novel also formally manages to represent the mother's point of view. This is accomplished with dialogue and also via Jack's heightened powers of observation when it comes to reading his mother ("Her face is gone flat, that means I said a wrong thing but I don't know which" [14]). The novel also justifies and deploys the clever device of "parroting," a game Ma has designed in which Jack repeats utterances he hears on the television, on a news program, for example, that he doesn't understand. He needs to repeat them perfectly. Formally, this game justifies his repetition of adult utterances in other contexts, but this potentially minor detail also allegorizes (wonderfully) every child's relationship to adult language (or every subject's relationship to language per se).

18. Sigmund Freud, *Beyond the Pleasure Principle,* vol. 18 of *The Standard Edition of the Complete Psychological Works of Sigmund Freud,* ed. and trans. James Strachey (London: Hogarth Press, 1955), 15.

19. Ibid., 14.

20. In an extended and privileged scene, after the ordeal is over, Ma is interviewed by a TV reporter while Jack looks on. In the midst of the interview, the woman says to Ma,

> "You breastfed him. In fact, this may startle some of our viewers, I understand you still do?"
> Ma laughs.
> The woman stares at her.
> "In this whole story, that's the shocking detail?"
> The woman looks down at her paper again. "There you and your baby were, condemned to solitary confinement—"
> Ma shakes her head. "Neither of us was ever alone for a minute" (233).

Room also, of course, comments here on the still-controversial status of "prolonged"—or by extension public—breastfeeding. See, for example, the Facebook page "If breastfeeding offends you, put a blanket over YOUR head!," accessed December 1, 2016, https://www.facebook.com/If-breastfeeding-offends-you-put-a -blanket-over-YOUR-head-444758635156/.

21. "We choose, instead, *not* to choose the Child, as disciplinary image of the Imaginary past or as site of a projective identification with an always impossible future." Lee Edelman, *No Future: Queer Theory and the Death Drive* (Durham, N.C.: Duke University Press, 2004), 31.

22. Elizabeth Freeman, *The Wedding Complex: Forms of Belonging in Modern American Culture* (Durham, N.C.: Duke University Press, 2009), 178–209. See also Roland Barthes's essay "The Great Family of Man," in *Mythologies*, trans. Annette Lavers (New York: Noonday Press, 1972), 100–102, in which photography is implicated in the very category of the human.

23. André Green, *On Private Madness* (Madison, Conn.: International Universities Press, 1993), 245.

24. Lenny Abrahamson attempted to represent the "wild" side of maternal relation in his film version of Donoghue's novel (A24, 2015). In a 2016 interview with the Irish *Independent*, Donoghue comments, "[T]he film is such a masterpiece of naturalism. I remember [Lenny] saying to me to write it like a wildlife documentary." Aoife Kelly, "'It's Amazing Beginner's Luck with My Very First Screenplay': Emma Donoghue on Oscar Nomination," Independent.ie, January 15, 2016, http://www .independent.ie/entertainment/movies/its-amazing-beginners-luck-with-my-very -first-screenplay-emma-donoghue-on-oscar-nomination-34367084.html.

25. Emmanuel Levinas, "Ethics as First Philosophy," in *The Levinas Reader*, ed. Sean Hand (Oxford: Blackwell, 2009), 75–87.

26. Jessica Benjamin, *The Bonds of Love: Psychoanalysis, Feminism, and the Problem of Domination* (New York: Random House, 1988), 68.

27. Jessica Benjamin, "Two-Way Streets: Recognition of Difference and the Intersubjective Third," *differences: A Journal of Feminist Cultural Studies* 17, no. 1 (2006): 116.

28. Ibid, 117.

29. Jessica Benjamin, *Shadow of the Other: Intersubjectivity and Gender in Psychoanalysis* (New York: Routledge, 1998), 99 (emphasis in original).

30. Benjamin, "Two-Way Streets," 140.

31. Ibid., 133.

32. Jacques Lacan, *Freud's Papers on Technique 1953–1954*, bk. 1 of *The Seminar of Jacques Lacan*, ed. Jacques-Alain Miller, trans. John Forrester (New York: Norton, 1998), 217.

33. Benjamin, "Two-Way Streets," 126. For a different theoretical elaboration of this, see Jean Wyatt, "Giving Body to the Word: The Maternal Symbolic in Toni Morrison's *Beloved*," *PMLA* 108, no. 3 (May 1993): 474–88. See also Judith Butler's critique of collapsing accounts of *the* Symbolic with a poststructuralist understanding of kinship in *Antigone's Claim: Kinship between Life and Death* (New York: Columbia University Press, 2000).

34. Benjamin, "Two-Way Streets," 131.

35. D. W. Winnicott, quoted in ibid., 134.

36. D. W. Winnicott, *Playing and Reality* (New York: Routledge, 1991), 47. Winnicott insists that "[p]laying is a doing" that "*has a place* and a time." It is not "*inside*," nor is it "*outside*" (41). Psychoanalysis has mistakenly concerned itself only with "the use of play" (its content), whereas Winnicott would like to turn our emphasis to play's *form*. "*Psychotherapy*," Winnicott adds, "*takes place in the overlap of two areas of playing. . . . [W]here playing is not possible then the work done by the therapist is*

directed towards bringing the patient from a state of not being able to play into a state of being able to play" (38; emphases in original).

37. In terms of "presentness," one might also think about one of the distinctive anxieties of contemporary parenthood: "being there." See Joan C. Tronto, "The 'Nanny' Question in Feminism," *Hypatia* 17, no. 2 (2002): 34–49.

38. Winnicott, *Playing and Reality*, 14–15.

39. Ibid., 5.

40. Irina Aristarkhova's insightful account of what the philosophical tradition has both employed and failed to acknowledge provides another route for thinking about Ma's accomplishment in *Room*: "The woman is not any more a *space* for generation and nursing than the man or the machine. The work of the matrixial/maternal is indeed the active making of space for and careful nourishment of the gestating child." See *Hospitality of the Matrix: Philosophy, Biomedicine, and Culture* (New York: Columbia University Press, 2012), 28.

41. See Leo Kanner, "Autistic Disturbances of Affective Contact," *Nervous Child* 2 (1943): 217–50; Bruno Bettelheim, *The Empty Fortress: Infantile Autism and the Birth of the Self* (New York: Free Press, 1967); and Philip Wylie, *Generation of Vipers* (New York: Rinehart, 1955). It is hard not to be intrigued by the fact that the daughter of the author of *Generation of Vipers* would later write an influential book on breastfeeding!

42. Thomas Hobbes, *Leviathan* (Peterborough, Ont.: Broadview Press, 2002), 151. I will return to the figure of the Hobbesean mother in my chapter on Morrison's *A Mercy*. However, see also my discussion here of Soran Reader's odd relationship to this figure.

43. Judith Jarvis Thomson, *Rights, Restitution, and Risk: Essays in Moral Theory*, ed. William Parent (Cambridge, Mass.: Harvard University Press, 1986), 2.

44. Ibid., 5. In the course of her argument, Thomson comes up with many imaginative scenarios. A particularly interesting one (in relationship to *Room*) involves a woman and a growing child confined to the space of a small house. As the child keeps growing, he eventually crushes the woman to death: "For what we have to keep in mind is that the mother and the unborn child are not like two tenants in a small house which has, by an unfortunate mistake, been rented to both: the mother *owns* the house" (7).

45. Ibid., 13.

46. Ibid., 19. Early fetal viability is one scenario that presents us with new questions that were not pressing when Thomson's essay was published, in 1971, just before *Roe v. Wade*. It is tempting to think about how changes in neonatal medicine and reproductive technology might have shifted her argument. Whereas the liberal feminist theorist finds herself contemplating the "child" who might be "detach[ed]" alive, new assisted reproductive technology has introduced us to complex legal and ethical questions concerning frozen embryos. See Liza Mundy on the "embryo glut" and on the difficult situation of many fertility patients. And, of course, this is an extremely explosive political issue in the context of abortion debates. If a court should rule that embryos are human lives that merit legal protection, it would provide antiabortion

activists with effective precedent ("If *Roe* does topple, it could be reproductive tech-nology that provides the push"). *Everything Conceivable: How Assisted Reproduction Is Changing Men, Women, and the World* (New York: Knopf, 2007), 292, 297. For a brief but compelling personal account of deciding what to do with frozen embryos, see Paul Ford, "Determining the Fate of Frozen Embryos: Do You Know Where Your Children Are?," *Elle*, September 30, 2013, http://www.elle.com/life-love/sex-relationships/advice/a12594/freezing-embryos/.

47. Soran Reader, "Abortion, Killing, and Maternal Moral Authority," *Hypatia* 23, no. 1 (2008): 134. Further references will be cited parenthetically.

48. Toni Morrison, *Beloved* (New York: Vintage, 1987).

49. Here again, it is worth underlining the strong intertextual connection between *Room* and *Beloved* that I anticipated with the epigraph to this chapter. Ma tells the journalist that she was "saved" when Jack was born, and that his birth was "the best thing" that she has ever done (233); the echo of *Beloved* here is unmistakable.

50. Thomson, *Rights, Restitution, and Risk*, 18.

51. Guenther, "'Like a Maternal Body,'" 131–32.

52. Plato, *The Republic*, trans. Christopher Rowe (New York: Penguin, 2012), 514a. All further references will be parenthetical.

53. The feminist poststructuralist account that I articulate here is entirely in line with Karen Barad's account of "agential realism" as a critique of "representational-ism": "Representationalism separates the world into the ontologically disjointed domains of words and things. . . . [R]epresentationalism is a prisoner of the prob-lematic metaphysics it postulates." "Posthumanist Performativity: Toward an Under-standing of How Matter Comes to Matter," *Signs: A Journal of Women, Culture, and Society* 28, no. 3 (2003): 129–30.

54. Guenther writes, "[T]he ethics of maternal substitution in particular calls for a feminist politics of reproduction and motherhood, even if this feminist politics also returns to the ethical encounter for its inspiration." "'Like a Maternal Body,'" 131.

55. The space of Room is archaic, and Old Nick's fantasy is a form of archaic patriarchalism. "Outside," most men can't or don't assume that there's a space like this anymore, but, of course, little versions reappear. See, for example, the documen-tary *The Wolfpack*, directed by Crystal Moselle (Dolby, 2015), depicting the family of a man who fantasizes an extreme form of patriarchal control in twenty-first-century New York.

56. Plato's emancipated and enlightened individual appears not to be affected by any ambivalence about his escape: "As he remembered the place he lived in first, what counted as wisdom there, and his former fellow prisoners," Socrates asks Glau-con, "don't you think he would call himself happy for his change of residence, and pity the others?" (516c). But, as we shall see, Plato does make him go back for one last visit.

57. "As soon as there is sovereignty, there is abuse of power and a rogue state." Jacques Derrida, *Rogues: Two Essays on Reason*, trans. Pascale-Anne Brault and Michael Naas (Stanford, Calif.: Stanford University Press, 2000), 102.

58. Ma tells Jack one poorly timed and unmanageable story after they leave Room, a story about Harry Harlow and his rhesus monkeys: "[A] scientist took them [the baby monkeys] away from their mothers," Ma tells Jack, "and kept each one all alone in a cage—and you know what, they didn't grow up right. . . . It turns out they needed the love as much as the milk" (221). Ma attempts to reassure Jack, who wants to revisit the story: "Don't think about the baby monkeys anymore, OK? They're OK now." Jack responds (like the boy in Cormac McCarthy's novel), "I don't think they're OK" (228). Donoghue's fleeting reference to Harry Harlow would repay extended consideration in this context. For a discussion of Harlow's appearance in a CBS documentary (entitled *Mother Love*), see Donna Haraway, *Primate Visions: Gender, Race, and Nature in the World of Modern Science* (New York, Routledge, 1989).

59. Donoghue's most recent novel, *The Wonder* (Boston: Little, Brown, 2016), set in mid-nineteenth-century Ireland and concerned with a "fasting girl," Anna, and an English nurse, Lib, appointed to watch over her to verify that she is indeed miraculously surviving without food, revisits some of the crucial tropes and concerns of *Room*. Anna is ultimately rescued by Lib, and this rescue involves a complex relationship between care and violence. Anna's death is ultimately staged—as is Jack's in *Room*—and she lives on in a new and uncertain world.

60. Sara Ruddick begins *Maternal Thinking* with reference to precisely this passage from Plato's *Republic*. She retells the story of her education as a philosopher in the 1950s: "[I]n that context, I learned that literature was thought to be effeminate. . . . It was philosophy's Reason that abetted my desire to free myself from the fate of wife-and-mother with its messy, fleshly children and dull duties. . . . While I was certainly not about to take a woman for a model, there was always a danger that in an emotional, uncontrolled moment I might turn 'womanly'" (5).

2. Postapocalyptic Responsibility

1. A crucial precursor text for *The Road*, I would suggest, is Nathaniel Hawthorne's "Roger Malvin's Burial." Hawthorne's tale is the son's story; *The Road* is the father's. "Roger Malvin's Burial" encodes the prehistory of the United States; *The Road* is about its apparent end. Hawthorne's story thus offers us an account of the formation of the (national) superego that is simultaneously an account of melancholia, that deadly refusal of mourning. A certain masculine fantasy of nonviolence (which can result in the worst forms of violence) also informs *The Road*, as does a powerful, if less complex, mapping of internal and external space. In McCarthy's world, a sense of founding guilt has been transformed into a sense of relentless (undeserved) persecution. See Nathaniel Hawthorne, "Roger Malvin's Burial," in *Nathaniel Hawthorne's Tales*, ed. James McIntosh (New York: Norton, 1987), 17–31.

2. Cormac McCarthy, *The Road* (New York: Vintage, 2006), 286. All further references to this text will be parenthetical.

3. Another fascinating text to place in conversation with *The Road* is David Vann's *Sukkwan Island*, in *Legend of a Suicide: Stories* (New York: HarperCollins, 2008), 36–208. Although Vann's novella is also about a father and son who must

survive in the wilderness, the very idea of starting civilization all over again is clearly marked as the destructive and pathological fantasy of the father character. Indeed, the father's destruction manages an impossible feat (and rupture of narrative form): he becomes solely responsible for his son's suicide.

4. One might consider McCarthy's effort to imagine the end of patriarchy in relationship to Nancy Armstrong's account of the British postdomestic, postfamilial contemporary novel. See "The Future in and of the Novel," *Novel: A Forum on Fiction* 44, no. 1 (2011): 10. My effort here will be to read McCarthy's turn *toward* the family as something other than merely resistant, conservative, and symptomatic.

5. Emma Donoghue, *Room* (Toronto: HarperCollins, 2011), 317.

6. Cormac McCarthy, "Hollywood's Favorite Cowboy," interview by John Jurgensen, *Wall Street Journal*, November 20, 2009.

7. Melanie Klein, *The Selected Melanie Klein*, ed. Juliet Mitchell (New York: Free Press, 1986), 151.

8. Jessica Benjamin, *Like Subjects, Love Objects: Essays on Recognition and Sexual Difference* (New Haven, Conn.: Yale University Press, 1995), 113.

9. Judith Butler, *Frames of War: When Is Life Grievable?* (London: Verso, 2009), 44, 177. See, too, Butler's *Precarious Life*: "Is there something to be gained from grieving, from tarrying with grief, from remaining exposed to its unbearability and not endeavoring to seek a resolution for grief through violence? . . . To foreclose that vulnerability, to banish it, to make ourselves secure at the expense of every other human consideration is to eradicate one of the most important resources from which we must take our bearings and find our way." *Precarious Life: The Powers of Mourning and Violence* (London: Verso, 2004), 30.

10. McCarthy, "Hollywood's Favorite Cowboy."

11. In her reading of *The Road* as grail narrative, Lydia Cooper suggests that "[t]he apocalypticism of *The Road* seems to be a response to an immediate and visceral fear of cataclysmic doom in the United States after the terrorist attacks on 9/11." "Cormac McCarthy's *The Road* as Apocalyptic Grail Narrative," *Studies in the Novel* 43, no. 2 (2011): 221.

12. There are no references to the man's mother in the text. There are, however, two brief references to his father and to an idealized day spent with his uncle; we also encounter the community represented as an all-male archaic society in a recollected scene of mass snake burning (188). So, although both *Room* and *The Road* feature a parent and a child in an extreme situation, in *The Road,* on the one hand, the violence can be read as a faceless environmental projection or externalization and disavowal of Oedipal conflict that works by effacing the maternal or killing it in order to find it dead (mourn its loss). In *Room*, on the other hand, the violence has a face, and it is the face of the gothic patriarch—the father.

13. Hanna Rosin quotes biologist Ronald Ericsson ("Did male dominance exist? Of course it existed. But it seems to be gone now. And the era of the firstborn son is totally gone") and social worker Mustafaa El-Scari, who addresses his weekly class on fathering for men who have failed to pay child support: "What is our role? Everyone's

telling us we're supposed to be the head of a nuclear family, so you feel like you got robbed. It's toxic, and poisonous, and it's setting us up for failure." "The End of Men," *Atlantic*, July/August 2010, https://www.theatlantic.com/magazine/archive/2010/07/the-end-of-men/308135.

14. Thomas Carlson's Heideggerian reading of *The Road* similarly locates a certain ethical possibility in what he calls "the suspension of the world." "With the World at Heart: Reading Cormac McCarthy's *The Road* with Augustine and Heidegger," *Religion and Literature* 39, no. 3 (2013): 59. See Phillip Snyder, who traces the significance of a Derridean and Levinasian account of hospitality, for another version of an ethical reading. "Hospitality in Cormac McCarthy's *The Road*," *Cormac McCarthy Journal* 6 (2008): 83.

15. For a very different rendition of a parent–child relationship stripped bare, see Lydia Millet's *My Happy Life* (Brooklyn: Soft Skull Press, 2006). In this text of parenting in extremity, the nameless female protagonist is radically deprived of relation and ultimately placed in solitary confinement. With no access to the proper way to name her own child, she comes to refer to him as "Brother": "Because I have been sure of one thing in my life: and that was Brother. He did not speak yet but in other ways he was clear to me. . . . Brother and I had a code of feeling. So I stuck to him like glue, and only left him alone to go to sleep. Even then, sometimes I would curl up on a chair next to him. It is hard to say what Brother ever made of me, but I made a galaxy out of him. And all the lonely stars spiraled toward the center, glowing" (79–80).

16. It is surely no accident that the little bit of "paradise" the father and son encounter in their travels is a bomb shelter filled with "the richness of a vanished world." The father reassures his son that those to whom this shelter belonged were "good guys," "like" themselves. This scene registers nostalgia for Cold War America, of course, but it also illustrates the very way in which paranoia functions to produce, through splitting, the ideal or the good. For a real life and more markedly contemporary version of this fantasy, see Evan Osnos's article about billionaire survivalists "Doomsday Prep for the Super-Rich," *New Yorker*, January 30, 2017: "In recent years survivalism has expanded to more affluent quarters, taking root in Silicon Valley and New York City, among technology executives, hedge-fund managers, and others in their economic cohort" (36).

17. Sigmund Freud, "Mourning and Melancholia," in vol. 14 of *The Standard Edition of the Complete Psychological Works of Sigmund Freud*, ed. and trans. James Strachey (London: Hogarth Press, 1957), 253.

18. Ibid., 252.

19. The coin and the arrowhead also raise the question of what it means to think of this cultural inheritance as belonging to the (white) father.

20. Lee Edelman, *No Future: Queer Theory and the Death Drive* (Durham, N.C.: Duke University Press, 2004), 148.

21. Sara Ruddick, *Maternal Thinking: Toward a Politics of Peace* (Toronto: Demeter Press, 2009), 40.

22. See Barbara Katz Rothman's analysis of contemporary surrogacy arrangements and their relationship to "the historical legacy of patriarchy, which values 'seed' (now understood as egg as well as sperm) over relationships, including all other aspects of the maternal relationship, as the meaningful essence of the human." "The Legacy of Patriarchy as Context for Surrogacy; or, Why Are We Quibbling over This?," *American Journal of Bioethics* 14, no. 5 (2014): 36. See also Karin Lesnik-Oberstein: "Reproductive technologies in many cases would have no validity, or a different validity at the very least, without these assumptions: that the having of children is of a paramount importance, and that these children need to be 'biologically,' and preferably also 'genetically,' 'own' children." *On Having an Own Child: Reproductive Technologies and the Cultural Construction of Childhood* (London: Karmac, 2007), xxi.

23. Edelman, *No Future*, 3 (emphases in original).

24. Ibid., 27.

25. Ibid., 12. Edelman does distinguish this figure of the child from the lived experience of any historical/biological children: "Though that division is never stable, since the latter is constantly subject to cultural articulation as the former, it provides an important basis for trying to recognize the distinction between an ideological construct and the substrate (unknowable outside of ideology) on which the construct is etched." Lee Edelman, "Against Survival: Queerness in a Time That's Out of Joint," *Shakespeare Quarterly* 62, no. 2 (2011): 156. In other words, what is justified in the name of "the Child" may very well work against the interests of children; but at the same time, Edelman doesn't want to suggest that we can wholly or simply separate out ideal and material children.

26. For a more historical and socioeconomic account of this "secular theology," see Viviana Zelizer, *Pricing the Priceless Child: The Changing Social Value of Children* (Princeton, N.J.: Princeton University Press, 1985). Here, Zelizer writes of early twentieth-century prospective adoptive parents: "Experts now wrote about the dangers of 'seeking compensation in children for frustrated affections,' or unfulfilled ambitions. If child placing agencies were less often confronted by requests for a sturdy working child, they now faced new expectations, as the couple who applied to the New York State Charities Association for a three-month-old baby, 'who could eventually go to Princeton'" (195).

27. Edelman, *No Future*, 148.

28. William Shakespeare, *Hamlet,* quoted in ibid., 154.

29. Edelman, *No Future*, 166.

30. Ibid., 161. At stake here is the question of how to assess the gift or burden of the father's writing. "One can sign neither a child nor a work," writes Derrida. See Jacques Derrida and Maurizio Ferraris, *A Taste for the Secret*, ed. Giacomo Donis and David Webb, trans. Giacomo Donis (Malden, Mass.: Blackwell Publishers, 2001), 29. And how can one ignore McCarthy's publicly declared decision to reserve all autographed copies of *The Road* for his son John, who, he claims in an interview, is also the novel's "coauthor": "[A] lot of the lines that are in there are verbatim conversations my son John and I had. . . . There are signed copies of the book, but they all

belong to my son John, so when he turns 18 he can sell them and go to Las Vegas or whatever. No, those are the only signed copies of the book." McCarthy, "Hollywood's Favorite Cowboy."

31. This reads as a perfect little gloss on Derrida's *différance*. "Différance," Derrida writes, is what makes the movement of signification possible, "only if each so-called 'present' element, each element appearing on the scene of presence, is related to something other than itself, thereby keeping within itself the mark of a past element, and already letting itself be vitiated by the mark of its relation to the future element." "Différance," in *Margins of Philosophy*, trans. Alan Bass (Chicago: University of Chicago Press, 1982), 13.

32. See Arielle Zibrak, whose title says it all: "Intolerance, a Survival Guide: Heteronormative Culture Formation in Cormac McCarthy's *The Road*," *Arizona Quarterly* 68, no. 3 (2012): 103–27. See also Kevin Kearney, who argues for more nuance ("[T]he novel wavers in the dialectic between the hope of reproductive futurism and the Real of finitude"), although he ultimately comes down on one side: "This tension between the transcendental and the immanent, between 'the fire' and the 'coldly secular,' 'intestate' world, I argue, tends toward a universe without transcendence and without the assurance of a symbolic Other." "Cormac McCarthy's *The Road* and the Frontier of the Human," *Literature Interpretation Theory* 23 (2012): 174.

33. Jacques Derrida, *Archive Fever: A Freudian Impression*, trans. Erin Prenowitz (Chicago: University of Chicago Press, 1995), 2.

34. One might almost have expected the man to have connected with an abandoned answering machine. "A spectral response (thus informed by a *technē* and inscribed in an archive) is always possible," writes Derrida in *Archive Fever*; ". . . [A] bit like the answering machine whose voice outlives its moment of recording: you call, the other person is dead, now, whether you know it or not, and the voice responds to you, in a very precise fashion, sometimes cheerfully" (62).

35. Ibid., 72. See also Derrida's *Specters of Marx: The State of the Debt, the Work of Mourning, and the New International*, trans. Peggy Kamuf (New York: Routledge, 1994), 74.

36. Derrida, *Archive Fever*, 36. In *Learning to Live Finally*, Derrida speaks of a "double feeling" that his writing will only begin to be read in the future *and* that it will die with him in being reduced to its shelf life or death: "[O]n the one hand, to put it playfully and with a certain immodesty, one has not yet begun to read me, that even though there are, to be sure, many very good readers (a few dozen in the world perhaps, people who are also writer-thinkers, poets), in the end it is later on that all this has a chance of appearing; but also, on the other hand, and thus simultaneously, I have the feeling that two weeks or a month after my death *there will be nothing left*. Nothing except what has been copyrighted and deposited in libraries. I swear to you, I believe sincerely and simultaneously in these two hypotheses." *Learning to Live Finally: The Last Interview*, trans. Pascale-Anne Brault and Michael Naas (Hoboken, N.J.: Melville House, 2007), 34.

37. Derrida, *Archive Fever*, 79 (emphases in original).

38. McCarthy's play *The Sunset Limited: A Novel in Dramatic Form* (New York: Vintage, 2006) was published in the same year as *The Road* and reads as a kind of companion piece. One encounters here, too, questions of responsibility—"You run into people and maybe some of them are in trouble or whatever but it doesn't mean that you're responsible for them" (4)—belief in "cultural things," and a "world [that] is largely gone" (25). Indeed, the play more generally explores what might sustain or fail to sustain one as a living being. Problematically and unapologetically, however, *Sunset Limited* allegorizes all of the differences that it wants to explore through an opposition between its two characters: the faithless "White," a middle-aged college professor who has just attempted suicide, and the evangelical "Black," a man of a similar age who saved him and who subsequently attempts to talk him out of his depression. One could attempt, however, to tease out a more subtle thread by beginning with Black's final words after the still (presumably) suicidal White has departed. Black addresses God using a word, *okay*, that is crucial in the exchanges between father and son in *The Road*. Here, as in *The Road*, okay serves to defer a final cognitive/ethical assessment of the question under discussion while performing Jakobson's phatic linguistic function of repositing and reaffirming a linguistic channel of communication, or a relation.

39. Edelman, "Against Survival," 162.

40. Giovanna Borradori, *Philosophy in a Time of Terror: Dialogues with Jürgen Habermas and Jacques Derrida* (Chicago: University of Chicago Press, 2003), 113 (emphases in original).

41. Edelman, "Against Survival," 162.

42. The relationship between Edelman and Derrida is more complex than I have time or occasion to unpack here. Note, for example, how Edelman himself sets up an opposition with Badiou, Lacan, and the figure of "bin Ladenism" (as opposed to bin Laden), on one side, and Derrida, on the other.

43. Edelman's work thus seems to confirm Judith Butler's suspicion in *Antigone's Claim*: "Although Lacan's theorization of the symbolic is meant to take the place of those accounts of kinship grounded in nature or theology, it continues to wield the force of universality. . . . [D]oes this understanding of universalization work to usher in God (or the gods) through another door?" *Antigone's Claim: Kinship between Life and Death* (New York: Columbia University Press, 2000), 44–45.

44. See, for example, Claire Curtis, who argues that *The Road* is one of the exceptions to the genre in refusing "any sustained analysis of starting over." *Postapocalyptic Fiction and the Social Contract: "We'll Not Go Home Again"* (Lanham, Md.: Lexington Books, 2010), 12.

45. Amy Hungerford comments on what one might call McCarthy's faith in the performative capacity of language. She writes of the novel's final passage: "Who tells us this? . . . [T]he description of the trout are the father's words, the narrator's word, and God's words. Their lyricism, their sensuousness, flaunt the power of the word to evoke a world. . . . [T]he final wordfish of *The Road* feel like sheer assertion, without even the fiction of an immortal character to keep them pinned to the

world." *Postmodern Belief: American Literature and Religion Since 1960* (Princeton, N.J.: Princeton University Press, 2010), 136. For another effective reading of the enigmatic end of McCarthy's text, see Thomas Schaub: "McCarthy closes his novel with a master topos of western belief placed here as a kind of epitaph for the world's body." "Secular Scripture and Cormac McCarthy's *The Road*," *Renascence: Essays on Values in Literature* 61, no. 3 (2009): 152–67.

46. Donoghue, *Room*, 292.

47. Lisa Guenther, *The Gift of the Other: Levinas and the Politics of Reproduction* (Albany: State University of New York Press, 2006), 152.

48. Even as the "mix" differs, all of these registers appear in both *Room* and *The Road*. Colson Whitehead surely refers, tongue in cheek, to *The Road* with his novel *Zone One*'s account of parents as the most frightening figures one encounters in the midst of the zombie apocalypse: "A parent–child combo might pop up at the crest of the old country road, wan and wary, and Mark Spitz shrank from these, no matter how well outfitted they were. . . . [T]hey were paranoid he wanted to rape or eat their offspring. . . . The parents were dangerous because they didn't want your precious supplies. They possessed the valuables, and it hobbled their reasoning." *Zone One: A Novel* (New York: Doubleday, 2011), 140.

49. Jakobson writes of the phatic function, "There are messages primarily serving to establish, to prolong, or to discontinue communication, to check whether the channel works. . . . The endeavor to start and sustain communication is typical of talking birds; thus the phatic function of language is the only one they share with human beings. It is also the first verbal function acquired by infants; they are prone to communicate before being able to send or receive informative communication." *Language in Literature* (Cambridge, Mass.: Harvard University Press, 1987), 68, 69. See also Timothy Morton on the relationship between the phatic and ecocriticism: "Future ecocriticism must take the phatic dimension of language into account. . . . The environmental aspect of phatic communication explains the popularity in contemporary ambient electronic music of samples from radio talk shows ("Hello, you're on the air"), scanned telephone conversations and other phatic phenomena." *Ecology without Nature: Rethinking Environmental Aesthetics* (Cambridge, Mass.: Harvard University Press, 2007), 37.

50. See J. L. Austin's own dismantling of the constative/performative opposition at the end of his series of lectures, *How to Do Things with Words* (Cambridge, Mass.: Harvard University Press, 1962), 145–47.

51. Klein, *Selected Melanie Klein*, 189.

52. Edelman, "Against Survival," 162.

53. D. W. Winnicott, *Deprivation and Delinquency* (New York: Routledge, 2013), 105.

54. *Where the Wild Things Are,* directed by Spike Jonze (Warner Bros., 2009). For more on love as the end of the world, see Sigmund Freud, "Psychoanalytic Notes on an Autobiographical Account of a Case of Paranoia," in vol. 12 of *The Standard Edition of the Complete Psychological Works of Sigmund Freud,* ed. and trans. James

Strachey (London: Hogarth Press, 1955), 1–82. See also Derrida's accounts of the interrelationship between mourning, love, and the end of the world in *The Work of Mourning* (Chicago: University of Chicago Press, 2001) and *The Politics of Friendship* (London: Verso, 1997). For a specific contemporary fictional account of parental love figured as the end of the world, see T. Coraghessan Boyle, "Chicxulub": "My point? You'd better get down on your knees and pray to your gods," says the father who has nearly lost his teenage daughter to a car accident, "because each year this big spinning globe we ride intersects the orbits of some twenty million asteroids, at least a thousand of which are more than half a mile in diameter." *New Yorker*, March 1, 2004, www.newyorker.com/magazine/2004/03/01/chicxulub.

55. Barbara Katz Rothman in *Future Baby*, directed by Maria Arlamovsky (NGF, 2016).

56. Thomas Szasz reads the traditional religious prohibition of suicide as indicative of a profound human anxiety concerning abandonment: "I am suggesting that man's invention of a God from whom he must never be separated and the prohibition of suicide arise from and satisfy the same basic need—the child's need never to be separated from his parent." *Fatal Freedom: The Ethics and Politics of Suicide* (Syracuse: Syracuse University Press, 2002), 112.

57. The point here is not that the man is "bad"—he cares only about his own son—when he should be "good"—a humanitarian who cares about *all* children. Insofar as ethics is ethics and not merely morality, its commitments are dangerously ungrounded. See Derrida's *The Gift of Death*: "What binds me to singularities, to this one or that one, male or female, rather than that one or this one, remains finally unjustifiable. . . . And yet we also do our duty by behaving thus. There is no language, no reason, no generality or mediation to justify this ultimate responsibility." *The Gift of Death*, trans. David Wills (Chicago: University of Chicago Press, 1995), 71.

58. D. W. Winnicott, *Playing and Reality* (New York: Routledge, 1991), 90.

59. Ibid., 41.

3. Maternal Love / Maternal Violence

1. D. W. Winnicott, *Playing and Reality* (New York: Routledge, 1991), 10.

2. Barbara Johnson, *Mother Tongues: Sexuality, Trials, Motherhood, Translation* (Cambridge, Mass.: Harvard University Press, 2003), 85.

3. Ibid.

4. Toni Morrison, *Sula* (New York: Vintage, 1973), 48.

5. Derek Attridge, "Innovation, Literature, Ethics: Relating to the Other," *PMLA* 114, no. 1 (January 1999): 27.

6. Toni Morrison, quoted in Mervyn Rothstein, "Toni Morrison, in Her New Novel, Defends Women," *New York Times*, August 26, 1987.

7. Toni Morrison, *A Mercy* (New York: Random House, 2008), 10. All further references to this text will be parenthetical.

8. Valerie Babb, "*E Pluribus Unum?* The American Origins Narrative in Toni Morrison's *A Mercy*," *MELUS* 36, no. 2 (Summer 2011): 147.

9. John Updike, quoted in ibid., 148.

10. Babb, "*E Pluribus Unum?*," 148.

11. Ibid.

12. Jean Laplanche, *Essays on Otherness*, ed. and trans. John Fletcher (London: Routledge, 1999); Jacques Derrida, *The Gift of Death*, trans. David Wills (Chicago: University of Chicago Press, 1995). For accounts of the ethical that have a particular relationship to Morrison's "maternal ethics," see Thomas Keenan, *Fables of Responsibility: Aberrations and Predicaments in Ethics and Politics* (Stanford, Calif.: Stanford University Press, 1997); and Cathy Caruth, *Unclaimed Experience: Trauma, Narrative, and History* (Baltimore: Johns Hopkins University Press, 1996). Keenan, in an account of Paul de Man's reading of the "blessed babe" passage from book 2 of Wordsworth's *Prelude*, calls attention to the baby's cry and proto-speech act—a cry, so to speak, from the wilderness. "Why is the baby screaming?" asks Keenan. "Because, manifestly the attachment to the mother is something questionable, because the apparently natural legitimacy of the relation is not guaranteed by anything other than the most fragile of conventions. The baby has to claim what is so obvious because it threatens to disappear" (41). The baby's speech, Keenan concludes, is not performative, in the straightforward Austinian sense, because it also claims a fact, "the fact of a relation." "'We,'" Keenan adds, "are that child" (42). Caruth offers an account of Lacan's reading of Freud's "Dream of the Burning Child," an account that also concerns a child's cry (the cry of the dead child in the father's dream) and the parent's experience of his own failure to respond (Caruth, 9). For Caruth, it is the simultaneous experience of missing the death of the other and of nevertheless being called to witness that constitutes a kind of ethical relation.

13. Laplanche, *Essays on Otherness*, 170–71.

14. Ibid., 169. For an insightful and extended Laplanchean reading of *A Mercy*, see Jean Wyatt, "Failed Messages, Maternal Loss, and Narrative Form in Toni Morrison's *A Mercy*," *Modern Fiction Studies* 58, no. 1 (Spring 2012): 128–51. Wyatt's reading emphasizes Florens's developmental blockage and hence the way in which her relationship with the blacksmith traumatically repeats her relationship to her mother: "The many signs of Florens's arrested development that we witness throughout the novel—both linguistic and behavioral—constitute Morrison's indictment of slavery" (130).

15. Jacques Derrida, *Specters of Marx*, trans. Peggy Kamuf (New York: Routledge, 1994): 18.

16. Jonathan Elmer, *On Lingering and Being Last: Race and Sovereignty in the New World* (New York: Fordham University Press, 2008), 44. Elmer's book includes a chapter on Aphra Behn's play *The Widow Ranter* (1690), which is set, like *A Mercy*, in late seventeenth-century Virginia. "Virginia, in Behn's imagination," writes Elmer, "is a place in which private bodies and a 'mechanical' and senseless legality both run amok" (35–36). The New World setting, Elmer continues, "proved to be the most significant stage for the exhibition of this liminal space in which sovereign power and 'bare life' square off" (44).

17. For an account of reviews and responses to *A Mercy* that were determined to connect (the fantasy of) a "postracial" America (Barack Obama's America) with Morrison's "preracial" landscape, see Jessica Wells Cantiello, "From Pre-racial to Post-racial? Reading and Reviewing *A Mercy* in the Age of Obama," *MELUS* 36, no. 2 (Summer 2011): 165–83. Cantiello quotes Morrison at the Los Angeles Central Library in November 2008: "I have to tell you, I really like President-Elect Obama, but I wish he'd stay out of my book reviews and things" (167). Although *A Mercy* isn't "postracial," it is certainly contemporary in a number of ways. It has even, tragically, one might say, become more "contemporary" since its publication, as it aligns clearly with the pressing and present concerns of Black Lives Matter, which would call our attention to the social reproduction of black lives as more crisis ridden than ever.

18. Toni Morrison, *Beloved* (New York: Vintage, 1987), 10.

19. This resonates with Derrida's account of the spectral, "this instant that is not docile to time," in *Specters of Marx*, xix.

20. Quoted in Alan Taylor, *American Colonies* (New York: Viking, 2001), 148.

21. Russell Menard, "From Servitude to Slavery in the Chesapeake," in *Major Problems in American Colonial History*, ed. Karen Ordahl Kupperman (Lexington, Mass.: D. C. Heath, 1993), 110.

22. William Waller Hening, *Statutes at Large: Being a Collection of All the Laws of Virginia*, vol. 2 (Richmond, Va.: Samuel Pleasants, 1809–23), 170.

23. Ibid., 270.

24. Taylor, *American Colonies*, 157.

25. William Byrd, quoted in ibid. Edmund S. Morgan also cites the increased reliance in late seventeenth-century Virginia on the labor of those described as "a brutish sort of people." Quoted in Edmund S. Morgan, *American Slavery, American Freedom: The Ordeal of Colonial Virginia* (New York: Norton, 1975), 315. Indentured white labor, Morgan explains, proved very lucrative in the seventeenth century; but it also produced growing numbers of freedmen who were, in Morgan's words, "Virginia's dangerous men": "The substitution of slaves for servants gradually eased and eventually ended the threat that the freedmen posed" (308).

26. Thomas Hobbes, *Leviathan* (Peterborough, Ont.: Broadview Press, 2002), 151. This is also to suggest that when we enter 1682 Maryland with Morrison's slave mother and her child, we are also stumbling upon one of the founding scenes of modern political philosophy.

27. Ibid.

28. See, for example, Judith Daar, "Federalizing Embryo Transfers: Taming the Wild West of Reproductive Medicine?," *Columbia Journal of Gender and the Law* 23, no. 2 (2012): 257–325; and Meredith Leigh Birdsall, "The Wild West of Reproductive Technology: Ethical and Feminist Perspectives on Sex Selection Practices in the United States," *William and Mary Journal of Women and the Law* 17, no. 1 (2010): 223–47.

29. Dorothy E. Roberts, "Privatization and Punishment in the New Era of Reprogenetics," *Emory Law Journal* 54, no. 3 (2005): 1360.

30. Melinda Cooper, *Life as Surplus: Biotechnology and Capitalism in the Neoliberal Era* (Seattle: University of Washington Press, 2008), 136.

31. Dorothy Roberts refers to George W. Bush's promotion of an "ownership society" and quotes the Cato Institute's description of the concept: "An ownership society values responsibility, liberty and property. Individuals are empowered by freeing them from dependence on government handouts and making them owners instead, in control of their own lives and destinies. In the ownership society, patients control their own health care, parents control their own children's education, and workers control their retirement savings" ("Privatization and Punishment," 1349). For a fictional representation of the reproductive dilemmas of a fifteen-year-old African American girl left to negotiate her own way through the thickets and storms of a neoliberal state of nature, see Jesmyn Ward, *Salvage the Bones* (New York: Bloomsbury, 2011). Pondering the dilemmas that leave her with no choices, Esch concludes, "These are my options, and they narrow to none" (103).

32. Jacob Vaark's "sky vulgar with stars. . . . The silver that glittered there was not at all unreachable. And that wide swath of cream pouring through the stars was his for the tasting" echoes God's promise to Abraham regarding innumerable descendants in Genesis 15:5.

33. Sigmund Freud, "The Transformation of Puberty," in *Three Essays on the Theory of Sexuality*, vol. 7 of *The Standard Edition of the Complete Psychological Works of Sigmund Freud*, ed. James Strachey, trans. James Strachey and Anna Freud (London: Hogarth Press, 1953), 222.

34. See my "Mother's Milk and Sister's Blood: Trauma and the Neoslave Narrative," *differences: A Journal of Feminist Cultural Studies* 8, no. 2 (Summer 1996): 101–26.

35. For a particularly memorable representation of precisely this dynamic, see Herman Melville's *Benito Cereno*. Melville's American captain "discovers" "naked nature," a scene of an enslaved woman nursing her infant, at a moment of psychic crisis: "There's naked nature, now; pure tenderness and love, thought Captain Delano, well pleased." *Benito Cereno* (1856), in *Billy Budd and Other Stories* (New York: Penguin, 1986), 198.

36. Morrison, *Beloved*, 193.

37. Certainly, this commodification recalls contemporary scenes from the frontiers of reproductive politics in which the child is treated as a commodity and the mother's relationship to her child—the mother as "gestational carrier"—is disavowed. See Barbara Katz Rothman's "The Legacy of Patriarchy as Context for Surrogacy; or, Why Are We Quibbling over This?," *American Journal of Bioethics* 14, no. 5 (May 2014): 36–37. "And yes, in this brave new world," Rothman writes, "empowerment for women in poverty can mean selling these services, can mean prostitution, can mean selling organs. It truly can be better to do these things than not. As it could truly be better for a woman in Auschwitz to give sexual services to a guard in exchange for another bit of gruel. The problem lies not with the woman making the 'choice,' but with the situation. We of the wealthy world profit from the exploitation of poor women, men and children with almost every shirt we put on our backs, almost every

bite of food we take. We exploit people in poverty and never have to think about it. And now we can profit in our motherhood—but unlike the shirt and the food, this time the product is going to grow up and demand an explanation" (37).

38. Schoolteacher and his "ethical" solution are very much in line with what Cary Wolfe calls humanist philosophy's "desperate attempt to maintain the species barrier." See Wolfe's insightful account of this "desperation" in *Animal Rites: American Culture, the Discourse of Species, and Posthumanist Theory* (Chicago: University of Chicago Press, 2003), 41.

39. Julia Kristeva, "Freud and Love: Treatment and Its Discontents," trans. Leon S. Roudiez, in *The Kristeva Reader*, ed. Toril Moi (Oxford: Blackwell, 1986), 257.

40. Sigmund Freud, quoted in Ernest Jones, *Sigmund Freud: Life and Work*, vol. 2, *Years of Maturity, 1901–1919* (London: Hogarth Press, 1955), 468.

41. Jacques Lacan, *Écrits: A Selection*, trans. Bruce Fink (New York: Norton, 2002), 300.

42. This representation of blocked, suspended, yet insistent engagement contrasts powerfully with the logocentric fantasy of purified communication represented in *The Road* (the father's voice preserved like the sacred fire that the "good guys" carry).

43. William Faulkner, *Absalom, Absalom!* (New York: Random House, 1990).

44. Contemporary reproductive technology might prompt a rereading of some of these scenes, as genetic testing of the most minimal bit of signifying materiality would now seem to allow us to answer the question of paternity, while simultaneously the status of the mother has been rendered newly uncertain. See Rachel Bowlby, *A Child of One's Own: Parental Stories* (Oxford: Oxford University Press, 2015), 4.

45. Toni Morrison, *Jazz* (New York: Vintage, 1992), 178.

46. An American literary history of this trajectory would want to turn to Nathaniel Hawthorne's *The Scarlet Letter* (1850), another important source text for Morrison.

47. Jacques Derrida, *Limited Inc.,* trans. Samuel Weber and Jeffrey Mehlman (Evanston, Ill.: Northwestern University Press, 1988), 8.

48. See particularly Morrison's *Sula*. Nel witnesses her mother's undoing, following a failed scene of recognition, and resolves "to be on guard—always" (28). This repeats Shadrack's story with a difference and thus aligns the trauma of war—shell shock—with the trauma of racial subject formation in the United States in the 1920s. See also the paired set of mirror scenes, which offer first to Shadrack and then to Nel the image as a compensatory form.

49. See also the significance of birds for scenes of maternal abandonment and protection in *Beloved*: "Little hummingbirds stuck their needle beaks right through her headcloth into her hair and beat their wings. And if she thought anything, it was No. No. Nono. Nonono. Simple. She just flew. Collected every bit of life she had made, all the parts of her that were precious and fine and beautiful, and carried, pushed, dragged them through the veil, out away, over there where no one could hurt

them. Over there. Outside this place, where they would be safe. And the humming-bird wings beat on" (163).

50. Here, one might consider Freud's relationship to folk interpretations of dreams with regard to his new psychoanalytic method. Unlike the modern scientists and philosophers who Freud claims regard dreams as meaningless, the "common" people have always known that dreams are meaningful structures. In fact, the very last words of *The Interpretation of Dreams* mark both Freud's continuity and his distinction from this older tradition. Freud claims with a rhetorical flourish that dreams do, in a certain sense, predict the future: "By picturing our wishes as fulfilled, dreams are after all leading us into the future. But this future, which the dreamer pictures as the present, has been moulded by his indestructible wish into a perfect likeness of the past." *The Interpretation of Dreams*, part 2, and *On Dreams*, vol. 5 of *The Standard Edition of the Complete Psychological Works of Sigmund Freud*, ed. and trans. James Strachey (London: Hogarth Press, 1953), 621.

51. Jean Laplanche, "Transference: Its Provocation by the Analyst," trans. Luke Thurston, in *Essays on Otherness*, 222.

52. Morrison, *Beloved*, xiii.

53. Derrida, *Specters of Marx*, 9.

54. One of the striking things about *Beloved* is that Sethe makes a different choice the second time around; but for Beloved, her infant, it means the same thing, it repeats the same message. This is because the trauma in question is abandonment, not death as such. Beloved is a figure for trauma, and so, by definition, in a sense, she cannot have a future. Instead, this possibility is split off onto Denver and perhaps Sethe herself.

55. Jacques Derrida, *Given Time: I. Counterfeit Money*, trans. Peggy Kamuf (Chicago: University of Chicago Press, 1995), 14.

56. Derrida, *Gift of Death*, 41.

57. Morrison's meditations on survival in *A Mercy* and *Beloved* (and certainly also elsewhere) could be considered together with Derrida's writing on survival and "*survivance*" ("That is what the self is, that is what I am, what the *I* is, whether I am there or not"), particularly in his last published seminar, *The Beast and the Sovereign*, vol. 2, trans. Geoffrey Bennington (Chicago: University of Chicago Press, 2011), 131. In *The End of the World and Other Teachable Moments: Jacques Derrida's Final Seminar* (New York: Fordham University Press, 2014), Michael Naas articulates the connection between the archive (or the trace) and survival in a way that particularly resonates with Morrison's work: "No immortality of the soul, therefore, no authentic experience of death or facing up to death as such, only a finite and contingent survival in the archive, a survival—and thus an archivization—that begins with the first trace and that thus takes place always and from the beginning *without me.*" (140).

58. Winnicott, *Playing and Reality*, 10.

59. I'm reminded here of Harriet Jacobs's / Linda Brent's complex relationship to agency in *Incidents in the Life of a Slave Girl*, ed. Jean Fagan Yellin (Cambridge,

Mass.: Harvard University Press, 1987); and of the story that Jonathan Safran Foer tells of his starving grandmother at the end of World War II in *Eating Animals* (New York: Little, Brown, 2009). In the former book, Linda Brent defends herself against rape or a mock-consensual relationship with her owner, Dr. Flint, by "choosing" a relationship with Mr. Sands. In *Eating Animals*, Foer tells the story of his starving grandmother's refusal to eat the piece of meat that a Russian farmer offers to her:

"'He saved your life.'

"'I didn't eat it.'

"'You didn't eat it?'

"'It was pork. I wouldn't eat pork.'

"'Why?'

"'What do you mean why?'

"'What, because it wasn't kosher?'

"'Of course.'

"'But not even to save your life?'

"'If nothing matters, there is nothing to save'" (16–17).

60. Emma Donoghue, *Room* (Toronto: HarperCollins, 2011), 236.

4. "Monstrous Decision"

1. See Lauren Sandler, "The Childfree Life: When Having It All Means Not Having Children," *Time*, August 12, 2013, http://content.time.com/time/subscriber/article /0,33009,2148636,00.html; and Meghan Daum, *Selfish, Shallow, and Self-Absorbed: Sixteen Writers on the Decision NOT to Have Kids* (New York: Picador, 2015). In 2012, the American Society for Reproductive Medicine removed the "experimental" label from "egg freezing," or, as it is known, "vitrification." This "revolutionary" technique has made it easier to send "sex cells and embryos ping-ponging around the globe"— presumably to the advantage of some and the disadvantage of others. Vitrification can also be used to facilitate "fertility preservation," and in 2014 both Apple and Facebook announced that vitrification would be offered as a benefit to their employees: "Some observers saw it as benefitting women: more reproductive freedom in a male-dominated industry. Others saw it as avoidance of a greater challenge: integration of work and family life." Egg freezing, it would seem important to note, fosters the illusion of an infinitely deferrable decision. See Kate Allen, "Take One Egg. Cool to Minus 196 C. Revolutionize Fertility," *Toronto Star*, November 26, 2016, https:// www.thestar.com/news/world/2016/11/26/take-one-egg-cool-to-196-c-revolutionize -fertility.html.

2. See Michelle Goldberg, *The Means of Reproduction: Sex, Power, and the Future of the World* (New York: Penguin, 2009), for a complicating argument. Goldberg suggests that, contrary to the antifeminist position of notorious Christian conservatives who associate women's freedom with depopulation, "women's liberty" and the necessary accompanying social supports result in "healthy fertility rates" (222).

3. Reproductive "choice" is, of course, bound up with and complicated by racial and class hierarchies. On the racial politics of reproduction, see Dorothy Roberts,

Killing the Black Body: Race, Reproduction, and the Meaning of Liberty (New York: Vintage, 1997); Rickie Solinger, *Pregnancy and Power: A Short History of Reproductive Politics in America* (New York: New York University Press, 2005); and Judith Stadtman Tucker, "Is Motherhood a Class Privilege in America? An Interview with Historian Rickie Solinger, author of *Beggars and Choosers*," *Mothers Movement Online*, October 2004, http://www.mothersmovement.org/features/solinger/solinger_p1.htm. Roberts writes, "Reproductive liberty must encompass more than the protection of an individual woman's choice to end her pregnancy. It must encompass the full range of procreative activities, including the ability to bear a child, and it must acknowledge that we make reproductive decisions within a social context, including inequalities of wealth and power. *Reproductive freedom is a matter of social justice,* not individual choice" (*Killing the Black Body,* 6). See also Alys Eve Weinbaum, *Wayward Reproductions: Genealogies of Race and Nation in Transatlantic Modern Thought* (Durham, N.C.: Duke University Press, 2004): "Although the sexual economy of reproduction has begun to budge . . . the racial economy of the new reproduction within which the sexual economy is imbricated remains quite static" (232).

4. Lionel Shriver, *We Need to Talk about Kevin* (New York: Harper Perennial, 2006). Future references to this text will be parenthetical.

5. *Thursday* is a kind of nonname that functions like a name, somewhat analogous to "9/11." See Derrida on this particularly charged naming in Giovanna Borradori's *Philosophy in a Time of Terror: Dialogues with Jürgen Habermas and Jacques Derrida* (Chicago: University of Chicago Press, 2003): "But this very thing, the place and meaning of this 'event,' remains ineffable, like an intuition without concept, like a unicity with no generality on the horizon or with no horizon at all . . . reduced to pronouncing mechanically a date, repeating it endlessly, as a kind of ritual incantation, a conjuring poem, a journalistic litany or rhetorical refrain that admits to not knowing what it's talking about" (86).

6. See Andrew Solomon's *Far from the Tree: Parents, Children, and the Search for Identity* (New York: Scribner, 2012), on the tenacity and complexity of parental feelings of responsibility. Solomon interviews, among many others, the parents of children who have committed violent crimes. He is astonished by his meeting with the Klebolds (the parents of Dylan Klebold, one of the two shooters at Columbine High School in April 1999): "I set out to interview Tom and Sue Klebold with the expectation that meeting them would help to illuminate their son's actions. The better I came to know the Klebolds, the more deeply mystified I became" (587). See also "The Reckoning," Solomon's portrait of and interview with Peter Lanza, the father of Adam Lanza, who killed twenty-six people at Sandy Hook Elementary School as well as his mother and himself. Andrew Solomon, "The Reckoning," *New Yorker,* March 17, 2014, http://www.newyorker.com/magazine/2014/03/17/the-reckoning.

7. Lionel Shriver, "Failed Novels, Maternal Ambivalence, and the Orange Prize," supplementary material in *We Need to Talk about Kevin,* 9.

8. Bruno Bettelheim, "Feral or Autistic Children," *American Journal of Sociology* 14, no. 5 (1959): 467. See, too, Bettelheim on the "living soul . . . with death for a

master," whether it be the infant with an unloving mother or the inmate of a concentration camp. *Surviving the Holocaust* (London: Fontana Paperbacks, 1986), 103.

9. Christine Overall, *Why Have Children? The Ethical Debate* (Cambridge, Mass.: MIT Press, 2012), 3; David Benatar, *Better Never to Have Been: The Harm of Coming into Existence* (Oxford: Clarendon Press, 2006). Further references to these texts will be parenthetical.

10. Benatar's work calls to mind a more poignant engagement with the nonconsensual dimension of being in Marilynne Robinson's *Housekeeping* (New York: Farrar, Straus & Giroux, 1980): "Of my conception I know only what you know of yours. It occurred in darkness and I was unconsenting. . . . My ravishers left their traces in me, male and female . . . and oblivion expelled me. . . . By some bleak alchemy what had been mere unbeing becomes death when life is mingled with it. So they seal the door against our returning" (215).

11. "Lest it be thought that the arguments I advance are intended as mere philosophical games or jokes," Benatar adds, "I should emphasize that I am entirely serious in my arguments and I believe the conclusions" (5). Benatar is also a self-proclaimed "pro-death" proponent of abortion: "[T]he failure to abort is what must be defended" (133).

12. Overall could be said to overemphasize the one-off nature of this decision. One might suggest instead that the parent-guardian is always remaking this decision.

13. Jacques Derrida, *The Gift of Death*, trans. David Wills (Chicago: University of Chicago Press, 1995), 24.

14. Jacques Derrida, "Force of Law: The Mystical Foundation of Authority," *Cardoza Law Review* 11, nos. 5–6 (1990): 961.

15. Derrida, *Gift of Death*, 34.

16. Derrida, "Force of Law," 965.

17. L. A. Paul, "What You Can't Expect When You're Expecting," *Res Philosophica* 92, no. 2 (April 2015): 20–21. Parenthetically, Paul suggests that "[t]he rhetoric of the debate over abortion and medical advances in contraceptive technology have probably also contributed to the framing of the decision to have a child as a personal choice" (21). But it is precisely the "modern conception of self-realization" through "making reflective rational choices about the sort of person one wants to be," Paul continues, that is undone by the decision about reproduction.

18. This wildness or irreducible trace of the madness of decision is also registered in Andrew Solomon's work via the figure of the "horizontally identified" child—the child who will form relations of similarity outside of the "vertical" structure of familial reproduction. See also Shriver's invocation of the groundlessness of reproduction in "Be Here Now Means Be Gone Later," which speculates that although "[n]umerous factors have contributed to the Incredible Shrinking Family . . . I believe all of these contributing elements may be subsidiary to a larger transformation in Western culture no less profound than our collective consensus on what life is for." "Be Here Now Means Be Gone Later," in Daum, *Selfish, Shallow, and Self-Absorbed*, 80.

19. There's something particularly strange about categorizing coming into existence as "an unusual case"!

20. Jacques Derrida, *Adieu to Emmanuel Levinas* (Stanford, Calif.: Stanford University Press, 1999), 23.

21. See Colson Whitehead's account of reproduction and the zombie apocalypse in *Zone One*: "'Enough babies,' she said. Before the plague, he'd always thought it weird when people said that, as they croaked about overpopulation, the millions of kids in want of a good-home, ever-shrinking planetary resources. . . . Now Mark Spitz understood plainly what they had meant by 'What kind of person would bring a child into this world?' . . . The answer was, 'Only a monster would bring a child into this world.'" Colson Whitehead, *Zone One* (New York: Anchor, 2011), 246.

22. On the belated or repeated taking up of a maternal role, see Alice Munro's magisterial "My Mother's Dream," in *The Love of a Good Woman* (Toronto: McClelland & Stewart, 1998).

23. On wanting an "own child," specifically in relation to new reproductive technologies, see Karin Lesnik-Oberstein, *On Having an Own Child: Reproductive Technologies and the Cultural Construction of Childhood* (London: Karnac, 2007). Obviously, the feminist implications of the literary text do not necessarily align clearly with the professed views of the author. Shriver elsewhere displays a not atypical discomfort with the term *feminism* ("About the Author," supplementary material in Shriver, *We Need to Talk about Kevin*, 3). For more on the vexed patriarchal reproduction of the same, see the father in McCarthy's *The Road*, or Jacob Vaark in Morrison's *A Mercy* (discussed in chapters 2 and 3, respectively).

24. Lisa Guenther, *The Gift of the Other: Levinas and the Politics of Reproduction* (Albany: State University of New York Press, 2006), 11.

25. Ibid., 10–11.

26. Ibid., 10.

27. Ibid., 11.

28. Ibid., 57.

29. This passage, once again, recalls Lee Edelman's discussion of reproductive futurity as a form of deep nostalgia and conservatism. *No Future: Queer Theory and the Death Drive* (Durham, N.C.: Duke University Press, 2004). It is the father's childhood that Eva's husband wants to preserve in the life of his son. And in this respect, Kevin's father also recalls many aspects of the father in McCarthy's *The Road*.

30. *We Need to Talk about Kevin*, in other words, is hardly a blame-the-mother narrative, even as blaming the father isn't really the point either. Rather, both Shriver and Winnicott use the maternal figure and maternal labor as the privileged site for working through the difficulties of all relation. See, too, Sara Ruddick, *Maternal Thinking* (Toronto: Demeter Press, 2009). Ruddick suggests that we think in terms of maternal labor whether it is men or women who perform this work. Winnicott has very little to say about fathers, although the presumption might be that fathers can mother, even if they take the male analyst (Winnicott), rather than the mother herself, as their model. See Adam Phillips on Winnicott and fathers in *Winnicott* (London: Fontana, 1988).

31. What would happen, Jessica Benjamin asks, if the infant didn't provide an early "glimmer of recognition as a sign of the mutuality that persists in spite of the

tremendous inequality of the parent–child relationship?" *The Bonds of Love: Psychoanalysis, Feminism, and the Problem of Domination* (New York: Random House, 1988), 14.

32. See, again, Munro's "My Mother's Dream," in which the crying baby is an axe-wielding murderer (figuratively speaking): "I sent a meat cleaver cry down on her head" (322); "My crying is a knife to cut out of her life all that isn't useful. To me" (319). There is a rich history (one that would include Rousseau and Freud, as well as Munro and Sendak) of equating infants and tyrants.

33. Referring to Franklin as a "liberal" father, Eva also suggests that Kevin is in some sense the product of a specific historical understanding of parenting and of the child: "I mean that when I was a kid, parents called the shots. Now I'm a parent, kids call the shots. So we get fucked coming and going" (107). Compare this with Philip Roth's Jerry Levov, in *American Pastoral*, berating his "liberal" brother, who is also the father to a destructive child: "Sure, it's 'liberal'—I know, a liberal father. But what does that mean? What is at the *center* of it? Always holding things together. And look where the fuck it's got you! . . . No you didn't make the war. You made the angriest kid in America. Ever since she was a kid, every word she *spoke* was a bomb." *American Pastoral* (London: Vintage, 1998), 279.

34. The infant Kevin exhausts two nannies, one of whom Eva reaches out to, asking if Kevin "responds" to her. The nanny, Siobhan, answers with uncharacteristic bitterness: "*Respond?* . . . You could say that" (102). When Kevin begins to speak, after much delay, his first words are a sentence, uttered in response to the afterschool cartoons that Eva switches on as a form of stimulation: "'I don like dat.' . . . He repeated levelly, 'I don like dat'" (114). The idea that identity is formed in part through repeated performances of rejection is not a surprising one, but for Kevin this negativity is exclusive and unrelenting.

35. In an earlier scene, Eva slaps Kevin and is told by her horrified husband, "There's a consensus—that violence is no way to get your point across" (128). Franklin's exclamation is, of course, deeply ironic in the context of this story.

36. D. W. Winnicott, "Hate in the Counter-Transference," *International Journal of Psychoanalysis* 30 (1949): 72.

37. D. W. Winnicott, *Playing and Reality* (New York: Routledge, 1991), 92.

38. Ibid., 91.

39. Benjamin, *Bonds of Love*, 68.

40. Much of what occurs here I have glossed in my earlier discussion of Spike Jonze's *Where the Wild Things Are* (see the Introduction). In the film, Max anxiously fears that he has destroyed his mother, but he takes a passage through an alternate world to rediscover that she is still there; however vulnerable she is, she has survived his destruction (in the book, her survival is represented by the hot supper waiting for him).

41. Winnicott, *Playing and Reality*, 91.

42. Winnicott crucially deploys the term and concept of "use" in the way that one might expect him to deploy the word *relate*. Indeed, he crucially reverses the

significance of these two terms. This conceptual shift is inseparable from Winnicott's more general critique of psychoanalytic thought as concerned with the isolated subject—he refers to "the world of difference that there is between relating and usage." And this "world of difference" is the *world*: "If I am right in this, then it follows that discussion of the subject of relating is a much easier exercise for analysts than is the discussion of usage, since relating may be examined as a phenomenon of the subject and psychoanalysis always likes to be able to eliminate all factors that are environmental" (ibid., 88). Winnicott's "use" might be associated with the poststructuralist and posthumanist critique of "relation" as reciprocal and consensual.

43. It's worth recalling that the narrative is entirely from Eva's perspective, and this means that suspecting her reliability is structurally part of the event of reading the text. In other words, rather than dismissing either "the bad seed" or "the monstrous mother," Shriver's novel cleverly keeps both in play.

44. Note that Eva's affinity for empty form twins her with Kevin, whose monstrousness repeatedly takes on this same characteristic: "Kevin was a shell game in which all three cups were empty" (234). Eva searches Kevin's face, looking for her husband, but instead encounters her own reflection.

45. Winnicott, "Hate in the Counter-Transference," 72.

46. Recall here the man's first words to his son in *The Road* ("I'm right here" [5]) and Ma's assertion in *Room* ("I think what babies want is mostly to have their mothers right there" [233]).

47. Winnicott writes, "Now I want to add that in certain stages of certain analyses the analyst's hate is actually sought by the patient, and what is then needed is hate that is objective. If the patient seeks objective or justified hate he must be able to reach it, else he cannot feel he can reach objective love" ("Hate in the Counter-Transference," 72). See also the story Winnicott tells in the same article about how he barely managed to refrain from hitting a runaway nine-year-old boy who was in his care: "The important thing is that each time, just as I put him outside the door, I told him something; I said that what had happened had made me hate him. This was easy because it was so true. I think these words were important from the point of view of his progress, but they were mainly important in enabling me to tolerate the situation without letting out, without losing my temper and every now and again murdering him" (73).

5. "Dis-ap-peared"

1. Hannah Arendt, "The Crisis in Education," in *Between Past and Future: Six Exercises in Political Thought* (New York: Viking, 1961), 191.

2. Ibid.

3. Michael Grossberg, "Liberation and Caretaking: Fighting over Children's Rights in Postwar America," in *Reinventing Childhood after World War II*, ed. Paula S. Fass and Michael Grossberg (Philadelphia: University of Pennsylvania Press, 2012), 19–37.

4. Arendt, "Crisis in Education," 192–93.

5. Grossberg, "Liberation and Caretaking," 22.

6. Ibid.

7. See, for example, Richard Farson, *Birthrights* (New York: Macmillan, 1974); and John Holt, *Escape from Childhood: The Needs and Rights of Children* (New York: Dutton, 1974).

8. Grossberg, "Liberation and Caretaking," 22.

9. Bruce C. Hafen and Jonathan O. Hafen, "Abandoning Children to Their Rights," *First Things,* August–September 1995, 18–24, https://www.firstthings.com / . . . /001-abandoning-children-to-their-rights.

10. Grossberg, "Liberation and Caretaking," 29. Article 3.2 of the Convention on the Rights of the Child states, for example, that "States Parties undertake to ensure the child such protection and care as is necessary for his or her well-being, taking into account the rights and duties of his or her parents, legal guardians, or other individuals legally responsible for him or her, and, to this end, shall take all appropriate legislative and administrative measures." Article 12.1 asserts that "States Parties shall assure to the child who is capable of forming his or her own views the right to express those views freely in all matters affecting the child, the views of the child being given due weight in accordance with the age and maturity of the child." See the website of the UN High Commissioner for Human Rights for the full text of the convention: http://www.ohchr.org/en/professionalinterest/pages/crc.aspx.

11. Elizabeth Young-Bruehl, *Childism: Confronting Prejudice against Children* (New Haven, Conn.: Yale University Press, 2012), 12–13.

12. Ibid., 13.

13. Ibid., 15. For more on this development, see Rebecca Dingo, "Securing the Nation: Neoliberalism's U.S. Family Values in a Transnational Gendered Economy," *Journal of Women's History* 16, no. 3 (2004): 173–86.

14. Young-Bruehl, *Childism,* 16.

15. Ibid., 131.

16. Ibid., 139.

17. Paula S. Fass, "Is There a Story in the History of Childhood?," introduction to *The Routledge History of Childhood in the Western World,* ed. Paula S. Fass (New York: Routledge, 2013), 14.

18. Steven Mintz, *Huck's Raft: A History of American Childhood* (Cambridge, Mass.: Belknap Press of Harvard University Press, 2004), 337. For the origin of discourses of child protection, see Viviana A. Zelizer, *Pricing the Priceless Child: The Changing Social Value of Children* (Princeton, N.J.: Princeton University Press, 1985). For a recent intriguing take on zombie fiction as a discourse of child protection, see James Berger, "Propagation and Procreation: The Zombie and the Child," in *Race, Gender, and Sexuality in Post-apocalyptic TV and Film,* ed. Barbara Gurr (Houndmills, U.K.: Palgrave Macmillan, 2015), 149–63.

19. Young-Bruehl, *Childism,* 212. For a more recent "confusion" of politics and pedophilia and another version of the "politicized pedophile," see "PizzaGate": Gregor Aisch, Jon Huang, and Cecilia Kang, "Dissecting the #PizzaGate Conspiracy

Theory," *New York Times,* December 10, 2016, https://www.nytimes.com/interactive
/2016/12/10/business/media/pizzagate.html?_r=0. "In the span of a few weeks, a false
rumor that Hillary Clinton and her top aides were involved in various crimes snow-
balled into a wild conspiracy theory that they were running a child-trafficking ring
out of a Washington pizza parlor."

20. See Jacques Derrida's invocation of the autoimmune in, among other places,
"Autoimmunity: Real and Apparent Suicides," in *Philosophy in a Time of Terror: Dia-
logues with Jürgen Habermas and Jacques Derrida* (Chicago: University of Chicago
Press, 2004), and *Rogues: Two Essays on Reason* (Stanford, Calif.: Stanford University
Press, 2005).

21. Rony Brauman, "Contradictions of Humanitarianism," trans. Bridget Conley
and Emily Apter, *Alphabet City* 7 (2000): 47. For a series of approaches to critical
human rights theory, see Ian Balfour and Eduardo Cadava, eds., "And Justice for
All? The Claims of Human Rights: An Introduction," special issue of *South Atlantic
Quarterly* 103, nos. 2–3 (2004). For discussions of children's rights in particular, see
Jacqueline Bhabha, "The Child—What Sort of Human?," *PMLA* 121, no. 5 (2006):
1526–35; and Julia O'Connell Davidson, *Children in the Global Sex Trade* (Cambridge,
U.K.: Polity Press, 2005). Davidson writes, "Is the utopianism embodied in dominant
children's rights talk, with its emphasis on children's universal right to 'childhood,'
likely to address the structural inequalities and oppressions that affect particular sections of humanity, both child and adult?" (63).

22. *Prisoners,* directed by Denis Villeneuve (Warner Home Video, 2013), DVD. A
"final" version of the script (which nevertheless differs from the final film version)
can be found online, at http://www.pages.drexel.edu/~ina22/splaylib/Screenplay
-Prisoners.pdf.

23. A. O. Scott, "After Two Children Vanish, Agony Begets Recklessness: Review
of *Prisoners* by Denis Villeneuve," *New York Times,* September 19, 2013.

24. Guzikowski's screenplay came out in the same year as Jane Mayer's masterful
account of the Bush-Cheney regime's "war on terror," *The Dark Side.* "In the day and
age we live in," Mayer quotes Cheney as saying, "with the threats we face, I believe
in a strong, robust executive authority, and I think the world we live in demands it."
Jane Mayer, *The Dark Side: The Inside Story of How the War on Terror Turned into a
War on American Ideals* (New York: Doubleday, 2008), 59. Marc Redfield refers to
this characteristic gesture, whereby the questionable actions of the American state
are framed as responses to a demand coming from the enemy (or from a "world"
or an "age" of danger), as the "*fort-da* game" that the sovereign plays with himself,
"relegat[ing] sovereignty to the other in order to take it back." Marc Redfield, *The
Rhetoric of Terror: Reflections on 9/11 and the War on Terror* (New York: Fordham
University Press, 2009), 130. The almost unbearable loss that this *fort-da* game would
presumably try to master is the loss of the idea of America itself. Guantanamo Bay,
wrote Thomas Friedman in the New York Times, "is the anti–Statue of Liberty"
(quoted in Mayer, *Dark Side,* 313).

25. Scott, "After Two Children Vanish."

26. French Canadian Villeneuve was best known, previously, for *Incendies,* an adaptation of Wajdi Mouawad's play set during the Lebanese civil war; and *Polytechnique,* a haunting retelling of the massacre of women engineering students at Montreal's *École Polytechnique* in 1989. *Incendies* made the *New York Times* list of the top ten films of 2011 and was nominated for the Academy Award for Best Foreign Language Film. *Polytechnique* was screened at Cannes in 2009 and was named the best Canadian film of 2009 by the Toronto Film Critics Association. The Guzikowski script for *Prisoners* was completed in 2009 and won several screenwriting competitions in the years before Villeneuve finally succeeded in bringing it to the screen. If *Prisoners* exemplifies the paranoid "paternal" narrative I've invoked in these pages, Villeneuve's critically acclaimed 2016 film, *Arrival* (with a screenplay by Eric Heisserer and based on a short story by Ted Chiang), tells the "maternal," depressive story.

27. Scott, "After Two Children Vanish." Scott continues: "*Prisoners* is the kind of movie that can quiet a room full of casual thrill-seekers. . . . It absorbs and controls your attention with such assurance that you hold your breath for fear of distracting people on the screen."

28. David Denby, "Search Missions: *Prisoners* and *Salinger,*" *New Yorker,* September 23, 2013; online at http://www.newyorker.com/magazine/2013/09/23/search -missions.

29. Christine Overall, *Why Have Children? The Ethical Debate* (Cambridge, Mass.: MIT Press, 2012), 17.

30. Werner Hamacher, "The Right to Have Rights (Four-and-a-Half Remarks)," *South Atlantic Quarterly* 103, nos. 2–3 (2004): 343–56.

31. This is clearly a portrait of what Rebecca Dingo calls "familial individualism" (see "Securing the Nation"). See also Villeneuve's comments on *Prisoners* as akin to a western (in an online interview for *Télérama* in 2013): "*Prisoners* traite d'une certaine paranoïa propre aux États-Unis, d'une tension entre l'individualité et les institutions, d'une fragilité du tissu social, de la déresponsabilisation par rapport à la torture et la violence. Pour moi, c'est un film douloureusement américain, proche d'un western." "Denis Villeneuve: 'Prisoners' est un film douloureusement américain, proche d'un western," interview by Jacques Morice, *Télérama,* September 10, 2013, http://www.telerama.fr/cinema/denis-villeneuve-prisoners-est-un-film -douloureusement-americain-proche-d-un-western,103305.php. These remarks also recall McCarthy's *The Road,* a text surely "proche d'un western" in more than one sense, and McCarthy's own relationship to that which is "douloureusement américain." Part of what is distinctive about *Prisoners* is its characteristic deployment of Hollywood modes of identification, even as one might think—and this is borne out by Villeneuve's comments—that it is up to something else. Here, I have in mind the way in which Keller Dover is simultaneously a Christian survivalist and a kind of everyman American father figure. Note how the racial identity of the African American friends and neighbors, the Birches (played by Viola Davis and Terrence Howard), is supposed to be of absolutely no significance. They merely happen to be the

cultured and well-educated (she is a veterinarian) family next door. Their race is, however, used to raise Keller Dover above the level of the merely right-wing fringe subject.

32. Brauman, "Contradictions of Humanitarianism," 48.

33. The look of *Prisoners* tends to contribute to this almost apocalyptic sense of "no future"; the "somber cinematography" of Roger A. Deakins (who also filmed *Fargo* and *No Country for Old Men*, among many others), writes A. O. Scott, "turns the Keystone State into a study of grays and browns, dead leaves and bare trees, under a sky like wet metal" ("After Two Children Vanish").

34. Denby, "Search Missions."

35. "Keller" is quite interesting as a name, beyond its proximity to *killer*. Primarily a last name, in German it means "cellar" or "basement," and, of course, such spaces have a particular significance in *Prisoners*. Also, this word seems to be used in several suggestive common figurative phrases, such as *im Keller sein* ("to reach rock bottom"), or *eine Leiche im Keller haben* ("to have a skeleton in the closet").

36. Denby, "Search Missions."

37. Hamacher, "Right to Have Rights," 350. All further references to this text will be parenthetical.

38. Hamacher's critique of human rights theory resonates with certain posthumanist theories of the political. See, for example, Jane Bennett's *Vibrant Matter: A Political Ecology of Things* (Durham, N.C.: Duke University Press, 2009): "[I]f human intentionality can be agentic only if accompanied by a vast entourage of nonhumans, then it seems that the appropriate unit of analysis for democratic theory is neither the individual human nor an exclusively human collective but the (ontologically heterogenous) 'public' coalescing around a problem" (108).

39. Alice Munro, "My Mother's Dream," in *The Love of a Good Woman* (Toronto: McClelland & Stewart, 1998), 293–340.

40. Cormac McCarthy, *The Road* (New York: Vintage, 2006), 87.

41. Ibid., 77. There is some indication in *Prisoners* that the family is also struggling economically. Although financial security might be said to be beside the point for the father in McCarthy's novel, in both instances, on the one hand, a certain security discourse and a regressive patriarchal fantasy may be seen as responses to economic and symbolic precariousness (in the era of "the end of men"). On the other hand, an excess of financial security produces similar fantasies among certain survivalist billionaires!

42. Lee Edelman, *No Future: Queer Theory and the Death Drive* (Durham, N.C.: Duke University Press, 2004), 216.

43. See Elaine Scarry, *The Body in Pain: The Making and Unmaking of the World* (New York: Oxford University Press, 1985); and Jonathan Elmer, "Torture and Hyperbole," *Law, Culture, and the Humanities* 3, no. 1 (2007): 18–34.

44. Keller Dover laments, along with Cormac McCarthy's protagonist, "On this road there are no godspoke men. They are gone and I am left and they have taken with them the world" (*The Road*, 32).

45. Absolute protection (as the other narratives examined in this study would seem to know) precludes a relation with the very child to be protected; hence David Benatar's insistent refrain in *Better Never to Have Been: The Harm of Coming into Existence* (Oxford: Clarendon Press, 2006): if you really want to protect a child, don't have a child! See also Tim Kreider's "The End of the Line," an essay in a collection devoted to writers writing about choosing not to be parents: "[O]ne of the reasons I don't want children is fear. I'm afraid that if I ever did have children of my own I would love them so painfully it would rip my soul in half, that I would never again have a waking moment free from the terror that something bad might ever happen to them." Tim Kreider, "The End of the Line," in *Selfish, Shallow, and Self-Absorbed: Sixteen Writers on the Decision NOT to Have Kids*, ed. Meghan Daum (New York: Picador, 2015), 271.

46. Early in the movie, the children show an interest in the RV that Alex has parked in their neighborhood; we later learn that he gave the daughters a ride and that it was his "aunt," Holly Jones, who decided to turn this into a kidnapping: "You should know," Holly tells Dover, "Alex didn't lay a hand on the girls, just wanted to give them a ride in the RV. I was the one who decided they should stay." This remark deserves its own reading: Why would Holly Jones, the film's terrifying nihilist, feel the need to defend or exonerate Alex here? Is it she or the film that needs to make this clear to Dover and the audience? It could be thought of as a final maternal gesture on her part, protecting Alex from guilt and taking it all upon herself, even as it also exposes the film's misogynist determination to displace guilt onto the monstrous mother. The script also tells us that Holly's comments have the appropriate effect on Dover: "Guilt creasing his forehead, Keller starts to look a little sick" (Guzikowski, *Prisoners*, 199).

47. Jean Laplanche, "Seduction, Persecution, Revelation," in *Essays on Otherness*, ed. and trans. John Fletcher (London: Routledge, 1999), 191.

48. In chapter 4, I noted a similar structure at work in Lionel Shriver's *We Need to Talk about Kevin*: Kevin's uncertainty regarding the grounds for his being manifests as a desire to randomly end the lives of others. Compare, too, Ben's father's apparent ambivalence with respect to his son's conception in Kenneth Oppel's *Half Brother* (New York: Scholastic, 2010) (see Afterword); and the prayerlike address to a child concerning the excessive desire—the wanting-in-advance—that preceded his or her coming into being in Maggie Nelson's *The Argonauts* (Minneapolis: Graywolf Press, 2015). David Grossman's words, quoted in George Packer, "The Unconsoled: A Writer's Tragedy and a Nation's" (profile of David Grossman), *New Yorker*, September 27, 2010, 1–11, and used as an epigraph to chapter 3 (on Morrison's *A Mercy*), describe a maternal refusal (also expressed by Ma in *Room*) to play into a patriarchal game of sacrifice (the fantasy of an all-justifying and fully realizable paternal promise). The murder of children (in *Prisoners* and *We Need to Talk about Kevin*) expresses a destructively nihilistic response to the exposure of the emptiness of this sacrificial, promissory logic. There is something antisacrificial, in other words, about

a maternal, posthumanist ethics of relation that combines a commitment to social reproduction with a refusal of the fantasy of absolute redemption or protection.

49. Although Munro's story is both of and about an earlier historical moment, its affective economy is similar to that of *Room*, and thus we could say that "Miles City, Montana" is to *Prisoners* as *Room* is to *The Road*.

50. Jean Laplanche, *New Foundations for Psychoanalysis*, trans. David Macey (Oxford: Basil Blackwell, 1989), 90.

51. Ibid., 90–91.

52. *Future Baby*, directed by Maria Arlamovsky (NGF, 2016).

53. This promise harks back to the depressive possibility that I explored in my reading of McCarthy's *The Road* in chapter 2. More generally, it would be fair to say that a maternal ethics is intimately associated with reparative possibility, partly as a response to patriarchal paranoid-schizoid tendencies. See Melanie Klein, *The Selected Melanie Klein*, ed. Juliet Mitchell (New York: Free Press, 1986); and Eve Sedgwick, "Paranoid Reading and Reparative Reading; or, You're So Paranoid, You Probably Think This Essay Is about You," in *Touching Feeling: Affect, Pedagogy, Performativity* (Durham, N.C.: Duke University Press, 2003), 123–51.

54. Alice Munro, "Miles City, Montana," in *The Progress of Love* (London: Vintage, 1985), 87. All further references to this story will be given parenthetically.

55. Laplanche, *New Foundations for Psychoanalysis*, 18.

56. "Steve Gauley," as a repeated signifier, on the one hand, at once inscribes an unredeemable, unbound, and enigmatic excess and constitutes a (maternal?) attempt, on the part of the narrator, to bind this excess into signification. On the other hand, providing maternal grief would seem to be the lifelong and monstrous task taken up by Holly Jones, the bereaved mother in *Prisoners*.

57. See Munro's autobiographical sketch "The Eye" for another unforgettable "gift of death." When a beloved babysitter dies in an accident, Munro's mother takes her young daughter to visit the parents and see the body: "Come now," [my mother] said to me. Her gentleness sounded hateful to me, triumphant. . . . I looked straight into the coffin and saw Sadie. . . . Something moved. I saw it, her eyelid on my side moved. . . . I was not surprised then and not in the least scared. Instantly, this sight fell into everything I knew about Sadie and somehow, as well, into whatever special experience was owing to myself. And I did not dream of calling anybody else's attention to what was there, because it was not meant for them, it was completely for me." Alice Munro, "The Eye," in *Dear Life* (Toronto: McClelland & Stewart, 2012), 269. The story of the "I" here is the story of receiving and resisting the gift of death. Instead of "I think, therefore I am," the Munrovian scene of selfhood gives us something more like "I encounter the death of the other as a gift from my mother, and therefore I/eye am."

58. "Parental love," Freud suggests, "which is so moving and at bottom so childish, is nothing but the parents' narcissism born again, which, transformed into object-love, unmistakably reveals its former nature." *On Narcissism*, vol. 14 of *The*

Standard Edition of the Complete Psychological Works of Sigmund Freud, ed. and trans. James Strachey (London: Hogarth Press, 1957), 91. Narcissism as the fantasy of self-completion is, in a sense, the gift given to and then taken away from each new human life: no one is born having consented to life's terms. "Has anyone supposed it lucky to be born?" asks Whitman in "Song of Myself." *Leaves of Grass* (New York: Penguin, 1961), 30. This curious narcissistic economy is exacerbated, of course, by the historical specificity of Munro's story, which records a woman's ambivalence toward motherhood, particularly insofar as it endangers her "real work": self-production, or "a wooing of distant parts of [one's]self" (88). Munro, here and throughout her work, depicts the very moment when, with the rise of feminism and innovations in reproductive technology, the inevitability of producing more life would be, and is still being, called into question.

59. Compare the perspective of the narrator here (and her experience of an excess of unprocessable affect) with that of the narrator at the end of Munro's "Trespasses," in *Runaway* (Toronto: McClelland & Stewart, 2004), 197–235, who has just, in a certain sense, witnessed her own funeral.

60. See, too, the passage in Munro's 1997 story "The Children Stay," in *The Love of a Good Woman*, 181–213, in which Brian tells Pauline that when she leaves the marriage she will not be able to take Caitlin and Mara (their children) with her: "'The children,' he said, in the same shivering and vindictive voice. Changing the word 'kids' to 'children' was like slamming a board down on her—a heavy, formal, righteous threat. 'The children stay,' Brain said. 'Pauline. Did you hear me?'" (212).

61. For more on the ethical dimension of Munro's fiction, see my essays "The Baby or the Violin? Ethics and Femininity in the Fiction of Alice Munro," *Literature, Interpretation, Theory* 14, no. 2 (2003): 69–97, and "Seduction and Subjectivity: Psychoanalysis in the Fiction of Alice Munro," in *Critical Insights: Alice Munro*, ed. Charles May (Ipswich, Mass.: Salem Press, 2012), 68–86.

62. The narrator recalls the adults "saying the Lord's Prayer in their unnaturally weighty voices" (104). *Prisoners* opens with Keller Dover reciting the same words as his son kills his first deer.

63. Deer, that is, dead deer, signify a whole unspoken dialogue on mortality and on responsibility for the death of the other in both "Miles City, Montana" and *Prisoners*. In Munro's story, the narrator's daughters notice a dead deer strapped to a car on the car ride, and one of the children refers back to this deer in a back-seat guessing game of "Who Am I?":

> Cynthia was somebody dead, and an American, and a girl. Possibly a lady. She was not in a story. She had not been seen on television. Cynthia had not read about her in a book. She was not anybody who had come to the kindergarten, or a relative of any of Cynthia's friends.
> . . . "It's the deer," said Meg, who hadn't been playing. (95–96)

The screenplay for *Prisoners* includes a conversation between the teenage son and daughter of the Dovers and the Birches, Ralph and Eliza, in which the boy refers to deer hunting as a form of population control (5–6).

64. Significantly, all the scenes of torture depicted in or referred to by the film take place in "homes."

65. Jacques Derrida, "Signature, Event, Context," in *Limited Inc*, trans. Samuel Weber and Jeffrey Mehlman (Evanston, Ill.: Northwestern University Press, 1988), 17.

66. Holly Jones is finally confronted by detective Loki in the act of injecting poison into the arm of Dover's daughter. "Make sure they cremate me," she says. "I don't want to be buried in some box."

67. Jacques Derrida, *The Gift of Death*, trans. David Wills (Chicago: University of Chicago Press, 1995), 76.

68. Ibid.

Afterword

1. Alice Munro, "My Mother's Dream," in *The Love of a Good Woman* (Toronto: McClelland & Stewart, 1998), 324.

2. Immanuel Kant, *Anthropology from a Pragmatic Point of View*, ed. Robert B. Louden (Cambridge: Cambridge University Press, 2006), 168.

3. Jacques Derrida, *The Animal That Therefore I Am*, trans. David Wills (New York: Fordham University Press, 2008), 98.

4. Ibid.

5. Ibid., 99.

6. Kant, *Anthropology*, 238n13b.

7. Derrida, *The Animal That Therefore I Am*, 98, 106.

8. Kant, *Anthropology*, 182n36. See Jean Itard, *The Wild Boy of Aveyron*, trans. George Humphrey and Muriel Humphrey (New York: Meredith, 1962), and François Truffaut's filmic representation, *The Wild Child* (United Artists, 1970), for an echo of the conviction that a sense of justice represents the essence or foundation of the human social order. Perversely enough, Itard is pleased when he attempts to punish Victor unjustly and Victor bites him: "How could I be other than delighted? It [the bite] was a very legitimate act of vengeance; it was an incontestable proof that the feeling of justice and injustice, that eternal basis of the social order, was no longer foreign to the heart of my pupil" (95). All further references to this text will be parenthetical.

9. Karen Joy Fowler, *We Are All Completely beside Ourselves* (New York: Penguin, 2014); Colin McAdam, *A Beautiful Truth* (New York: Penguin, 2013); Kenneth Oppel, *Half Brother* (Toronto: HarperCollins, 2010). All further references to *Half Brother* will be parenthetical.

10. McAdam, *Beautiful Truth*, 112.

11. Elizabeth Hess, *Nim Chimpsky: The Chimp Who Would Be Human* (New York: Bantam, 2008), 13.

12. Although it is addressed to a young audience, this fiction performs work that is very much in line with the deconstructive reconsideration of the human–animal opposition as explored by Derrida in *The Animal That Therefore I Am*: "It is *not just* a matter of asking whether one has the right to refuse the animal such and such a

power (speech, reason, experience of death, mourning, culture, institutions, tech-
nics, clothing, lying, pretense of pretense, covering of tracks, gift, laughter, crying,
respect, etc.—the list is necessarily without limit, and the most powerful philosophical tradition in which we live has refused the 'animal' *all of that*). It *also* means asking
whether what calls itself human has the right rigorously to attribute to man, which
means therefore to attribute to himself, what he refuses the animal, and whether he
can ever possess the *pure, rigorous, indivisible* concept, as such, of that attribution"
(135).

13. *Project Nim*, directed by James Marsh (BBC Films, 2011), DVD.

14. Terrace planned both to raise a male chimp in a human family (or rather
planned to *have* him raised in a human family) and to teach him American Sign Language. Terrace had been a student of Noam Chomsky's rival B. F. Skinner, and he set
out to challenge Chomsky's claim ("[H]uman language appears to be a unique phenomenon, without significant analogue in the animal world." *Language and Mind*
[New York: Harcourt Brace & World, 1968], 59) and accompanying alpha status. See
Hess's *Nim Chimpsky*. Nim's story is a primary source, if not the primary source, for
Oppel's narrative.

15. Roger Shattuck, *The Forbidden Experiment: The Story of the Wild Boy of
Aveyron* (London: Secker & Warburg, 1980), 155. Shattuck's study both retells and is
closely identified with Itard's own account.

16. For another version of a humanist insistence on the transcendence of imitation and an accompanying lived critique, see Ron Suskind, *Life, Animated: A Story
of Sidekicks, Heroes, and Autism* (New York: Kingswell, 2014) and the documentary
of the same name by Roger Ross Williams (Orchard, 2016). Suskind's son, Owen,
stopped speaking just before his third birthday and was diagnosed with autism.
Owen's speech would eventually reemerge via an imitation of the words of characters
from various Disney films. Although Suskind and his wife were at first jubilant—it
would seem that Owen has begun to speak again—their hopes are deflated by
experts who explain that Owen's repetitions are meaningless. Owen's parents, then,
might be said to misread ethically, as they gradually draw their son back into a world
of shared signification; they assist Owen as he remakes the world into a place he can
inhabit. We see in this instance, and more generally in representations of autism,
how the human is "contaminated" by both the "animal" and the "machine." When
Truffaut did research for his film *The Wild Child* and contemplated the representation of Victor, he both read about autism and watched footage of autistic children.
See Dudley Andrew and Anne Gillian, *A Companion to François Truffaut* (Oxford:
Wiley-Blackwell, 2013), 237.

17. Jonathan Culler, *The Literary in Theory* (Stanford: Stanford University Press,
2007), 164.

18. Judith Butler, *Giving an Account of Oneself* (New York: Fordham University
Press, 2005), 70.

19. See the William Steig cartoon "I M A U-M B-N. U R N N-M-L," in *CDB!*
(New York: Simon & Schuster, 1968).

20. Jacques Derrida, "A Certain Impossible Possibility of Saying the Event," *Critical Inquiry* 33, no. 2 (2007): 447.

21. Another particularly intriguing moment occurs when Ben attempts to write a school composition using only Zan's words. The human beings, interestingly, differ in their interpretation of just what this shows. The teacher gives Ben a C– and comments, "Stop messing about." Ben's father says it is "gibberish," whereas Ben's mother is amazed by Zan's power of expression. Ben himself says that he "was trying to prove something": the problem is not with what Zan is learning but with what they are choosing to teach him (250, 251). See also the reference to one of Zan's favorite games (which is a version of Freud's *fort da*—the game that ushers a child into culture [89]).

22. Hess, *Nim Chimpsky*, 242. Still, Terrace betrayed some ambivalence in publishing his scientific results simultaneously in the form of a repudiation and in a book meant for more popular consumption that celebrated Nim's accomplishments.

23. Derrida, *Animal That Therefore I Am*, 128–29.

24. Accounts of Nim's life and education reveal a contradictory relationship to the imitative or repetitive. Here is Hess describing the routine established by Nim's ASL instructor: "Upon entering the classroom, he was required to hang his coat on a hook, sit down at his little desk, and pay attention—no screeching, bouncing, biting, or joking around. If he misbehaved, as chimps are wont to do, Stewart stuffed him into a specially constructed four-foot-square box that sat in the corner of the room for what Terrace described as a 'time-out' period" (103–4). Nim's adoptive "sister," Jenny, comments on the gross inconsistency between raising Nim "as a human" and "locking him in a box when he was bad." Bob Johnson, a Columbia psychology student who was helping to look after Nim, comments, "There was an incredible level of basic stupidity about the nature of chimpanzees. Do chimps really learn sitting at a desk? Why did Nim have to hang his jacket up on a hook? What did any of this have to do with language?" (107). The complication here is that, Johnson's excellent question aside, pure repetitive behavior—hanging one's coat on a hook—is indeed a crucial part of learning to "speak."

25. Timothy Morton, *Ecology without Nature: Rethinking Environmental Aesthetics* (Cambridge, Mass.: Harvard University Press, 2007), 37.

26. McAdam, *Beautiful Truth*, 15.

27. J. L. Austin, "Performative Utterances," in *The Norton Anthology of Theory and Criticism*, ed. Vincent B. Leitch et al., 2nd ed. (New York: Norton, 2010), 1296 (emphasis added).

28. Derrida, "Certain Impossible Possibility," 458.

29. David Benatar, *Better Never to Have Been: The Harm of Coming into Existence* (Oxford: Clarendon Press, 2006), 13.

Index

abandonment, ethics of: destruction and, 1–2; maternal, 61; Nim Chimpsky's violence and, 199–200; in *Prisoners*, 167; in *The Road*, 77, 92–99, 114, 236n57. *See also* maternal ethics

abortion, 40, 57–59, 61–62, 224n13, 227n46, 244n11, 244n17

"Abortion, Killing, and Maternal Moral Authority" (Reader), 57–62

Abrahamson, Lenny, 226n24

Absalom, Absalom! (Faulkner), 115

absolute protection, fantasy of, 98, 165, 173, 174, 188, 252n45

accident motifs, 179–80, 184–85

Adler, Felix, 9

adoptive parents, 232n26

"Against Survival" (Edelman), 88–89

agential realism, 228n53

aggression. *See* violence

Alaimo, Stacy, 213n19

allegory of the cave: Plato's, 63, 68–71, 228n56; in *Room*, 62–71, 114

Allen, Kate, 242n1

All Joy and No Fun (Senior), 11–12

alpha male, 195. *See also* masculinity

American Pastoral (Roth), 18, 219n70, 246n33

American Sign Language: teaching chimp in, 194, 198

American Society for Reproductive Medicine, 242n1

Anderson, Laurie, 32, 222n114

Andrew, Dudley, 256n16

Anglo–Dutch Wars, 106

animal: border between signification and, 112, 116; child as, 192–207; the human and the, 2–3, 192, 195, 255n12; Schoolteacher's lesson in *Beloved*, 112, 240n38

Animal That Therefore I Am, The (Derrida), 191, 255n12

anthropomorphizing, 220n85

Antigone's Claim (Butler), 234n43

anxiety: about postpatriarchal parental responsibility, 14–15; about reproduction, 18. *See also* cultural anxiety

Archard, David, 159, 215n45

archive: Derrida on meaning of, 86–87, 88, 233n34, 241n57

Archive Fever (Derrida), 86–89

Arendt, Hannah, 159–60, 222n111, 247n1; on international human rights policy, 169, 170

Argonauts, The (Nelson), 221n103, 252n48

Ariès, Philippe, 4, 211n8

Aristarkhova, Irina, 218n62, 221n107, 227n40

Aristotle, 171

Arlamovsky, Maria, 213n31, 214n43, 216n53

Armstrong, Nancy, 230n4

Arrival (film, Villeneuve), 250n26

assisted reproductive technology (ART), 3, 124, 227n46; collateral effects of, 12–13, 213n30

259

Nixon, Richard, 162, 163
No Future (Edelman), 82

Obama, Barack, 238n17
object relating to object use: Winnicott on, 24–26, 98, 150, 246n42
Oedipal theory, 21, 22, 50–51; apocalypse and, 79; Half Brother as Oedipal story, 202–3; historical contingency of, 177; We Need to Talk about Kevin as Oedipal fantasy, 139
omnipotence: of child, 18, 24–25, 26, 28, 46, 49, 150; fantasy of, 46, 49; good-enough mother and, 101–2; maternal power and state of nature, 56–62; of Old Nick in Room, 67, 228n55
On Education (Kant), 3
On Liberty (Mill), 9
Oppel, Kenneth, 120, 192, 193–96, 252n48. See also Half Brother
Origins of Totalitarianism, The (Arendt), 169
orphanhood: in A Mercy, 106; orphaned children as inscriptions of "writing," 115–17
Osnos, Evan, 231n16
other, the: Butler on, 200; Derrida on, 137; dispossession for the sake of, 140; distinction between responsibility to and responsibility for, 102–3; duality of relationship to, 94–95; gift of full recognition from, 151; mother as surviving, 46–56, 67, 148, 150, 155, 156–57; patriarchal othering of the maternal, 187; pushing the other outside the self, 148; unmaking of in Prisoners, 166, 167, 173. See also Road, The
Otherwise Than Being (Levinas), 41, 42
Our Posthuman Future (Fukuyama), 8
Overall, Christine, 128, 130, 132–35, 140, 165, 244n9, 244n12, 250n29
ownership society, 239n31
Ozick, Cynthia, 223n131

Packer, George, 252n48
paranoid post-9/11 fantasy, 74. See also Prisoners; Road, The
parental address: child constituted by, 113–14, 115, 118; enigmatic messages of, 22–23, 33, 104–5, 114–15, 118–19, 122, 178–79, 186, 206. See also communication; language
parenting: attachment, 214n40; bonds of parent–child relations, 16; burden of responsibility of, 11–15, 84, 123–24; paradox of modern parenthood, 11–12; posthumanist parent–child relations, 221n103; at the social limit, 29–38; surrogate, 11, 13–14, 124, 215n43, 216nn52–53, 232n22, 239n37
"parroting" game in Room, 225n17
particularity of relation to child: consent and being-in-relation, 156; representational abstractions vs., 141–43
Pateman, Carole, 45, 216n52, 225n16
patriarchy: cultural script of patriarchal sex right, 43–44; at end of world in The Road, 73–99, 193; in Half Brother, 195; late-patriarchal terror, 96; of Old Nick in Room, 67, 228n55; patriarchal motherhood, 45; patriarchal sacrificial economy, 36–38, 96–98, 188, 252n48; post-9/11 crisis of, 77–79; in Prisoners, 166, 167, 173–75, 176, 193; violence and self-undoing of, 44
Paul, L. A., 131–32, 244n17
Payne, Alexander, 215n43
pedophiles, 248n19
Pee-wee's Playhouse (television show), 51
performativity, 200, 204n45; animal/human distinction and, 201–2; Austin's speech-act theory and, 199, 203–5, 235n50; constative-performative opposition, 70, 92, 153, 205–6, 235n50; Derrida's account of the future and, 87–88, 89, 95; ethics as performative, 41; McCarthy's faith in performative

cultural artifacts in, 81–82; depictions of placelessness, 87; Derrida's *archons* in, 87; endings of, 74–75; ethics of abandonment in, 77, 92–99, 114, 236n57; father–son relationship in, 78–80, 83–84, 87, 172, 247n46; final passage of, 234n45; as grail narrative, 230n11; the man's dependence on the boy for meaning in, 201; mirror scene in, 76–77, 94; mother in, 77–78, 82–83, 175, 187, 230n12; as paranoid post-9/11 fantasy, 74; performative force of familial bonds in, 89–92; poetics of remains, 80; precursor text for, 229n1; psychopolitical terrain of, 75–77; ruined library in, 86; sacrifice-as-seduction in, 36–37, 188; trauma of birth in, 77–84; utopian dimension of, 91; vision of the future in, 74, 84–92, 95, 99

Roberts, Dorothy E., 109, 223n126, 238n29, 239n31, 242n3

Robinson, Marilynne, 244n10

Roe v. Wade, 13, 213n30, 227n46

"Roger Malvin's Burial" (Hawthorne), 229n1

Room (Donoghue), 31, 34, 36, 37, 39–71, 120, 173, 187, 188, 195, 247n46; allegory of the cave and, 62–71, 114; ambivalence toward postcaptivity world in, 64–66, 228n56; compared to *The Road*, 75, 90, 230n12; as domestic novel, 43–44; escape plan in, 69–70, 71; intertextual connection with *Beloved*, 59, 228n49; Jack's narration of, 45, 225n17; linguistically rich world created by Ma in, 51; Ma's suicide attempt, 62, 64; maternal power and the state of nature in, 56–61, 66; mother as hostage in, 40–45, 67–68; mother as surviving other in, 46–56, 67; mother–child relationship in, 34, 39, 45, 55, 65–71, 230n12; Old Nick,

43–45, 52, 55, 56, 66, 67–68, 225n14; as study of "ethics as first philosophy," 49; utopia of, 39, 48; as weaning narrative, 40, 46–49, 51–56

Room (film), 226n24

Rosin, Hanna, 230n13

Roth, Philip, 18, 219n70, 246n33

Rothman, Barbara Katz, 12–13, 29, 214n43, 216nn52–53, 232n22, 236n55, 239n37

Rothstein, Mervyn, 236n6

Rousseau, Jean-Jacques, 211n9, 246n32

Ruddick, Sara, 30, 45, 101, 221n107, 225n15, 229n60, 231n21, 245n30; definition of mother, 30, 84, 194

Runaway (Munro), 254n59

Sacks, Oliver, 222n113

sacrifice, maternal, 56–62, 101, 188–89; abortion debate and, 57–59, 61–62; of being's irreducible relationality, 62; gift of death and, 69–70

sacrificial economy, patriarchal, 36–38, 96–98, 188, 252n48

sadism, moral, 76

Sandler, Lauren, 242n1

Sandy Hook Elementary School shooting, 243n6

Saunders, George, 32, 222n112

saying and said, distinction between, 90–91

Sayles, John, 215n43

Scarlet Letter, The (Hawthorne), 32–33, 222n118, 240n46

Schapiro, Tamar, 3, 8, 211n7

Schaub, Thomas, 235n45

Scott, A. O., 164, 249n23, 250n27, 251n33

Scott, Ken, 214n43

Sears, Martha, 214n40

Sears, William, 214n40

seduction theory: Laplanche on Freud's, 104–5

self-ownership, 54

Wolfe, Cary, 6–7, 212n13, 212n19, 217n59, 240n38
Wolfpack, The (documentary), 228n55
Wonder, The (Donoghue), 229n59
Wong, Virgil, 221n107
Wordsworth, William, 237n12
Work of Mourning, The (Derrida), 236n54
world, meaning of, 99
"World Child Welfare Charter" (League of Nations), 215n44
World Congress of Families IV (2007), 10
writing: deconstructive account of, 118;

as iterative structure, 115; orphaned children as inscriptions of, 115–17
Wyatt, Jean, 226n33, 237n14
Wylie, Philip, 55, 227n41

Young-Bruehl, Elizabeth, 161–63, 164, 248n11

Zähle, Max, 215n43
Zelizer, Viviana A., 9, 213n25, 224n135, 232n26, 248n18
Zibrak, Arielle, 233n32
Zone One (Whitehead), 235n48, 245n21

NAOMI MORGENSTERN is associate professor of English at the University of Toronto.

CPSIA information can be obtained
at www.ICGtesting.com
Printed in the USA
FFHW010829240219
50647112-56055FF